VISUAL DISPLAY TERMINALS

Usability Issues and Health Concerns

John Bennett, Donald Case,
Jon Sandelin, Michael Smith
editors

Prentice-Hall, Inc., Englewood Cliffs, New Jersey 07632

Library of Congress Cataloging in Publication Data

Main entry under title:

Visual display terminals.

    Includes bibliographies and index.
    Contents: Developing and implementing VDT-based
systems : usability issues. The VDT as an agent of
change / by Peter Keen. The concept of usability / by
Brian Shackel. Designing the VDT interface for human-
computer productivity / by James Bair. Human limits and
the VDT computer interface / by Stuart Card. Managing to
meet usability requirements : establishing and meeting
software development goals / by John Bennett—[etc.]
    1. Machinery in industry—Addresses, essays, lectures.
2. Information display systems—Addresses, essays,
lectures.   3. Data processing personnel—Diseases and
hygiene—Addresses, essays, lectures.   I. Bennett, John L.
HD6331.18.D37V57   1984   001.64/43   83-17748
ISBN 0-13-942482-2

10 9 8 7 6 5 4 3 2 1

Printed in the United States of America

ISBN 0-13-942482-2

This book is available at a special discount when ordered in
bulk quantities. Contact Prentice-Hall, Inc., General
Publishing Division, Special Sales, Englewood Cliffs, NJ 07632.

Prentice-Hall International, Inc., *London*
Prentice-Hall of Australia Pty. Limited, *Sydney*
Prentice-Hall Canada Inc., *Toronto*
Prentice-Hall of India Private Limited, *New Delhi*
Prentice-Hall of Japan, Inc., *Tokyo*
Prentice-Hall of Southeast Asia Pte. Ltd., *Singapore*
Whitehall Books Limited, *Wellington, New Zealand*
Editora Prentice-Hall do Brasil Ltda., *Rio de Janeiro*

CONTENTS

PREFACE

Human productivity and quality of worklife will be increasingly affected by computer and communications technologies. The visual display terminal (VDT) provides access to the tools and services these technologies provide. The VDT is the physical device the human sees and touches. It shows the commands of the user and the subsequent responses of the system. For people unfamiliar with the internal details of computer systems, the VDT in essence *is* the system.

The ideas that form this book grew out of a conference held at Stanford University in the spring of 1982. Visual display terminals (VDTs) were chosen as the focus of the gathering because they are the symbol and the embodiment of computer systems. The book is divided into two sections that correspond to the original conference format. The first section, edited by John Bennett, explores usability issues in the design, development, and implementation of VDT-based computer systems. The second section, edited by Michael Smith, examines health concerns related to the use of VDTs. An introduction to each section previews the articles to follow, highlighting ideas or issues of special importance.

In Section One, the authors examine issues arising from the intricate interplay between the human and the VDT. The focus is not on functionality of VDT-based systems—not on *what* a system can do—but rather on a system's usability—*how* the user achieves useful results. A recurrent theme is that product usability increases when the user/system interface reflects principles founded on human factors and behavioral science research. Usability and productivity are interrelated, and many people have been disappointed with the productivity of workers using current generation VDT-based systems. Improving usability is therefore becoming an important consideration in designing, building, and implementing such systems. The authors in Section One propose specific ways to approach this goal.

1

Section Two focuses on visual display terminals and human health. Concern about the possible adverse health consequences of using visual display terminals has triggered a number of research studies in Europe and the United States. The major areas of concern are visual problems, musculo-skeletal discomfort, emotional disorders, and psychosocial disturbances. The authors in this section review published research on terminal-related health complaints, describe contributing factors, explain possible causes, and recommend what can be done to minimize or avoid potential health hazards. Visual discomfort, the most frequently-expressed complaint, is probed in considerable depth. The authors also review the respective responsibilities of the equipment manufacturer, the employer, and the employee in creating a safe VDT work environment, citing the efforts of one company (IBM) to inform and protect employees who use visual display terminals.

The objective of this book is to disseminate updated information useful to people who are involved in the design, development, or implementation of systems using visual display terminals. The authors hope that this shared knowledge will lead to more useful, usable, and safer VDT-based computer systems that truly help people become more effective in their jobs and other endeavors.

AUTHOR PROFILES

This book represents the collective wisdom and experiences of its ten contributors. A brief profile of each author follows:

James Bair is Manager of Office Systems Research at Bell Northern Research, Inc., where he is responsible for studies of user needs and user behavior related to office automation. While a Senior Information Scientist at Stanford Research Institute (now SRI International), he was the leader of their Office Automation Consulting and Research Program. He has taught courses or been an invited lecturer at many universities, including MIT, Stanford, and University College in London. He is the co-author of the books *Office of the Future* and *Emerging Office Systems*, and he has published numerous articles on evaluation, design, and implementation of computer-based office systems. He is an editor of the ACM journal *Transactions on Office Information Systems* and serves on the editorial board of the journal *Behavior and Information Technology*.

Walter Baker is Manager of Environmental Health and Safety on the corporate staff of IBM Corporation in Armonk, New York. He is responsible for providing guidance and strategic direction in the areas of ergonomics, toxicology, health data systems, and medical administration within the IBM Corporation. In his 25 years with IBM, he has held various management positions in research, development, and manufacturing of semiconductor materials and devices. His publications and patents are in the semiconductor field.

John Bennett is a member of the research staff at the IBM Research Laboratory, San Jose, California, where he conducts studies on user interface design for office systems. Since joining IBM in 1961, he has served in various research and management positions, with primary focus on interactive software systems supporting professionals. He is editor of the recently published book *Building Decision Support Systems*.

3

Stuart Card is a member of the research staff at the Xerox Palo Alto Research Center, where he conducts studies on human-computer interaction. He is also an affiliated associate professor for the Carnegie-Mellon University Cognitive Psychology Program in Human-Computer Interaction and a member of the editorial board of the journal *Human-Computer Interaction*. He and his colleagues, Thomas Moran and Allen Newell, are co-authors of the book *The Psychology of Human-Computer Interaction*.

O. Bruce Dickerson is Corporate Director of Health and Safety for IBM Corporation. He has served in a similar position with Fairchild Camera and Instrument Corporation and was on the faculty of the University of California Medical School. He is a past President of the American College of Preventive Medicine and has published several articles in the field of occupational health and safety.

Phyllis Grey Johnston is a Research Associate at the School of Optometry, University of California at Berkeley. Her recent work includes establishing a research project on the possible relationship between working at a video display terminal and measurable decrements in visual performance. She has been a Research Assistant in the Department of Physiology at Stanford University, and a Research Associate and an NIH Postdoctoral Research Fellow in the Department of Psychology at the University of California.

Peter G. W. Keen is Chairman of Micro Mainframe, Inc., Cambridge, Massachusetts. He has been an Associate Professor of Management Science at the Sloan School of Management at MIT, and he has been on the faculty of the graduate schools of business at Stanford, Harvard, and the University of Pennsylvania (Wharton). He is co-author of the book *Decision Support Systems: An Organizational Perspective*, and editor of the journal *Office Technology and People*. He has conducted research in and taught telecommunications and business policy, strategic computing education, and managing organizational change. He has consulted in the United States, Europe, and Latin America on top management policies for using technology.

Brian Shackel is Research Professor in the Department of Human Sciences at the University of Technology, Loughborough, England. He recently completed a concurrent appointment as Head of the Department and as Dean of the School of Human and Environmental Studies. His teaching and research have focused primarily on the ergonomics and human factors issues involved in the use of computer-based technologies. He led the Ergonomics Department at EMI Electronics from 1954 until he joined the University of Technology in 1969. He has served as advisor to the British government and has been editor of the journals *Applied Ergonomics* and *Journal of Occupational Psychology*. He is editor of the books *Man-Machine Interaction* and *Man-Computer Communication*.

Michael Smith is Chief of the Motivation and Stress Research Section in the Applied Psychology and Ergonomics Branch of NIOSH. His research group identifies work related health problems, develops methods to reduce or eliminate such problems, and designs and evaluates motivational techniques to create a safer work environment. He holds adjunct faculty positions at both Xavier University and the University of Cincinnati, where he teaches courses on human factors and occupational safety.

Lawrence Stark is Professor of Physiological Optics and of Engineering Science at the University of California, Berkeley and also Professor of Neurology (Neuro-ophthalmology) at the University of California, San Francisco. His research and teaching interests reflect his background both in medicine and in electrical engineering. He has brought engineering control system theory and information theory to bear on research issues in neurology, visual perception and pattern recognition, neural coding and biological evolution, and simulation of biocontrol models. He is author of the book *Neurological Control Systems: Studies in Bioengineering*, and has published over 200 scientific articles in various journals.

Acknowledgments

The editors and authors wish to thank those people who reviewed draft versions of the articles that form this book. Their critiques helped bring greater coherence to a broad spectrum of material.

Much of the administrative work so crucial in producing this book was expeditiously and competently dealt with by the project secretary, Ruby Lai. Ruby's efforts were a major contribution in meeting a very ambitious production schedule.

Bonnie Bernstein, Patricia Clappison, and Claire Delgado served as editors and production managers. While indexing the book, Sue Riggs also coordinated the final copyediting and proofing. Dikran Karagueuzian led the TEX and typesetting team, assisted by Chip Haven and Jonni Kanerva. Susan True, the designer, did a remarkable job of meeting the tight deadlines resulting from doing all the production work at Stanford.

We also wish to acknowledge the financial assistance of AT&T Bell Laboratories, Boeing Computer Services, Emerson Electric, the IBM Corporation, the Illuminating Engineering Society, Memorex, and Optical Coating Laboratory, Inc. This support made possible both this book and the conference from which many of the concepts and ideas contained herein first emerged.

SECTION 1

Developing and Implementing
VDT-Based Systems:
Usability Issues

INTRODUCTION

The authors in this section suggest that considerable improvement can and should be made in providing useful and usable VDT-based products. Their articles provide insights into past mistakes and misdirections in the evolution of VDT-based systems and provide a foundation of knowledge from which to draw in developing better products.

The articles progress from the social and organizational issues that implementors of VDT-based systems must consider to the specific techniques that design and development teams can employ as they produce VDT-based products. Following Keen's initial article on implementation issues, Shackel discusses concepts of usability. Shackel's article provides a framework for understanding Bair's field observations on failures of VDT-based systems to improve human productivity to the levels anticipated. A central theme in these first three articles is that product designers and developers must have a better understanding about how people function and that mechanisms are needed to identify product characteristics that frustrate users and hinder productivity. Card proceeds to establish a framework for incorporating what we are learning about human factors into product design. Learning experiences, observations, and new scientific knowledge are forming a knowledge base about usability. Bennett closes the section with a methodology for tapping this usability knowledge base in the product design and development process.

Peter Keen analyzes the social and organizational problems VDT-based products can cause when introduced into enterprises. He notes three prerequisites for successful introduction:

1. an underlying infrastructure for VDTs similar in nature to that supporting our telephone systems;
2. design of the physical device and its supporting software to meet requirements of people in organizations; and
3. an implementation strategy that considers the immense social and organizational changes these devices imply.

Keen then focuses on implementation issues as he reviews the experiences encountered in introducing data processing to organizations, noting lessons to learn and mistakes to avoid. Managing the implementation process requires that we understand the political issues of ownership and control over information and also the changing nature of work as VDTs alter traditional modes of communication between people. Introducing fundamental and significant change within organizations affects the status quo, and resistance manifested in "counter-implementation" is a natural reaction. Keen examines the causes of resistance and suggests ways to deal with them. He then provides ideas on developing a knowledge base for successful implementation. His extensive annotated references serve as a roadmap for the reader who wishes to explore a particular issue in greater depth.

Brian Shackel identifies user, task, tool, and environment as essential elements to consider in system design. His careful distinctions between useful function ("the capability offered by the system has potential value") and usability of function ("I can use the function as provided to produce results valuable to me") lead into a detailed definition and discussion of usability. Usability considerations are shifting the emphasis in system design. Formerly design was focused on functional power delivered to experts. Although the need for powerful function continues, we now see an increasing sensitivity to "the process of use" (the steps the user must take to attain beneficial results from the system) for people who are professionals in their work but not computer professionals.

Shackel provides a scholarly review of current literature to support his contention that issues concerning user capability, task analysis, VDT capability, and user environment must be considered in design. He shows how to move beyond slippery phrases such as "user friendly" by describing parameters that allow objective measurement of "usability." These parameters are given values by specifying the level of performance to be achieved, selecting the sample of intended users employed in tests, determining the time allotted for user training, specifying the time allotted for task performance by trained users, and establishing an acceptable error rate for the anticipated user environments. These objective measures can be given operational definitions that developers can consider when they make the technical, economic, and scheduling trade-offs customary in the design and development process.

Jim Bair opens his chapter with a case in which using traditional manual methods proved more cost effective than using an electronic office system to prepare a lengthy report. The example suggests that a worker's potential for increased productivity when using a VDT-based computer system is not automatically realized. After defining the terms "productivity" and "design," Bair reviews organizational levels that affect potential productivity change. These levels include the overall organization and its business context, divisional units of the organization, groups of users within a division, an individual interacting with a machine, and the machine itself. Each has a number of variables that influence productivity. Bair then proceeds to focus his chapter on the individual user interacting with the machine, an entity he labels the human-computer dyad.

Within his focus on the human-computer dyad, Bair illustrates some of the computer-demanded steps that many office systems require users to perform even though the steps are irrelevant to office-related results. Despite the excessive overhead associated with their use and the fact that they are relatively unproductive, computer-based systems continue to be acquired. Bair analyzes why by considering the perspectives of the system buyer (what can I afford?), the system user (what do I like?), and the system supplier (what will sell?). Then, from the perspective of the human factors scientist concerned with "what will increase human effectiveness and productivity," Bair reviews pertinent issues. He devotes considerable attention to the problems of measuring human-computer performance. His observations on the importance of quantitative and qualitative measurement when designing for productivity complement and support the observations of Keen and Shackel. Bair concludes with three specific recommendations for removing barriers to user productivity when using VDT-based systems.

Keen observed the need for VDTs that are designed to match actual user work patterns and requirements. Stuart Card in his chapter shows how we may use techniques from cognitive psychology to obtain information which can then be applied to improve a product design. He describes a model of the human as an information processor. This model, robust and simple enough to be used in practical calculations, highlights the physical and cognitive limits of the human user. Card provides examples that show how to use the model to predict at the time of system design what human performance to expect in tasks associated with use of VDT-based systems. He then gives a calibration of the model by showing how closely it approximates observable behavior. Finally, he shows how the model can be expanded to include different variables which may be of interest in a particular design situation.

Card focuses on the expert user's goal to minimize the time required to obtain desired results. This leads to a review of various pointing devices and their time dependencies in accomplishing common VDT-oriented tasks. He demonstrates that the mouse is not limited by the design of the device (the speed with which one can use a mouse for pointing operations), but rather by the information processing rate of the user's hand-eye coordination system. Thus, the mouse will perform at least as well as any alternative pointing device. Such empirical results are obviously important when the design criteria for a user/system interface include using a pointing device.

In the closing chapter of this section, John Bennett draws on both his research experience and his work within the industrial development community to outline an approach for managing trade-offs in the design and development process. His central thesis is that everyone on the development team must have an explicit frame of reference for usability. Once established, this frame of reference can be used to support definitive planning and focused discussions about usability trade-offs during new product development. A widely held impression in the development community is that usability is a "soft, subjective" topic, and this impression is reinforced by use of such undefined terms as "user friendly." It is therefore important to develop usability goals that are measurable in terms of desired standards and relatable in terms of ultimately effective product features. The development challenge is to assign agreed-upon target values for usability attributes and to allocate resources to meet the goals during the development process.

Bennett reviews and adapts the observations of Keen, Shackel, and Bair, thereby demonstrating the synthesis process that development groups must undertake when establishing performance goals. He then illustrates how the goals and their attributes can be represented in a hierarchical matrix format as one way of keeping the goals before the team. Research results, such as Card's human processor modeling, can then be used to provide technical knowledge about user capabilities when considering trade-offs in design and development decisions.

The issues addressed in this section are dynamic, not static. We are increasing our knowledge of social and organizational issues, of fundamental human factors, and of what constitutes good interface design in the intricate connection between a human and a VDT-based system. At the same time, hardware components (processors, storage systems, display terminals) are becoming more reliable and cheaper, and software is becoming more powerful. The challenge is to integrate these developments in the design of new products that will better serve those who need and use them. This section is intended to foster that goal.

THE VDT AS AN
AGENT OF CHANGE

Peter G. W. Keen

INTRODUCTION

This book as a whole discusses how people and computers can get along together. A visual display terminal (VDT) is something entirely new to many managers, clerks, and secretaries. It may be useful to them in terms of access to services and information, but it needs to be usable, too—not intimidating, disruptive, inconvenient, or hard to learn and operate. The underlying question the first section of this book addresses is:

> *How much does a designer or implementor need to know about people's thought processes, skills, attitudes, work, and the context of work in order to provide VDTs that are both useful and usable?*

One obvious analogy to the VDT is the telephone receiver. Behind each is a complex infrastructure of communication lines and switches. Telephone users take this infrastructure for granted. They are aware of it only when it is not working adequately—for example, when there is noise on the line, congested circuits, or some other malfunction. They see only the receiver, and it is this interface between themselves and the telephone network that determines their view of the whole system. They need not understand how that system works to use it comfortably and effectively.

It took decades of complex planning, capital investment, and technical innovations to build this hidden infrastructure. Now that it is in place, receivers can be put into new locations very quickly. Wherever there is a phone jack, a handset can be plugged in.

In a way, VDTs are compressing the social history of the telephone from several decades to several years. We are now at a stage where the infrastructure for computer services has been put in place. We are starting to plug in VDTs—like phone receivers—in new places at short notice. Some people adapt to them easily. Others, though, are taken by surprise, having never expected to be direct users of computers. For them, this technical change represents a social change. Their jobs suddenly require them to converse with computers via VDTs, and they may be unprepared, uneasy, or even unwilling to do so.

There are three main issues that will determine the speedy and successful adoption of VDTs:

1. **The infrastructure**. Data communications networks, private and distributed data processing systems, network protocols and architectures; a supply of skilled technical managerial staff for development and operations.
2. **Design of the physical device and its supporting software**. Factors contributing to effective design include multifunctionality, human engineering and ergonomics, ease of access and use, and economics of purchase and operations.
3. **Implementation**. Managing the introduction of VDTs and the immense social and organizational change they imply.

The first of these three processes, building the infrastructure, is primarily technical in focus. Few users need to understand how it works; like the phone system, they will take it for granted.

The second area, the design of the VDT, has often been viewed in technical terms, not behavioral ones. The common thread linking the varied topics discussed in Sections I and II of this book is that effective design and use requires a fusion of the technical and the behavioral. *People* use VDTs. The VDT must be adapted to their needs and processes, and not vice versa.

The technical tradition has often overlooked behavioral aspects of the third area of concern—implementation—the subject of this introductory section. Implementation is defined here in a broader sense than most computer scientists use the term. Implementation is not just the installation of a technical system in an organization, but the institutionalization of its use in the ongoing context of jobs, formal and informal structures, and personal and group processes. Installation does not guarantee institutionalization. Implementation includes the technical process of installation and the behavioral process of managing change.

The focus of this chapter is almost entirely behavioral. I look at VDTs from the viewpoint of people in organizations and address four main questions:

1. What lessons can we take from other efforts to introduce information technology?

2. How do users perceive VDTs?

3. What do we know about effective management of technical change?

4. What is the knowledge base needed by those involved in the large-scale introduction of VDTs?

The chapter highlights the need to see the user as a real person, rather than as an abstraction. Technical specialists are often isolated from the user's world—both psychologically and physically. They often demonstrate their naïveté about the user by making simplistic assumptions or by imposing their own preferences and work habits on the design of the tools they build. If they do not show a need to understand the users' perspectives, they are unlikely to feel a sense of responsibility to them.

It is instructive to substitute the word *colleague, client,* or *customer* for the word *user.* Individuals have an ethical responsibility to colleagues and a contractual one to clients. In both instances, they are flesh and blood people; specialists talk to and negotiate with them, and adapt a technical design to them, not the other way round.

Other chapters in this book present a sophisticated model of the user as an information processor, as part of a system. Cognitive psychology, ergonomics, and human factors research have made a substantial contribution to the physical design of VDTs and the development of "user-friendly" software. The goal of this chapter is to present a sophisticated model of the user as a real person in a real organization. Implementation of VDTs can be only as effective as the model of the user is comprehensive, accurate, and clear. Social psychology and organizational theory add to cognitive science in enriching our understanding of what happens when VDTs and users come together.

THE LESSONS OF DATA PROCESSING

It is useful to begin any discussion of VDTs and organizational change by reviewing the experiences of data processing (DP). Until fairly recently, data processing was characterized by a technocentric focus on hardware and a disregard for organizational and behavioral issues. This narrow view contributed to frequent failures in implementation.

A rich selection of literature, dating from the 1960s, explores factors that have contributed to success and failure in implementing computer systems and management science models. Representative studies are briefly summarized in the annotated bibliography at the end of the chapter. Many of the conclusions and recommendations made in these studies have become part of the conventional wisdom, but the commonplaces of today were innovative insights even in the late 1970s and early 1980s:

- The vital need to ensure meaningful involvement;
- The highly political nature of decisions about and impacts of information technology;

- The substantial effort and resources needed to manage technical change: understanding jobs, people, organizational structures, and group processes; building new roles and skills in facilitation, education, and communication; identifying and responding to potential resistance.

Out of this research tradition has emerged a clear picture of the relationship between technical change and organizational change. The lack of understanding about the dynamics of implementation caused expensive failures and disruptions for data processing and for users. Only in the past few years has DP recovered from its reputation as unresponsive, unable to deliver on its promises, and ill-suited to the workings of an organization. There has been an obvious culture gap between builders and users of information systems—an adversarial relationship of "we" versus "they."

New developments, such as VDTs, networks, end-user software, data base technology and application development tools, add up to a far more flexible, usable, and reliable technical base than was available in the 1960s and 1970s. However, even this improved technology still requires as a complement—but obviously not as a substitute—effective management of the change process. Designers of systems using VDTs must learn more to successfully implement this new technology. In some ways, their job is even more difficult than that of DP, because VDTs imply even more radical and rapid change. Once again, the telephone system is a useful analogy. The telephone receivers and the computer conversations of the mid-1980s are the multifunction workstation, personal computers, electronic mail, CAD/CAM, word processing, Decision Support Systems, end-user computing, and so on. The combination of cost-effective technology and substantial potential economic gains in productivity and efficiency have accelerated the pace and scope of change. In the past two decades, DP affected comparatively few organizational cultures. In 1975, few managers, professionals and secretaries had direct contact with computers. In 1985, few will not.

THE VDT FROM A USER'S VIEWPOINT

Like the phone receiver, a VDT is used by people who are interested in conversations. It is an access device and, from the user's perspective, it is the entire system—reached through an invisible infrastructure. Its introduction is often also a disruption because it allows people in organizations to redistribute information, thus breaking up traditional relationships and responsibilities; it requires new skills and attitudes and an active involvement with computers; and it can arrive very quickly.

The last point is key. What is new about VDTs is not that they are in themselves difficult, threatening, or complex. The evidence suggests otherwise: if they are carefully implemented, people take them in stride. They are a new type of TV or typewriter (that may even be seen as having the advantage of quietness), or just another device in the office landscape. What is strikingly new is the pace of change; VDTs can lead to a form of culture shock. Figure A–1 illustrates this. In the inner circle are programmers, accountants, and data entry staff. These are the people who had direct contact with computers before telecommunications pushed VDTs out into new cultures. The other people in the organization—secretaries, managers, and staff in functional areas like personnel or marketing—were indirect users, buffered from the computer. They are a far more heterogeneous culture than that of the inner circle. In most cases, they did not expect to make hands-on use of terminals, and their education and career paths rarely prepared them for the arrival of VDTs.

Zuboff (1982a) has looked at how people make sense of this arrival. Their work becomes computer-mediated, but not necessarily automated. The VDT is one aspect of the job, and the major concern of workers is to make sense of the new situation. Zuboff asks a range of questions that, less explicitly, people in the outer circle ask themselves:

1. What does it mean to "do a good job?" Neither physical effort nor interpersonal interaction is very relevant to job performance when much of the work centers on the VDT. Sustained attention becomes the norm for good work.
2. What will organizational life be like, or more specifically, "will this still be a good place to work?"
3. How do you make sense of the work you do as it becomes more abstract? Zuboff points out that messages, documents, money, and paper—which used to be concrete and processed visibly—become abstract and partially hidden when VDTs are used.

This increasing abstraction of work is perhaps the major single impact of VDTs. Zuboff provides many examples and then proceeds to address yet another organizational consequence of VDTs: "What is an organization if people do not have to come face to face to accomplish their work?" The longer-term potential applications of VDTs include teleconferencing, the traveling office, working at home, and a 24-hour time window for business operations (for example, in international banking). The organization's information flows and control systems will be designed in terms of logical processes and relationships instead of physical and geographical constraints. This means that the answer to Zuboff's question is: "The organization becomes an abstraction, too."

MANAGING CHANGE: IMPLEMENTATION DYNAMICS

Established procedures, job definitions, traditions, and structures built up over time lead to organizational "homeostasis." A homeostat, like a thermostat, adapts to change by trying to keep things working as they were before,

Throwing Terminals into New Cultures

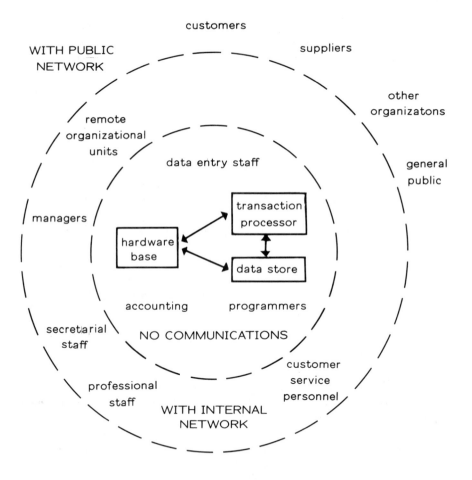

Figure A–1. Throwing terminals into new cultures. Heterogeneous
cultures unprepared; lack vocabulary to participate.

to stay on track. When a middle level manager operates an efficient work unit
within budget constraints, the status quo is encouraged. The better the per-

formance, the fewer the incentives to change. The more status and influence depend on existing processes and structure, the greater the cost of changing. The homeostatic nature of many of the middle levels of organizations, especially, leads to a social inertia.

Introducing information technology can disturb the delicate equilibrium of an organization. The costs of change may be perceived by those affected as greater than the benefits. Resistance, passive or active, is often a natural response to the intrusion of unproven innovations. When outsiders introduce VDTs, resistance can be even greater due to past experiences with badly implemented computer projects. People are threatened because the computer is *here*, on the desk, and a response must be made *now*.

Many technical specialists do not recognize social inertia. Companies that build VDTs and development teams that install them have grown used to rapid change as a norm. In fact, they benefit from change. They assume that new technology has a momentum of its own and that change is a logical process. Resistance then seems irrational to them.

The issue of homeostasis is central to the whole process of managing change. Overseeing implementation is equivalent to facilitating change; it begins by unblocking the status quo. Figure A–2 summarizes the steps involved in managing change, applying definitions from two models of change widely used in studies about the implementation of information systems (Schein 1961; Kolb and Frohman 1970). According to these models, effective change most depends on:

1. Building momentum for change: "unfreezing" the status quo and reducing homeostasis.
2. Recognizing the evolutionary rather than revolutionary pace of change: acknowledging that cultures must be able to assimilate the change and adapt to it comfortably.
3. Providing resources and roles to facilitate change: presenting the implementer as a change agent.
4. Focusing on institutionalization: making the system mesh with the other components of the organization such as tasks, formal and informal structures, and people.

In another model, Leavitt's "diamond" (1964), TECHNOLOGY, TASK, PEOPLE, and STRUCTURE are the basic and interdependent components of an organization (Fig. A–3). The pieces have to be in balance for equilibrium to exist. Change in one affects the others. For example, a technological innovation—VDTs used for customer service—may affect:

1. **Task**: job descriptions; what it means to "do a good job" (i.e. the operational definition of "productivity").
2. **People**: skill profiles; workers' attitudes about and comfort with their work.

LEWIN-SCHEIN MODEL	KOLB-FROHMAN MODEL
UNFREEZE: – alter the forces inhibiting change in order to disturb equilibrium and status quo and to create a need for, rather than resistance to, innovations	**SCOUTING:** – match the capabilities of the change agent/implementor to the needs of the situation; – avoid "have solution, will travel"
	ENTRY: – build felt need for change – define operational goals – create contract for change – recognize and respond to any resistance – build joint team
MOVE: – create the program for change	**DIAGNOSIS, PLANNING, AND ACTION:** – design and make operational the change program – corresponds closely to technical conception of implementation
REFREEZE: – integrate the change into the ongoing activities of the organization – reinforce the equilibrium	**EVALUATION:** – monitor progress in terms of the plans and goals defined in ENTRY – identify when the system is complete and self-sustaining
	TERMINATION: – hand over the system to the user group – integrate it into the organization – ensure it has a home and a manager

Figure A–2. Managing change.

LEAVITT DIAMOND

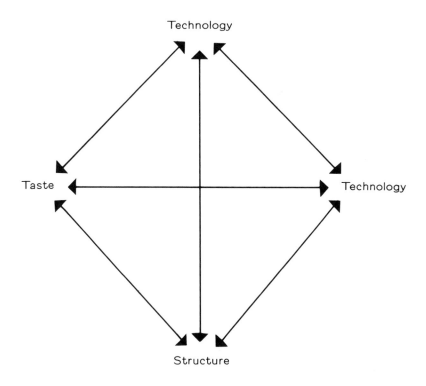

Figure A–3. Leavitt's "diamond" of organizational components.

3. Structure: informal contacts; reporting relationships; supervision.

So long as the current equilibrium is acceptable, *why* change? The VDT is only a disruption. This simple example explains why there is so much social inertia in organizations. When things are working well, there is no reason for TASK, PEOPLE, or STRUCTURE to adjust. Rather, there is every reason to resist technology, even if only passively through inaction. Where technical change is dampened by the *lack* of change in the other components, the entire system is frozen.

Implementation begins by unfreezing the status quo. A major conclusion of research on individual, group, social, and organizational change is that planned change must be self-motivated. If change is introduced by outside forces, frozen personalities, groups, and organizations respond by resisting.[1]

Organizations can be "unfrozen" in many ways, each of which builds a "felt need" to change:

1. A recognition of environmental trends, competitive problems, or valuable business opportunities that alter the cost-benefit ratios; the perceived cost of change may still be high, but the benefits or costs of *not* changing are even higher.
2. The commitments and actions of an innovater who can mobilize peers and subordinates.
3. A person who can bridge the gap between "us" and "them" and act as a translator and facilitator. This change agent can significantly reduce the uncertainty, fear of computers and computer people, and miscommunication which in themselves can lead to automatic resistance to potentially beneficial technological innovation.

Figure A–2 labels as ENTRY the process by which a change agent/implementor unfreezes the status quo. Figure A–4 summarizes the steps involved and gives references to case studies and articles providing more detail about how to handle ENTRY.

Major goals in the ENTRY process are to build joint commitment and trust between designers and users, and to define clear operational goals, which take into account needed adjustments to other components of the organizational diamond. In addition, resistance is actually encouraged. A technocentric definition of implementation as simple installation too easily dismisses resistance or tries to work around it; our definition of implementation as the management of change regards resistance as a signal about the costs of change and the lack of felt need. It must not be ignored or pushed underground.

Once the organizational system is unfrozen, movement is inevitable. The focus of the implementation effort must be to direct that movement and build on ENTRY through:

- Project management and control.
- Meaningful user involvement in planning, design, testing and installation.
- First-rate technical work.

The middle stage in Figure A–2, MOVE, ends with installation. What may be the most difficult step, REFREEZE, follows. Refreezing creates a new status quo and restores the equilibrium. It institutionalizes what has so far been a temporary system used as an organizational experiment in order to mesh it with TASK, other TECHNOLOGY, PEOPLE, and STRUCTURE.

Institutionalization occurs through education and ongoing support. The system must have a home and a manager in the users' own environment; its value must be firmly established. The more the innovation alters the

STAGES IN ENTRY

Build credibility and trust.

- Learn how the organization works.
  - forces pro/con change
  - key actors
  - history
- Become familiar with the culture.
  - people
  - norms and traditions
  - politics
- Build a line of credit.
  - find out concerns, opportunities
  - select a small visible problem the people care about
    and solve it
- Demonstrate personal, professional, or political basis
  for working together.

Build "felt need."

- Identify or create benefits from the change program.
- Explain and justify the rationale for change.
- Use education, information, and consulting to reduce
  uncertainty about the change.

Respond to resistance.

- Identify potential resisters; listen, educate, negotiate,
  and, where necessary, back off or push forward.
- Provide forums where resisters can express concerns and
  feel they have influence.
- Adjust the objectives, design, and phasing in response to
  reasonable resistance.

Define operational goals.

- What are we trying to accomplish (e.g., change the
  budgeting process, not build a planning model)?
- How will we know we've been successful; what will people do
  differently? How will the organization look different?
- What do we do first? If we can't phase it, can we ever
  build it?

Build meaningful involvement.

- Define formal liaison roles.
- Get good people assigned from user environment, not
  those who are expendable or mediocre.
- Define clear mutual responsibilities and review process.

Useful References:
Kolb and Frohman (1970); Lucas and Plimpton (1972); Schultz and Slevin (1975).

Figure A–4.   Managing the entry process.

status quo, the more effort, time, and top-level support may be needed to institutionalize it. Such innovation may, for instance, create new reporting relationships and staff positions, change criteria for performance appraisal, or require reassigning senior people. Without proper institutionalization, it is not at all unusual to find that after a year a new system sits idle and is finally removed. It may be far easier to build momentum for change than to cement it. Many applications of VDTs—for communication, text-handling, processing, and customer service—are intended to redesign work and to alter the organization. Plugging in VDTs can be done comparatively quickly. Institutionalizing their use may take much more time and effort.

This brief discussion describes the tactics of change and applies mainly to single projects. We know less about directing larger-scale strategic change. The best approach is incremental and bottom-up. In fact, there are very few examples in the implementation literature of successful large-scale change led from the top. The implementation research reveals one major reason for this failure—the intensely political nature of computer-based systems—a fact surprising to many technical specialists and, in some cases, distasteful to them.

The Politics of Information Technology

Ownership and control of information are closely linked to influence, authority, autonomy, and evaluation. Powerful information monopolies exist in many organizations. Building a data base and, more importantly, providing VDTs to access data previously the exclusive property of one person can be a political act. Many case studies on information systems illustrate this point:[2]

1. In a manufacturing plant, the introduction of a basic information system for operations and scheduling reduces the authority of plant managers and increases that of central staff.

2. Divisions resist the development of a planning model which they see as intruding on their autonomy and as increasing the ability of corporate staff to inspect their work.

3. In state government agencies, information is a critical resource; control of data enables agencies to preempt the policy debate, so they actively resist efforts to break open their monopoly.

4. A senior executive uses an information system to monitor his organization and his subordinates' decisions.

5. Police agencies pull out of cooperative ventures with other law enforcement agencies (and give up significant budgets) rather than lose control of their own data (Laudon, 1974).

A VDT is an access device; in effect it redistributes information and creates new nodes of influence in the organization. The VDT thus intrudes on traditional territories. Add to this the obvious battles over control of the technical resource—for example, DP struggling to maintain its old monopoly over hardware and development priorities—and it seems clear that the politics of computing is a central issue for implementation. VDTs are, in a way, a fifth column. Like phone receivers, VDTs can be undramatically, even casually, introduced; they may then substantially change key aspects of influence, authority, and ownership of data before those affected realize it. Failures to implement office technology using VDTs are less often due to technical problems than to social and political ones.

The topics discussed above may be summarized as the unanticipated organizational consequences of technical change. The lesson from implementation research is that such consequences and the counter-implementation they elicit (resistance, conflict, and even overt sabotage) are central features of information technology—not a minor, second order effect. If this is true for past innovations, it will surely be more so with VDTs because they push access to previously unobtainable information deep into and across the organization.

VDTs also seem to eliminate the old dichotomy between centralization and decentralization (Keen, 1981b). Centralization sacrifices time for control; decentralization does the reverse. In a large organization VDTs can be used to push an activity or process out to decentralized units and at the same time to coordinate it centrally via the communications network. A British-based company with 30 foreign divisions decided to decentralize responsibility for day-to-day money management (disbursements, timely cashing of cheques, overdrafts, etc.). At the same time it needed central coordination; if one division had a 10-day overdraft of 3 million pounds, the central unit needed to net this out, avoid overdraft charges, and invest the surplus. VDTs linked to a banking network allowed the company to run the 30 decentralized bank accounts as if they were one, located in New York. Is that increased centralization or decentralization?

Other examples show how VDTs provide centralization-with-decentralization:

1. The head of Research and Development accesses cost data from geographically dispersed labs and can oversee them far more effectively. He calls this "integration" and "coordination." The labs call it "control" and "intrusion."
2. A chief executive in a highly decentralized company uses a VDT to access yesterday's key performance data from operating units and to view an overall picture of the business. He can adjust the central plan, pinpoint problem areas, and send directives anywhere in the organization.
3. Dealers for an automobile company can use a VDT to locate specific car models or parts anywhere in the United States. This effectively transforms them from a set of independent units to a "federal" organization and allows the manufacturer's staff to access the dealers' financial and operating data.

These are fragmented examples, but they strongly suggest that the unanticipated organizational consequences of VDTs will be substantial:

- More and more of the planning and control processes will rely on the communications network;
- Key political, budgetary, executive, and liaison functions will be changed by the provision of VDTs;
- The possibility of decentralization-with-centralization must lead to major redesign of the formal and informal structure of organizations, especially multinationals with widely dispersed units.

Much of the conceptual and empirical base for implementation research now comes from political science. Section V of the Appendix lists examples. It may seem to many technical designers that VDTs and politics have little to do with each other. Even behavioral researchers in this and related areas tend to focus on the individual (e.g., cognitive psychology and the use of VDTs) or on fairly small groups (the impact of technical change on a work unit). With VDTs the focus will need to be larger. The experiences of DP can alert us to unanticipated organizational consequences; for VDTs, these will be transorganizational consequences.

The focus of implementation research has generally been on the impacts upon users. But VDTs are also part of an immense organizational change for the suppliers of information systems. We are moving from a period of supply-side economics and management of computing, when DP had a monopoly, to what is basically a free market. Quite often, VDTs (and even more so, microcomputers) are brought into the organization through the initiative of line managers outside the DP budget and outside DP's control. In many instances VDTs are part of a broader commitment to information technology—the communications infrastructure, data resource, and office technology tools—as the basis for major productivity gains and competitive advantage. In service industries, especially banking, telecommunications is a central aspect of long-term market initiatives for leading companies.

In such situations, the issue of authority is key. When companies start to use VDTs as the access mechanism for integrated, company-wide services and resources, then information technology becomes critical, instead of peripheral, to the main activities of the business. Direction, control, and leadership become crucial issues: who decides? DP can assume the information systems function of the organization, but only if it has both a leader who has the necessary managerial and business skills and a mandate from the top. Often the whole management structure for dealing with information resources is under strain (Keen, 1982) and these strains can compound the political ramifications of VDTs. They include:

1. Conflicts in authority and its concomitant, accountability.
Who is in charge, with what mandate and responsibility? What are

the trade-offs between central direction by DP and local autonomy? Office automation provides a clear example. A complex conflict can exist between line units who want to install word-processors or minicomputers to meet their particular needs quickly and cheaply and DP, which perceives these as threats to long-term integration and compatibility.

2. **Rapidly growing demand for systems** at a time when existing backlogs are high and staff for development is scarce.

3. **The need for cooperation and meaningful involvement** at all levels, including liaison between developers and users, and coordination in planning.

4. **A much broader range of applications, requiring more differentiated roles** than the traditional programmer-analyst to project leader career paths. Roles include business-oriented analysts; substitutes for traditional programmers, such as staff analysts using end-user languages and packages; trainers and educators; and specialists in telecommunications.

Each of these subjects is integrally related to VDTs and merits longer discussion.

The experiences of DP indicate, as do the other lessons from implementation research, the organizational implications of VDTs in terms of impacts and development issues. If technical designers too often have a simplistic model of the individual users, then how much more incomplete is their model of organizational processes? How many failures of technically sound VDT-based applications will result from ignoring the important political issues and not understanding the dynamics of authority and influence?

Resistance to Change

Any combination of (1) the disruptions technical change can bring to a stable organizational equilibrium, (2) the political concerns information technology often raises, and (3) the social uncertainty computer-mediated work implies, is likely to create "resistance." The word needs to be in quotation marks because it is an attribution rather than a fact: a value judgment about motives and behavior. Resistance may take many forms:

- Indifference, misunderstanding, or ignorance of the goals of an innovation and a consequent lack of commitment to effort.
- An expression by reasonable people of legitimate fears that the introduction of VDTs will change their world in ways they cannot predict or influence.
- Deliberate sabotage of a good idea.
- Deliberate opposition to an ill-conceived idea.

This list covers a wide spectrum of intentions and actions. It is too easy to call any nonacquiescence resistance. It may be more useful to look instead at the choices people make or can make in responding to the introduction of VDTs. Implementation research stresses that, as often as not, apparent resistance is reasonable and not irrational or lazy. It is, therefore, important first to provide a forum in which people can express their concerns and then to respond to them by negotiating, sharing information, adapting technical designs, and above all, developing mechanisms for genuine user involvement.

Many commentators on office technology have expressed concern about its misuse or thoughtless application and have suggested that workers *should* resist. Section II of the Appendix lists sample views expressed by academics and practitioners. (See also Gregory and Nussbaum 1982). A common theme underlies their comments: technicians do not adequately understand or care about the impacts of their activities.

Because VDTs can have profound social and economic consequences, researchers and practitioners often take strong, even ideological, positions concerning them. Many of these positions are essentially deterministic; they assume that information technology has largely inevitable consequences. The utopians have a vision of "productivity," "the new industrial revolution," "the Information Society," and "the Office of the Future." Dystopians predict the dehumanization of work and relationships, workers' loss of autonomy, and the erosion of privacy.

To observers who hold a deterministic view, resistance to change is a relatively uninteresting concept. If the consequences, negative or positive, are inevitable, then people's responses make little difference; technology has its own imperative. Implementation research assumes—and, of course, it may turn out to be incorrect—that there is a potential for choice and action and that consequences are not predetermined. A group of pessimists sees differential benefits from the introduction of VDTs, with workers often losing out and management gaining. Zuboff (1982), who coined the phrase "computer-mediated work," backs up his cautionary views with substantial empirical data; his work is essential reading.

These pessimists see resistance as a countervailing power. Workers need to express their legitimate rights and not passively allow the technology to erode the quality of their work life. On the other hand, the optimists fill the ranks of management (and write chapters in books like this). They consider information technology on the whole as beneficial to society, businesses, and individuals. But they also prefer healthy scepticism to passive acceptance.

Resistance is an interesting and important concept to those who do not regard information technology as deterministic. To a large extent, one's whole perspective on implementation is reflected in one's view of resistance and how to handle it. Here are some representative perspectives:

1. **Utopians.** Resistance is largely irrational or irrelevant and should be ignored or bypassed.

2. **Optimists.** Resistance is often very rational and must be handled openly by facilitation and negotiation.
3. **Pessimists.** Resistance is necessary in many cases; it can only be handled by workers banding together to present a united front or by management rethinking how and where to apply VDTs.
4. **Dystopians.** Resistance will be largely unavailing, and there is no reason to expect management and technicians to change their tune. (See Hoos' comments in Section II of the Appendix.)

These perspectives are more an expression of personal values than intellectual belief. Whatever position one takes, it must surely be based on knowledge of research along the whole spectrum, from dystopian to utopian. Those who bring radical change are responsible for its impacts.

Strategic Aspects of Change

VDTs imply strategic change. An electronic mail system, terminals in every branch of a supermarket chain or a bank, a distributed processing system in manufacturing plants, office technology as the cornerstone for major productivity drives—these are interdepartmental changes that can affect everyone in the outer circles of Figure A–1.

The most obvious requirement for strategic change is now the conventional wisdom of DP and office technology: the need for top management commitment. "Commitment," like "user involvement," is often left undefined as a vague panacea which translates to messages of good will and pseudo-participation. Serious commitment from top management requires the following strategic protocol:

- Explicit policies, mandates, and directives from the top.
- A clear business message and operational definition of "productivity."
- Formal high-level mechanisms for coordination and communication, such as steering committees.
- The authority and non-technical resources needed to mobilize for change: education, facilitators, and formal liaison roles, especially.
- Both a clear long-term goal and clear criteria for phasing.

The literature on these topics consists mainly of assertions and anecdotal experiences, and it is largely to be found in management-oriented publications like *The Harvard Business Review* or the *MIS Quarterly* (Nolan 1982). Implementation research on large-scale programs and innovations comes mainly out of political science. Although there is significant experience introducing a single application using VDTs, little of it is relevant to integrated transorganizational applications.

Even if the experiences of DP and implementation studies do not provide answers, at least they point to the questions and, hence, to the knowledge base needed for implementors to develop their own solutions. The research raises questions that fall into three categories. Within each category, there are some obvious issues:

1. What are the forces for and against change?
   - What is the climate for change?
   - Are people satisfied or dissatisfied with the present state of affairs?
   - What are the factors acting to unfreeze the status quo?
   - What business, social, historical, or political issues will inhibit or accelerate change?
   - Who gains or loses—or rather, who perceives gain or loss from change?
2. What is the degree and pace of change?
   - How much of the organization will be affected and to what degree in terms of skill needs, relationships, job descriptions, seniority, influence, budget, etc?
   - Does this innovation change the way geographically dispersed units (e.g., corporate and divisional staff) communicate with each other?
   - Will the main planning, control, supervisory, and administrative process be very different as a result of the change?
   - How quickly will these changes occur? Can they be phased?
3. What should be the process of implementation? What choices should management make and how will people respond to them at all levels?
   - Whose perceptions and actions will influence success or failure?
   - Are existing mechanisms for project management and user involvement adequate to handle this innovation?
   - Who are the credible implementors—those knowledgeable about the technology, applications, users, and uses?
   - Must top management play an active role to guarantee success?
   - Where are the likely sources of resistance? What has to be done to reduce them?

Although an incomplete list, these questions at least suggest the range of issues implementors of VDTs must handle, and thus the knowledge base they need.

A KNOWLEDGE BASE FOR IMPLEMENTING VDTS

The articles in this book define a knowledge base for designing VDTs, including cognitive psychology, ergonomics, and the principles of human engineering. No designers ignorant of such basic material can be considered qualified.

Innovations come into an organization through:
- "gatekeepers," who provide a link between the suppliers and potential users of new technology (Allen, 1977)
- innovators who are often loners
- "early adopters," influential figures whose acceptance gives the innovation visibility and credibility

Successful technological innovation is driven by "demand-pull," not "technology-push" (Von Hippel, 1979).

Managers assess innovations in terms of value and felt need, not formal cost-benefit analysis (Keen, 1981).

Other References
Rogers and Shoemaker, 1971; Utterbach, 1974.

Figure A–5. Dynamics of innovation.

Similarly, the implicit argument of this article is that anyone involved in the application of VDTs must be qualified in the organizational as well as technical aspects of implementation.

There are three main components to such a knowledge base: the dynamics of change, the impact of information technology on work, and organizational information processing. The first component has been the main topic of this article. I have highlighted only a few aspects of a broad subject: the basic dynamics of technical change and of facilitating change. These should be supplemented with the research on how innovations come into organizations (Fig. A–5) and on participative design and user involvement (Appendix, section III). The references in sections I and III of the Appendix and the references for Figures A–4 and A–5 can serve as an introduction to the literature on managing technical change.

The second component—the relationship between information technology and work—is a fast-growing area of study, especially in Scandinavia where researchers pay more attention to these issues because their political, legal, and social structures make discussion of them a central policy concern (Braudel, 1982 and 1983). Section IV of the Appendix lists useful U.S. and European references.

Those who focus on the negative impacts of information technology in general, and VDTs in particular, differ markedly from the optimists in that they stress the past rather than what is new. They argue that societies are more complex and that the pace of cultural change is slower than advocates of VDTs realize. They ask us to identify the historical forces that have shaped the present before we guess at the future. Zuboff (1982) makes the telling point that if indeed VDTs represent a new industrial revolution, it may be helpful to examine what happened in the last one. Stabell (1982), an optimist rather than a pessimist like Zuboff, also criticizes the focus on newness. Just because five-year-old descriptions of technology may be dated, that does not mean that fifty-year-old descriptions of its impact are irrelevant. The proponents of Office Technology look at the Office of the Future; they should look at the Office of the Past.

The last component is the most far-reaching for VDTs. It incorporates much from the other two components. They emphasize the points where people and VDTs actually meet, such as individual jobs, development projects, and the physical workplace; the last component is at a higher, more abstract level. It concerns the decisions to introduce VDTs to the workplace. It involves the issue of strategic change, especially the politics of change (Appendix, section V) and organizational design.

This last component has not been well treated in implementation studies. Tactical models of change do not generally look at the organization as a whole. If VDTs become as widely used across the organization as their designers intend and expect, they will provide access to the information and services that constitute the main mechanisms for planning, control, communication, inquiry, and reporting. In effect, they will define the very structure of the organization.

In general, technicians view organizations as tightly coupled hierarchies, in which information flows smoothly up and down. Theirs is almost a military model, with generals at the top and privates at the bottom. This, however, is an incomplete and generally inaccurate model of the organization. Much literature presents alternative views:

1. **The political model:** An organization is a collection of coalitions and units of shared or competing values, goals, and commitments. Negotiations are the major currency of political life, and the bottom and middle of this pluralistic society often has surprising power to resist directives from the top. This model has much to offer students of information technology implementation.

2. **Weick's model of "loosely coupled systems":** Far from being a hierarchy of tightly bound links, complex organizations are often a set of relatively independent units loosely coupled to each other. Weick uses the university as a model: the graduate schools of education and management may be parts of the university, but their links to each other are loose. Such a structure has several advantages. Each independent unit is freer to adapt to its special situation and is buffered from disasters in the others (Weick, 1969). Loose coupling means that information does not always flow directly or smoothly. Efforts to increase coupling via VDTs may be ineffectual or even undesirable.

3. **March's "garbage can" model:** A substantial randomness exists in organizations: solutions looking for problems, partial knowledge, incomplete and lost information, and problems that do not get

resolved. Such a view is far from the technician's idea of a tight hierarchy. Nothing is neat and tidy. If such is the case, efforts by computer specialists to "rationalize" information flows are likely to fail.

Each of these models implies different opportunities and problems for VDTs. The political model highlights the second-order consequences of alterations in information ownership, control, and access. In the "garbage can" and "loose-coupling" frameworks, VDTs may try to be coupling mechanisms, but they are unlikely to work unless they fit into the organizational structure and process. Section VI in the Appendix provides a list of key readings relevant to strategic implementation of VDTs.

SUMMARY

Earlier in this chapter, I summarized the experiences of data processing that reveal the unanticipated organizational consequences of technical innovations. Implementors must recognize that VDTs represent a disturbance to the fabric of the organization. Their introduction can threaten its social and political culture. VDTs create ambiguity and uncertainty, and they change the experience of work. They can redefine the long-term structure of the organization. However, all these forces can be predicted and analyzed and, in most situations, effective strategies can be devised in terms of design trade-offs, management, education, and implementation. Accomplishing this depends upon recognizing "users" as real people in real settings. It requires a combination of a cognitive science for design and an organizational science for implementation. This book presents that knowledge base. With this knowledge, implementors of VDT-based systems can anticipate and manage the consequences of change.

In DP and Management Science, we have seen too many unnecessary failures of sound technical designs. Those failures are a warning signal for implementors of VDTs. VDTs represent a flexible, reliable, and cost-effective technology with a growing range of proven applications and software. Improvements in VDT technology will continue, especially in terms of integration of tools. We can expect rapid, continued progress in this area. Implementation technology must keep pace with the ongoing revolution in information technology.

This brief article only provides a taste of the fascinating, complex, and critically important organizational side of the introduction of VDTs. Only the combination of good technology and effective management of change will proliferate VDTs across the office landscape and make them beneficial to the organization and the worker. Change is the issue; managing change is the key to people and computers getting along with each other.

APPENDIX

Section I: Implementation Studies

Ackoff (1960)

Identifies power as a key determinant of implementation success. Projects that lack a sponsor are often obstructed by others' ambitions and self-interest.

Ackoff (1967)

Designers assume managers know what information they need and will use it if it is made available. Uncovering their "needs" requires a systematic analysis of the organizational decision process.

Alter (1976)

Identifies factors, especially lack of involvement, that increase resistance to new systems. Highlights the value side of cost-benefit analysis.

Argyris (1971)

Management information systems (MIS) specialists are seen as a threat by managers, and lack interpersonal skills. Both sides talk in rational terms, and react in emotional terms.

Bean and Radnor (1979)

Identifies the need for translators and liaisons to bridge the culture gap between builders and users.

Churchman and Scheinblatt (1965)

Establishes lack of "mutual understanding" as a main cause of implementation problems. Later studies of differences in the way builders and users think, the role of the implementer, and the personal characteristics of technical specialists have reinforced this finding.

Grayson (1978)

Managers and management scientists are two separate cultures with minimal understanding of each other. We need to train people to have complementary technical and organizational knowledge.

Greenberger, Crenson, and Crissey (1976)

Case studies of the slow, complex, and rarely effectual process of implementing analytic models for public sector policy making. Concludes that the credibility of and trust in the spokesperson for the model is more important than the technical model itself in determining success. Managers validate the analyst, not the analysis.

Laudon (1974)

Detailed case studies that clearly demonstrate the political impact of redistributing information: "the process of technological innovation thus appears as a political process characterized by conflict and compromise among the parties involved."

Lucas and Plimpton (1975)

One of the first studies to apply the influential Kolb-Frohman model of managing change to explain the dynamics of unsuccessful and successful implementation. (See Fig. A–1.)

Mumford and Ward (1968)

Demonstrates the degree of impact and often disruption DP has on work units and how poorly these are anticipated and resolved. Mumford continues to be a leader in developing approaches to participative design.

Pettigrew (1976)

A study of the intensely political maneuvers involved in what seem to be purely technical choices; emphasizes the way programmers use their specialized knowledge to protect their status and maintain control.

Yin, Heald, and Vogel (1977)

An analysis of 140 case studies of public sector implementation; identifies local expertise, involvement, and management critical to the success of centrally-directed innovations. Views implementation as a bottom-up process dominated by pluralism.

Section II: Statements of Concern about the Impact of VDTs

The following quotations are Editorial Board Statements of Concern from *Office Technology and People* (1982, pp. 13–70).

Niels Bjorn-Andersen

"Short-term tactical productivity gains take priority over long-term strategic development."

"Quantitative evaluation takes precedence over qualitative. Employee technology instead of being exploited by it."

Franz Edelman

"The big question is: Will we again find ourselves in a cart-before-the-horse situation through undue and lopsided emphasis on technology, at the expense of end-user functionality?"

"At the moment the signs are mixed and the risk of having to repeat history is considerable."

W. Russell Ellis

"The possibilities for tight monitoring of employee performance afforded by recent office technology is, perhaps, the joy of management and the bane of classified personnel. But why must performance/productivity monitoring remain a hierarchically arranged enterprise?"

Martin C.J. Elton

"Experience with management information systems, telecommunication systems, and so on constantly reminds us that the process of implementation is much harder than is expected. It is as much a matter of art as one of science, and it is highly dependent on such qualities as leadership and trust."

"In the past, there has been too much thought about how people can be used inexpensively to support the smooth functioning of valuable machines."

Ida R. Hoos

"We are dealing with the same old Faustian bargain. Those with positive hopes for office technology stress efficiency, more work done better and faster with less human interference."

"But nowhere, except in the fanciful figuring of technological optimists, do these benefits show. Costs of processing paper have grown exponentially; productivity, however defined, is a national crisis. Coping with unresponsive technical systems is a national pastime. (Try correcting a credit card transaction.) By way of reply to the question as to whether the positive or the negative aspects of office technology will 'win,' I can only echo the words of the croupier at the gaming table, 'Les jeux sont faits.' "

"Implementors and sellers of office technology, marching to the only drum beat they can hear (or even heed appropriately, given the social environment in which they must operate), cannot be expected to respond sensibly to any of the issues; we are all guided by the lantern we carry in our hands and though we know that it makes the darkness darker, that knowledge seldom changes our course. Sellers and implementors have a personal stake in the acceptance and adoption of their services."

"There will be more applications. Changes in organizations will certainly continue; the handwriting was on the wall years ago; we are still learning its message. Like fish swimming in the sea, we will not be able to recognize the quality of wetness. Information technology will have dictated the paradigm. The civil liberties we are allowing to erode will have been lost and forgotten by a generation so brainwashed or cowed as to relinquish them as not being cost-effective."

"The issues for research range from the micro to the macro, from the personal to the social. They embrace a multitude of disciplines, among which the sociological, philosophical, psychological, and physiological demand just as much respect as the economic and technical."

Robert Johansen

"Evaluations of the use of new office systems over the last few years have shown that the 'culture' of an office must be understood in order to determine the optimum operation of a new system. The techniques of anthropology are perhaps the most relevant to such an inquiry, but very few persons involved with the implementation of new office systems have any training in anthropology."

Margrethe H. Olson

"Major productivity improvements through office automation have not occurred, however, for several reasons. We do not really understand how an office works except in a very superficial way."

Roger Pye

"The technology has always attracted attention; it is exciting, always changing and advancing at a fascinating rate. But people are another matter. They are slow, reactionary, and have strange superstitions concerning the way in which they work. The most exciting technology may get bogged down once it comes into contact with the people who operate or in other ways use it. This is the picture that can easily be put together from articles and papers on office technology. The picture is not usually presented in such blatant terms, but can be inferred from the juxtaposition of pieces on the capabilities of the latest technology and on trade unions' attitudes to visual display units. It is a picture which results from the separate consideration of the two components of what is ultimately a single system; technology and people. To consider one without the other is to lay open the conditions for failure and irritation."

James P. Ware

"This is a call to battle. I detest phe phrase 'Office Automation.' And I think it is time for us who care about building organizations that are both effective and humane to get back in control of the movement to improve office productivity. Because if we do not assert ourselves, the technologists, who are already well on the way to dominating this field, will certainly keep on trying to automate office and managerial work in the same blundering way they have attacked many data processing tasks for the past twenty years."

"The need is not for research but for teaching—for transmittance of what we already know about how to manage individual and organizational change."

Eleanor Herasimchuk Wynn

"Compared to the development and dissemination of technology, the development and dissemination of related social thought is extremely slow. The problem is not that the social science disciplines lack the tools and perspective required for the task, but that they have severe distribution problems. There is too little connection between the communities of people who design technology and those who devote themselves to studying society."

Shoshanah Zuboff

"If information technology is to be considered the technological infrastructure of the post-industrial society, its meaning must be located in terms of four key dimensions: zed.history of work, the nature of occupational life, the structure of collective behavior, and the psychological experience of productive activity."

"When work is abstracted its meaning tends to become thin."

Section III: Participative Design

The following articles appear in Bjorn-Andersen (1980) and include useful follow-on references:

Docherty, P.   User Participation in and Influence on Systems Design in Norway and Sweden.

Hedberg, B.   Using Computerized Systems to Design Better Organizations and Jobs.

"Socio-technical designing, on its own, is a dead end. It does not break the vicious circle in which people are replaced by computers, jobs are degraded, and powers are centralized."

"Organizational and individual needs must be the starting point for systems development. The problems must be defined from both managers' and workers' perspectives. Participative designing must replace designing by specialists. Socio-technical designs must be supported by changing values and rewards, and by changes in the power structures."

Mumford, E. The Participative Design of Clerical Information
Systems: Two Case Studies.
Another recommended source on participative
design is Mumford and Sackman (1975).

Section IV: Impacts of Information Technology

The writers cited below challenge many of the explicit and implicit assumptions of designers of VDTs. Their papers are theoretically and empirically sound, and—except for Brief's—backed up by many references and examples. The case they make is a very strong one. Although designers may not agree with it, their response should be informed disagreement.

Briefs (1980)
Presents a case for "deliberate social action" by workers and unions.

Gregory and Nussbaum (1982)
Review of surveys, case studies, claims and intentions about the impact of VDTs.

Zuboff (1982 b)
"Managers should heed the resistance, however, because it is telling them something about the quality of changes that are taking place [as a result of introducing VDTs]." Zuboff's term and frameworks for analyzing the psychology of computer-mediated work are becoming a reference point for assessing office technology.

Section V: Political Science Studies of Implementation

Bardach (1977)
Identifies "counter implementation," or games people play to prevent implementation.

Laudon (1975); Pettigrew (1976); and Greenberger et al. (1976)
Three books that present detailed case studies of the highly political nature of the implementation of information technology.

Pressman and Wildavsky (1973)
A classic justification of pluralism and a challenge to just about every assumption of the rationalist, technical tradition and of cost-benefit approaches. See also Wildavsky (1974).

Section VI: Organizational Literature Relevant to the Application of VDTs

Cyert and March (1963)
This remains the classic presentation of the Carnegie School's paradigms of decision making that have strongly influenced efforts to relate information technology to organizational processes.

Darnbusch and Scott (1975)

Highly relevant to VDT applications. Looks at the link between information and control; having information by which to evaluate performance is equivalent to having authority. Nurses dislike being evaluated through "objective," impersonal indicators; secretaries do, too (e.g. lines per hour, errors), and managers will as well as VDTs are used more and more to monitor, count, and even review their quality and quantity of work.

Galbraith (1977)

Defines the organization as an information-processing system and looks at ways to improve hierarchical and lateral coupling. A useful framework for thinking about where and how to apply VDTs to improve organizational information flows.

March and Olsen (1976)

An even more dynamic model than Weick's—the organization as "a garbage can."

Strauss (1978)

Views organizational decision-making and information flows as basically a process of negotiation and exchange in which information is a personal resource, not necessarily a public asset.

Weick (1969)

"Loose-coupling" in organizing (note "organizing," not "organizations"). Weick's model is a dynamic view rather than the static one embodied in organization charts. Emphasizes the limited and sometimes undesirable role of formal information systems as a coupling device.

NOTES

1. The terms "unfreezing" and "refreezing" were first used by Schein (1961) to explain the dynamics of brainwashing. The interrogator disrupts the stable sense of identity and personal reference in order to create a *need* to change; the only direction of change is that allowed by the interrogator. "Refreezing" institutionalizes the new personality through, for example, public statements of reformation and commitments to the new cause.

2. Several of the following illustrations come from unpublished case studies. The bibliography lists a number of published sources that address many aspects of the politics of information and information technology, notably Laudon (1974), Bardach (1977), and Pettigrew (1976).

REFERENCES

Ackoff, R. L. 1960. Unsuccessful case studies and why. *Operations Research* 8:259–63.

———. 1967. Management misinformation systems. *Management Science* 14:B147–56.

Allen T. J. 1977. *Managing the flow of technology.* Cambridge, Mass: M.I.T. Press.

Alter S. A. 1976. How effective managers use information systems. *Harvard Business Review* November 1976.

Argyris C. 1971. Management information systems: the challenge to rationality and emotionality. *Management Science* 17:B275–92.

Bardach E. 1977. *The implementation game: what happens when a bill becomes law.* Cambridge, Mass.: MIT Press.

Bean, A. S., and Radnor, M. 1979. The role of intermediaries in the implementation of management science. In *The Implementation of Management Science.* Amsterdam: North-Holland.

Bjorn-Andersen, N. 1980. *The human side of information processing.* Amsterdam: North-Holland.

Braudel, F. 1982 and 1983. *The Structures of Everyday Life*, vols. 1 and 2, New York: Harper and Row.

Briefs, V. 1980. The impact of computerization on the working class and the role of trade unions. In Bjorn-Andersen (1980).

Churchman, C. and Scheinblatt, A. H. 1965. The researcher and the manager: a dialectic of implementation. *Management Science* 11:B69–87.

Cyert, R. M., and March, J. A. 1963. *A behavioral theory of the firm.* Englewood Cliffs, N.J.: Prentice-Hall.

Darnbusch, S., and Scott, W. R. 1975. *Evaluation and the exercise of authority.* San Francisco: Jossey-Bass.

Docherty, P. 1980. User participation in and influence on systems design in Norway and Sweden in the light of union involvement, new legislation, and joint agreements. In Bjorn-Andersen (1980).

Galbraith, J. 1977. *Organizational Design.* Reading, Mass.: Addison-Wesley.

Grayson, D. J. 1978. Management science and business practice. *Harvard Business Review.* July-August 1978.

Greenberger, M. M.; Crenson, M. A.; and Crissey, B. L. 1976. Models in the policy process. New York: Russell Sage Foundation.

Gregory, J., and Nussbaum, K. 1982. Race against time: automation of the office. *Office Technology and People* 1:nos. 2 and 3:197–236.

Hedberg, B. 1980. Using computerized information systems to design better organizations and jobs. In Bjorn-Andersen (1980).

Keen, P. G. W. 1981. Information systems and organizational change. *Communications of the ACM*. January 1981.

———. 1981a. Value analysis: justifying decision support systems. *MIS Quarterly*. Spring 1981.

———. 1981b. Telecommunications and business policy. MIT Center for Information Systems Research, paper no. 81. September 1981.

———. (ed.). 1981c. *Office technology and people*. Editorial Board Statements of Concern, 1:13-70.

———. 1982. Managing information technology: authority and accountability. Proceedings of the 35th National Conference on the Advancement of Research. Arkansas, October 1982. Revised version available from author (1983).

King, J. L., and Kraemer, K. L. 1981. Cost as a social impact of computing. In *Telecommunications and Productivity*, ed. M. L. Moss. Reading, Mass.: Addison-Wesley.

Kolb, D. A., and Frohman, A. L. 1970. An organization development approach to consulting. *Sloan Management Review* 12. 1:51-56.

Laudon, K. C. 1974. *Computers and bureaucratic reform*. New York: Wiley.

Leavitt, H. J. 1964. Applied organization change in industry: structural, technical and human approaches. In *New Perspectives in Organization Research*, ed. W. W. Cooper, H. J. Leavitt, and M. W. Shelley II, pp. 53–71. New York:Wiley.

Lewin, K. 1952. Group decision and social change. In *Readings in Social Psychology*, ed. Newcomb and Hartley. New York: Henry Holt and Co.

Lucas, H. C., Jr., 1975. *Why information systems fail*. New York: Columbia University Press.

Lucas, H. C., Jr. and Plimpton, R. B. 1972. Technological consulting in a grass roots, action oriented organization. *Sloan Management Review* 14. 1:17-36.

March, J. A., and Olsen, J. P. 1976. *Ambiguity and choice in organizations*. Bergen: Universitets forlaget.

Mumford, E. 1980. The participative design of clerical information systems: two case studies. In Bjorn-Andersen (1980).

Mumford E., and Ward, T. B. 1968. *Computers: planning for people*. London: Batsford.

Mumford, E., and Sackman, H., eds. 1975. *Human choice and computers*. Amsterdam: North-Holland.

Nolan, R. L. 1982. *Managing the data resource function*. St. Paul, Minn.: West.

Pettigrew, A. 1976. *The politics of organizational decision making*. London: Tavistock.

Pressman, J. L., and Wildavsky, A. 1973. *The implementation game.* Berkeley: University of California Press.

Rogers, E., and Shoemaker, F. 1971. *Communication of innovations: a cross-cultural approach.* New York: Free Press.

Schein, E. H. 1961. Management development as a process of influence. *Industrial Management Review* 2.2:59–77.

————. 1969. *Process consultation: its role in organizational development.* Reading, Mass.: Addison-Wesley.

Schultz, R. L., and Slevin, D. P., eds. 1975. *Implementing operations research/management science.* New York: American Elsevier.

Stabell, C. B. 1982. A microeconomic framework for empirical research. *Office Technology and People* 1:91–106.

Strauss, A. 1978. *Negotiations.* San Francisco: Jossey-Bass.

Utterbach, J. M. 1974. Innovation in industry and the diffusion of technology. *Science* February 1974.

Von Hippel, E. 1976. The dominant role of users in the scientific instrument innovation process. *Research Policy* July 1976.

Weick, K. E. 1969. *The social psychology of organizing.* Reading, Mass.: Addison-Wesley.

Wildavsky, A. 1974. *Politics of the budgetary process.* Boston: Little, Brown.

Yin, R. K.; Heald, K. A.; and Vogel, M. E. 1977. *Tinkering with the system: technological innovations in state and local services.* Lexington, Mass.: D.C. Heath, Lexington Books.

Zuboff, S. 1982a. Computer-mediated work: the emerging managerial challenge. *Office Technology and People* 1:237-44.

————. 1982b. New worlds of computer-mediated work. *Harvard Business Review* September-October 1982.

THE CONCEPT OF USABILITY

Brian Shackel

"It is not the utility, but the useability of a thing which is in question."

Thomas De Quincey (1842, p. 730)

INTRODUCTION

Origins

The concept of utility and usefulness has ample history and lineage back to Greek and Roman times; indeed the Latin *utilis* and *utilitas* are adjective and noun with identical meaning to the modern *useful* and *utility*. But according to the *Oxford English Dictionary*, the first use of the word *usability* does not occur until 1842, in the above reference to De Quincey. Could any quotation be more fortunate and apposite?

It seems reasonable to suggest that the first industrial revolution created the concept of usability, or rather its underlying necessity, by the complexity and growing pace of technological change. This change has caused ever greater distance in time and space between designers and users, and so inevitably has resulted in the making of products which may be useful but are certainly not usable.

Modern technology and modern society are even more complex, further divorcing designers and users. The problem has since been recognized and corrective actions taken, and out of all this there has emerged a new discipline— the discipline and technology of Human Factors, or Ergonomics. Ergonomics has developed because many machines and systems are not easy to use and can be made more usable by the judicious application of knowledge from the human sciences, especially psychology. As a result, there is real concern to achieve ease of use; "user-friendly" has become a buzzword for salespeople; and the important criterion for design is now usability.

Of course, everyone seems to know what usability means; that is, until its recognition as a criterion implies evaluation, requiring measurement and operational definition. Then, as with terms such as *fatigue, work*, and *workload*—widely used but hard to define when applied to human situations— attention must be focused upon what the concept of usability actually means.

Context

The definition, content, and consequences of the concept of usability are of major importance for the whole field of Human Factors (Ergonomics). In this discourse, the subject of usability will be considered within the context and framework of interactive human-computer systems. The principal point of reference within this context will be the Visual Display Terminal (VDT) as the key device which most often provides the interactive interface between human and computer.

In one human generation of 30 years, this new technology of computing has progressed from an esoteric specialism for very few experts to a potential tool for very many ordinary people. With each successive computer generation of 7 to 10 years, the degree of specialized knowledge required by the user has decreased. But even today most people still believe that only "computer experts" can use computers usefully, and even the experts complain about usage problems (Gilb, 1980).

It is now 23 years since Licklider (1960) coined the term "man-computer symbiosis" to explain the anticipated very close cooperation between man and computer. Ten years later De Greene (1970, p. 291) said, "Licklider's paper has stimulated much thought and research, but we are still many years from operable, widespread man-computer symbiotic systems, mainly because of deficiencies in our understanding of psychological processes." De Greene's words are still valid today in 1983.

However, this does not mean that there has been no progress. Indeed, in view of the dearth of funding for Human Factors (compared with the computer industry), the growth of useful work has been remarkable in the last 12 years. Moreover, for our present context the logical starting date for references and review is appropriately marked 13 years ago by a noteworthy IBM report on human-ease-of-use criteria (Miller, 1971).

Aim

This chapter aims to provide a conceptual framework for understanding usability. The next three chapters will consider interface design; human performance using computer terminals; and approaches to evaluation, trade-offs, and implementation of usability goals in practical designs.

Although it draws extensively upon the relevant work of the last 11 years, this chapter does not intend to be a literature review. That need has been fully satisfied for various parts of the field by, among others, Bennett (1972), Martin (1973), Edwards and Lees (1972, 1974), Rouse (1975, 1977), Miller and Thomas (1977), Shackel (1979a), Gaines (1981), Ramsey et al. (1978), and Ramsey and Atwood (1979).

Instead, here we shall consider and speculate upon the importance of usability, meaning and definition, the components of usability, and the vital importance of usability of the VDT to the usage and acceptance of the whole computer system.

THE IMPORTANCE OF USABILITY

Is There Really a Problem?

In the last 10 years, the computer industry has succeeded both in growing at a phenomenal rate and in providing users with faster, bigger, cheaper computers. So what is the problem? The problem, briefly, is that the market and the users are both changing very rapidly. The market is becoming much more selective, partly as a result of poor usability experiences. The users are no longer primarily computer professionals, but are mostly *discretionary* users (see the next paragraph). As a result, the designers are no nonger typical of or equivalent to users; however, the designers do not realize how unique and, therefore, unrepresentative they are. Moreover, as Martin and Parker (1971) said, "No matter how hard he tries, a designer cannot really believe that people will be unable to use his system."

Indeed, in a sense, the industry is at real risk just because of its success, which tends to breed complacency and inertia. As Bennett (1979) has pointed out:

> For much of the history of computers, the development of products has been technology-driven. It has been up to the marketing people to put together a business case for a product that would make use of each new invention from the laboratory. The resulting product was typically placed in a working environment, the data processing installation, where it was used by computer professionals. In addition to their normal human ability to adapt, these people tended to be quite clever and to thrive on technical challenge. Thus it was cost-effective and good business to concentrate on providing high-function products and to rely on the gifted, dedicated users to come up with clever ways to make full use of the function. Now industry is interested in broadening its market by developing products which are attractive to less dedicated users. These *discretionary* users demand function and price, but they are also sensitive to usability. Typically they interact with computers to accomplish task results which can be accomplished in other ways (text editing, library search). If the usability of the computer terminal interface is not satisfactory, the task will be delegated, done another way, or not done at all.

The net result of such a failure in usability is likely to be a dissatisfied customer and no sale next time.

Usability Failures

Many specific studies of usability failures can be cited. For example, from a survey of 320 VDT workplaces, Stewart (1981) has recently reported: poor character spacing on the screen for 67% of the cases; poor character shape for 33%; poor image stability for 43%, and many other problems. If there are so many faults with straightforward hardware matters, are we mistaken to presume as many usability problems with documentation and software? While no similar analysis of software usability has been made, several authors have discussed various types of difficulties which have been found; e.g., Miller and Thomas (1977); Ramsey and Atwood (1979); Gaines (1981).

As a minor illustration at the simplest level, new users (with no great attraction to computers) are not only deprived of necessary diagnostic information but often feel rejected and insulted by such error messages as: "improper syntax" (meaning bad language—rude words?); or "illegal entry" (a criminal offence in most countries), often followed by the invitation "try again"! Some people become so disenchanted with these and other basic software difficulties that they never try again.

In an extensive survey, Eason et al. (1974) categorized responses by users to inadequate systems. Upon that work and another paper by Stewart (1976a), Ramsey and Atwood (1979) based a table summarizing such responses from which Figure B–1 is derived. These general findings, combined with the widespread desire of managers and others to control their own information, and the growing availability of cheap but powerful mini- and micro-computers, help to explain the considerable migration and growing discrimination of the market.

Market Value of Usability

One consequence of the rapid growth in the computer industry—especially with marked reduction in hardware costs, increased competition, and economic recession over the last few years—has been to take the industry into a buyer's market. The buyer and the user have become much more critical and demanding. For example, from its survey of users and user requirements, the British Computer Society (1978) reported that there is a general sense of exasperation among users, and gave examples of the numerous ways in which users believe that suppliers are failing to respond adequately and sensitively to their needs. For commercial reasons alone, it is worthwhile to spend time and money on market research about users. But what is the market and who are the users?

Many market forecasts have predicted further large increases in the production of mini- and micro-computers and especially in worldwide produc-

Response	Meaning	Comments
Disuse	100% reliance on and use of other information sources.	Needs other sources and (senior) discretionary users.
Misuse	"Bending the rules" to short-cut difficulties.	Needs "know-how." May damage system integrity.
Partial use	Use of only a limited subset of system capabilities.	Users may not learn to use the most relevant facilities.
Distant use	Use delegated to an operator.	Typical response of managers to bad usability.
Task modification	Changing the task to match capabilities of system.	Typical for rigid tools and unstructured problems.
Compensatory user activity	Compensation for system inadequacies by additional user actions.	Typical with users of low discretion, such as clerks.
Direct programming	Programming by user to make system suit needs.	Computer-sophisticated user, e.g., scientist or engineer.
Frustration and apathy	Response of user when above actions are inadequate or unsatisfactory.	Involves lack of user acceptance, high error rates, poor performance.

Figure B–1. Typical user responses to inadequate systems. (Derived from Ramsey and Atwood, 1979, based on Eason et al., 1974.)

tion of intelligent terminals. Market forecasts, however, are not real sales. If these growth projections are to be realized, there must be major increases in personal, domestic, and business systems and networks. But this growth will not occur unless the machines are acceptable to the users. For example, Dolotta (1976) predicted a growth in the number and variety of computer terminals, expected relatively more growth in display rather than typewriter terminals, and saw costs approaching that of a color television. Dolotta qualified the findings with one prerequisite: "software which is specifically tailored to make... terminals usable by (and useful to)... users."

However, to achieve the predicted growth in terminals the different needs of new users must be satisfied. Earlier users were committed to using computers either because of personal interest or job requirements. But potential new users are such people as managers, physicians, lawyers, and scientists who are committed to their task but not at all to the computer. They will only use computers if they are appropriate, useful, and usable.

So the market now contains important new categories of users. Moreover, some predict that "the *end user* will be the primary future acquirer of equipment and a major stimulus overall" to help the industry out of the present economic difficulties (Gartner, 1981). To respond to this new market presents a fundamental challenge to the system designer, involving a major reorientation in thinking. Designers must see the user as the center of the computer system instead of as a mere peripheral. This simple concept, easy to state but harder to achieve, is often expounded by ergonomists and human factors specialists, such as Nicholls (1979):

> In spite of changes in the nature of computing, remnants of old thinking remain with us. In former days, when the CPU was at the heart of a system, designers naturally talked of 'terminals' and 'peripherals.' I suspect it was in this period that people began to use the term 'end user.' The unconscious symbolism is both a symptom and a cause; the 'end' user at the 'terminal' was often the last person to be considered in the design of the system. It is important to develop a new view of computing systems, and to look at the user in a different light ... taking this view of computing, the centre of a system is the user.

So, if we are to improve the usability of interactive computer systems, then the former orientation of designers must be completely reversed. "The last shall be first"; designing must start with the end user. Therefore, because the VDT is the first part of the computer system (and quite often the *only* part) in contact with the user, it should be the first and salient unit in the whole design program. It is very likely that the VDT's poor usability will, in today's market place, prevent the sale of an otherwise functionally sound computer system.

Finally, the cost-benefit value of changing the orientation and concentrating centrally upon the human user (and therefore also upon the VDT) has been well illustrated by Gilb and by Doherty. Gilb (1980) projected from data by Phister (1976) to estimate that by the early 1980s the total personnel costs in data processing departments would be more than six times the cost of the hardware; in the rest of his paper he illustrates the need and the substantial pay-off in making computers more "humanized." Doherty (1979) presented similar data from IBM experience to conclude, "People costs are already very much greater than machine costs for over 95% of the man-made machine interactions. Furthermore, these two costs are diverging and, I believe, will continue to do so. Actions to reduce the human cost and simplify the human interface to computers will have the greatest impact on growth." Thus, both authors emphasize the direct market value of designing usability into systems.

MEANING AND DEFINITION

General Framework

Successful system design for usability will then, of course, require considerable attention to the user. However, the user must not be considered in isolation from other aspects of the situation—that would only perpetuate in reverse the all too common past fault of considering the technological tool in isolation from the user. Good system design depends upon solving the dynamic interacting needs of the four principal components of any system situation: user, task, tool, and environment (see Figs. B–2 and B–3). Likewise, usability depends upon the dynamic interplay of these four components (this framework is based upon earlier similar approaches by Bennett, 1972, 1979; and Eason, 1976).

The importance of the interactions between each of these four parts is gradually being recognized, but there are still many ways to overlook important aspects—sometimes with serious consequences. For example, engineering designers usually recognize the direct interaction between tool and environment, so equipment will usually be designed to fit the range of environmental temperatures. But similar interaction between tool and environment in

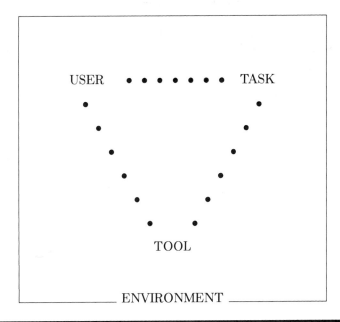

Figure B–2.   The four principal components in a human-machine system.

Figure B–3. Interactions between the four principal components. These joint authors as USERS are revising a paper (TASK) for an electronic journal using a computer and VDT (TOOL) in the ENVIRONMENT of a research group.

human or cultural terms is often overlooked. So, for example, a point-of-sale cash terminal for world-wide usage, designed with storage for currency notes the size of U.S. dollars only, will be a poor solution.

With this basic framework of the four principal components in a system in mind, we can now consider some meanings and definitions of terms.

Useful versus Usable

Perhaps not surprisingly, the dictionary does not help us greatly because the differentiation between these two concepts is not very clear. Both useful and usable have the definition "suitable for use." The distinction between them must be specified: "useful" means advantageous, profitable, fit for some desirable end, or having (latent) power to satisfy human wants; "usable" means able to be used, applicable to a purpose (i.e., the latent power to satisfy human wants can be harnessed).

Utility

So utility means usefulness or power to satisfy human wants. The utility, or usefulness, of a human-machine system will depend upon how well it fulfills its purposes and functions within the specified range of environments for which it was designed, and in relation to an assembly of cost factors.

Thus the working definition proposed for the utility of a system or equipment is "the capability in machine functional terms to fulfill the specified range of tasks within the specified range of environmental scenarios."

The usage of *utility* here, to mean the functional capability of the machine features, is equivalent in meaning to the word *functionality*, e.g., as used by Roberts (1979). However, *utility* will continue to be the term used here. This is different from the usage of *utility* to mean the final output from a "multi-attribute utility" assessment exercise, but for that meaning it may well be more appropriate to use the term *worth*, as do Hays et al. (1975). The terms *utility* and *usability* remain a contrasting pair to distinguish these two basic concepts with which we are concerned in this chapter.

Usability

With the framework of the four principal components in mind, we can now turn to the meaning of usability. Usability depends (a) upon the design of the tool (the VDT and the computer system) in relation to the users, the task, and the environments, and (b) upon the success of the user support provided (training, manuals, and other job aids such as online and offline "help" facilities). Usability for individual users will be judged (a) by subjective assessment of ease of use and (b) by objective performance measures of effectiveness in using the tool.

Therefore, for a tool to be claimed as usable, it must be proved to enable some required percentage of the appropriate range of USERS to carry out some required percentage of the range of TASKS within some required proportion of the range of usage ENVIRONMENTS and with flexibility and robustness permitting adaptation to a wider range of tasks and environments than originally specified. This must be accomplished by users (given the *user-support* provided) within some specified time from start of user learning, and within some maximum "relearning" time for intermittent users after some specified non-usage interval. Evaluation trials will measure:

- the success rate in meeting the specified ranges of users, tasks, and environments;
- ease of use in terms of judgments (e.g., learning, using, remembering, convenience, comfort, effort, tiredness, satisfaction);
- effectiveness of use in terms of performance (e.g., time, errors, number and sequence of activities, etc.) in learning, relearning, and carrying out a representative range of operations.

From the above suggestions, it is evident that usability involves not only "ease of use" but also "efficacy" (i.e., effectiveness in terms of measures of performance). Therefore, the working definition for the usability of a system or equipment is: "the capability in human functional terms to be used *easily* (to a specified level of subjective assessment) and *effectively* (to a specified level of performance) by the specified range of users, given specified training and user support, to fulfill the specified range of tasks, within the specified range of environmental scenarios."

A convenient shortened form for the definition of usability might be "the capability to be used by humans easily and effectively."

Related Concepts: Likeability, Cost, and Acceptability

Other closely related concepts require elucidation in relation to usability. When people judge whether a tool is acceptable, they probably consider whether it is likeable and how much it costs them in addition to whether it is useful and usable.

Without stating a precise relationship between the terms, we may suggest that the relevant factors are associated in some form of trade-off paradigm such as the following in Figure B–4.

This paradigm suggests that whether or not I accept something depends upon whether I believe it sufficiently useful, usable, and likeable in relation to what it costs me. If I do not accept something, then the combination of utility, usability, and likeability are not sufficient to satisfy my wants in relation to its human and financial costs.

Stated in this way, the concepts are simple and clear. However, the process of teasing out the determinants behind all these concepts is difficult and complex, especially when we try to analyze them in any given situation. I will further pursue only the question of usability in this chapter; even there the determinants are by no means clear.

Utility: *Will it do what is needed functionally?*
   +
Usability: *Will the users actually work it successfully?*
   +
Likeability: *Will the users* feel *it is suitable?*

   MUST BE BALANCED IN A TRADE-OFF AGAINST

Cost: *What are the capital and running costs; what are the*
               social and organizational consequences?

   TO ARRIVE AT A DECISION ABOUT

Acceptability:*on balance, the possible alternative for purchase.*

Figure B–4. The paradigm of usability and related concepts.

THE COMPONENTS OF USABILITY: INTRODUCTION

The definition of *usability* has been presented above without any of the analysis supporting it. In the space available, I can provide only an illustrative discussion rather than a comprehensive review of all relevant aspects within the four principal components (user, task, tool, environment). Other comprehensive reviews of the literature, despite compression, have required 140 pages (Ramsey and Atwood, 1979) and 300 pages (Shackel, 1979a).

As soon as we try to organize the available knowledge into a clear structure, we find the need for appropriate taxonomies, both to deal more comprehensively with all four principal components and to explain each one properly. Some implicit work on taxonomy has been done in each literature review; e.g., Shackel and Shipley (1969); Miller and Thomas (1977); Ramsey and Atwood (1979) by the structural organization of the review itself. But no very satisfactory taxonomies have been proposed and explicated. Shackel (1969) tried to define a first level of subdivisions and to relate them to various computer applications, but this was more an expository structure than a taxonomy. Shackel (1979a) and Ramsey and Atwood (1979) tried to classify the work so that it also provides the form and sequence of a design guide. Shackel (1979a) based his upon the checklist for the processes of "work station analysis" (Shackel, 1974, Chapter 2) already proposed for equipment design in general (see Appendix). Ramsey and Atwood (1979) structured their review directly to the sequence of their suggested design guide topics (see Fig. B–5).

However, far too little work has been done to develop the required taxonomies. The problem is that a taxonomic approach assumes, indeed needs for simplicity, a unidimensional or two-dimensional field with minimal interactions. As always with human activities, however, the situation is complex and multidimensional with many, probably nonlinear, interactions. Most research tends to deal with a very limited sample from the wide range of possible combinations of human characteristics and capabilities, tasks, types of computer application, and environmental scenarios.

With this difficulty in mind, we shall first consider each of the four principal components and then return to this problem of interactions. Each component needs to be considered fully under three major headings:

1. Basic characteristics
2. Specific factors regarding human-computer systems and usability
3. Interaction issues in relation to the three other components

However, this structure cannot be followed rigorously due to space limitations. Instead, we shall discuss basic characteristics briefly along with some usability-related aspects for each component, and then later discuss interactions as a separate topic.

Users:
  –their behavior in general
  –how to determine the properties of a particular user population
  –the implications of those properties for the interactive sysem
Tasks:
  –what tasks users perform
  –how to determine tasks involved in an application
Requirements analysis:
  –how to analyze information requirements
  –how to select appropriate types of problem-solving, clerical and
    support aids
  –allocation of basic tasks to user or computer
  –modeling of user-system interactions
  –evaluation of basic design
Interactive dialogue:
  –properties of different dialogue types
  –selection of appropriate dialogue type(s)
  –detailed design of command language, system access structures,
    tutorial aids, etc.
Output devices and techniques:
  –properties of display devices
  –implications of dialogue method for display device selection
  –selection or design of display device(s)
  detailed display design, formatting, coding techniques, etc.
Input devices and techniques:
  –properties of input devices
  –implications of dialogue methods for input device selection
  –selection or design of input device(s)
Evaluation of system performance:
  –use of subjective evaluations, objective performance measures

Figure B–5.   Possible section topics for a design guide (Figure 1 from
    Ramsey and Atwood, 1979).

USABILITY COMPONENTS: 1. THE USER

The User Defined

In discussing the user in the singular we are in danger of making a serious
error. There is not one user, but many different types and levels of user.
Indeed, in one sense, because each person sees him or herself as a unique
individual, the user defies definition. However, intuition and research have
indicated that one may reasonably group users together and design for them,

Computer 'Professionals'
- system analysts
- programmers
- hardware designers
- sales representatives

Non-'Professionals'
- managers
- secretaries, office staff, etc.
- specialists (e.g., in the professions)
- consumers and the public
- casual (inexperienced/infrequent users)

Figure B–6.   Different types of users.

in a number of broader categories related, for instance, to the types of task they perform or the jobs and roles they fulfill (Eason et al., 1974; Mumford and Sackman, 1975).

Several categorizations of user types have been published. From these a major distinction can be made between computer 'professionals' and non-computer professionals (see Fig. B–6). Under these broad headings several specific types of user have been identified. Further information about these types of users is given in a later section.

However, defining the user will not necessarily simplify designing to suit the user; nor necessarily will it limit the range of facilities that must be designed into a system for users. There is already evidence (Martin, 1973b; Eason et al., 1974, 1975) that any individual user may well use only a small subset of all the facilities or all the commands provided by a system, but that different users need and use different subsets.

User Characteristics

There is, of course, ample evidence from the relevant human sciences (anatomy, physiology, psychology, sociology) about the basic characteristics of people. The knowledge is organized under categories such as human size, strength, speed, errors, skills, intelligence, memory, training, experience, social behavior, group dynamics, etc. But these data are not related specifically to the situations of human-computer interaction. Particular information about any category can be shown to be relevant, but this will be done only in appropriate contexts later.

Three other human aspects—variability, motivation, and attitudes—will be briefly discussed here because they are particularly relevant.

With regard to *variability*, we all know that people vary from one another and that each person is variable from time to time, but the size of the differences is often not appreciated. Between different types of users, with different abilities, the variability in performance can be very large indeed. For example, Klemmer and Lockhead (1962) found there was a range of 2:1 in speed and 10:1 in errors between different operators in well-practiced computer input keying tasks. Sackman (1970) found a range of up to 15:1 difference in the completion times and interaction times for man-computer problem-solving tasks. Again, in a query language study using subjects from various backgrounds, Thomas (1977) found a factor of 6 in the times needed to train subjects to a standard level and, even then, a factor of 9 in the percentage of queries subsequently answered correctly. This enormous variability should be fully recognized and allowed for in the development of every human-computer system.

Methods to deal with this variability have not been explored systematically, but several researchers have proposed or tried various solutions. For example, Martin (1973b) pointed out the need for flexibility and a range of facilities in order to suit different levels of users. Martin (1973b) and Palme (1977) both propose the need for systems to be adaptive, both for different levels of users and for the same user at different times. Bennett (1979) and Martin (1973b) also urged the need for adaptive systems for a different reason: to help the user to learn by starting with a simpler interface, and then providing more facilities as the user becomes more sophisticated. Finally, Harris (1977) has emphasized how end users will naturally tend to formulate their inquiries of a data-base in many different forms; he then illustrated how his ROBOT natural language query system can cope with this human variability.

With regard to *motivation*, highly attractive tasks (such as games) and strong goal orientation can create user involvement and overcome poor usability. For example, computer analysts and programmers often tolerate system complexity and equipment inconvenience because of their motivation. At the other end of the spectrum, the controls of video games are often very unergonomic, but their success in the marketplace and game parlors demonstrates the value of motivation and ultra-simplicity. Indeed, many people are additionally motivated when faced with difficulties in order to demonstrate their additional skill.

Just how motivation can increase user tolerance of a computer system was illustrated by Harris (1977) in his report of the practical use of the ROBOT natural language query system. He states that "users with a real need to know the information in the database are more tolerant than users who do not care about the answers." He found this difference despite a very high success rate and user acceptability of the system.

This effect of motivation depends upon human adaptability; as a result, designers tend to assume that users will learn to adapt to whatever tool is provided. Experience shows that often this does not happen, or that market choice rapidly intervenes. Especially due to the spread of the microcomputer, users will not be willing to adapt themselves but will instead expect the computer to be adapted to them. As they become more sophisticated still, users will criticize more and demand more. The 'consumer movement' in Europe and the USA has also increased the level of criticism and expectation; people may not merely question, but may refuse to accept or work with certain equipment or procedures. At the organizational level this is already happening. For example, trade unions and union members in Europe have refused to work with VDTs or other terminals under various circumstances.

Refusal to use a system due to low motivation caused by frustration was illustrated experimentally by Melnyk (1972). Using an information retrieval situation, she presented different formulations of the task for experimental and control subjects, so as to generate different levels of frustration. The experimental subjects, who had less clear definitions of procedures and goals, reported significant levels of frustration, focused their frustration on difficulties with the computer interface, and expressed unwillingness to use the system in the future. This study shows some of the dynamics of motivation leading to rejection.

With regard to *attitudes*, a topic closely related to motivation, there have been surprisingly few attitudinal studies about computers. Zoltan and Chapanis (1982) refer to a study by Lee in 1963, who interviewed 3,000 American adults nationwide and reported these two major attitudes: (1) the computer is a beneficial tool of man, and (2) it may be a superhuman thinking machine that downgrades man. Attitudes may well have changed since then, but the only recent studies are those by Lucas and Zoltan and Chapanis.

Lucas (1977) developed a special attitude questionnaire to test the acceptability of a computer interview to medical patients. Out of 75 patients 67 returned the questionnaires (a high response rate); a large percentage (82%) had a favorable attitude to computer interrogation and 49% preferred it to interrogation by a doctor. The computer interview dialogue had been developed by the late Dr. C. R. Evans (UK National Physical Laboratory) deliberately to provide a chatty and user-friendly dialogue—clearly with some success. Zoltan and Chapanis (1982) studied four groups of professional persons: public accountants, lawyers, pharmacists, and physicians. They report both a positive and negative attitude toward computers. The positive attitude was similar to Lee's finding of the computer as a beneficial tool, but the negative attitude was different. The negative attitude took the form of discontent with the depersonalizing nature of computers and with the difficulty and complexity of computer languages. The results of this study "show that a great deal needs to be done to modify computers themselves to make them more readily acceptable to professional persons. Among other things, computers need to be easier to use and computer programs need to be simplified and altered to use language that is familiar to the professional."

Attitudes are probably related only indirectly to usability, except when the attitudinal measures directly investigate the users' opinions about ease of use. Essentially a subjective response, such attitudes may depend more upon the users' feelings about 'likeability.' However, Lucas and Zoltan and Chapanis employed fully established, scientific methods for gathering subjective attitude data. These methods certainly need to be adopted more widely to study the attitudes of users towards usability.

Types of Users

Despite preliminary categorization of user types (see Fig. B–6), studies of the work and needs of specific user classes have been all too limited. The most useful investigations so far have been the reports of the "MICA Survey" (Eason et al., 1974; Eason, 1976; Stewart, 1974, 1976b).

From these and related studies, some characteristics of nonprofessional users can be derived and are presented in Figure B–7. The first two categories (managers and secretaries/office staff) are self-evident; the next category (specialists) includes scientists, engineers, and professional persons such as lawyers, doctors, etc. (i.e., professionals but not computer professionals). The next category (consumers and the public) is again self-evident. The last (casual users) could in some sense be considered a different dimension from the others; any of the first three categories (managers, secretaries and specialists) may be inexperienced or infrequent users, and the fourth category will usually be so. I include the category of casual user separately here because it has been used extensively in the computer literature; also the thorough survey by Cuff (1980) reviews much of that literature usefully without subdividing to the previous three categories. From the paucity of references, clearly much more research is needed on this topic of types of users.

Models of Users

An excellent summary of modeling in relation to usage of interactive systems is presented by Ramsey and Atwood (1979, pp. 37–46); the following brief discussion adds some references and supplements their appraisal. The modeling discussed here is not strictly of users but of particular aspects of user performance.

Ting and Badre (1976) developed the familiar man-machine interactive loop into a formal flow model and used it to analyze mathematically the interactive process of learners with an audio-visual computer-aided learning system. Their results support the model and imply that the system characteristics were altered to adapt to the students' needs. By contrast, Brown and Klerer (1975) show how a simple change in dialogue design, for example using menu selection or a single key for a BASIC command instead of typing the whole command word, will change significantly the users' response time and also change the statistics of user demand upon a time-sharing system. Thus the model of the user changes significantly. Similar studies at the level of individual keystrokes have been carried out by Embley et al. (1978) in order to derive a model for predicting the session time at a terminal for program

Managers	Managers have highly variable information needs; current systems are often too constraining to meet the needs. Managers mostly expect minimum tedium and trouble for themselves, minimum learning time and maximum useful results. They are "discretionary" users, and so if dissatisfied resort to "distant use" (i.e. with operator between manager and system) or to partial use. See Eason 1976, Igersheim 1976, and Bennett 1979.
Secretary, Clerks, Office Staff	This group includes wide variety of jobs and tasks. Most jobs are characterized by routine, repetitive and well-defined use of computer. High risk of boring work and job dissatisfaction (best alleviated if computer use is only part of whole job). Need user support in order to help understand relation to whole system and thus maintain motivation and morale. See Mumford and Banks 1968, Eason et al 1974, and Damodaran 1976.
Specialists, e.g., in the professions	High proportion report dissatisfaction with available automated tools. These users often respond to such dissatisfaction by becoming personally involved in design or implementation of software tools, or by altering the task to match available tools. See Stewart 1974, 1976b.
Consumers and The Public	This group is very heterogeneous but has many common properties (e.g., little typing ability, etc.). These users benefit greatly from computer-initiated dialogue and usually require more tutorial features. A correct "mental model" of computer system and interactive dialogue cannot be assumed and must be explicitly conveyed by system. Dialogue design for these users needs much attention. See Card et al 1974, Eason 1980, Evans 1976, Ivergard 1976, Kennedy 1975, Lucas 1977, Malde 1977, 1978, and Maguire 1981 (see also below).
Casual (inexperienced/ infrequent) Users	The interactions of these users with the system are irregular in time and little motivated by job or social role. Tolerance of formal interaction dialogue is low. They are easily "disenchanted" by apparently trivial (to the computer designer) difficulties with terminals or dialogues. Learning and re-learning system usage must be very easy. Smooth transition from casual to experienced user/usage is not easy with current systems. See Cuff 1980, Eason et al 1974, Eason 1979, Martin 1973a, b, and Gaines 1981 (see also references for the last entry)

Figure B–7.   Some characteristics of non-computer professional users in human-computer interaction.

editing tasks, and much more extensively by Card et al. (1980a,b) to develop a model of the human user during the task of text editing. The results from this last work appear promising as a basis for developing a truly quantitative description of user behavior from the bottom upward.

However, this success is very modest; at the global level we are still at the stage of developing insightful speculation rather than quantifiable theories. Thomas (1978) has questioned the current view of communication at the man-computer interface. He proposes an alternative approach which stresses the game-theoretic aspects of communication, the importance of viewing message-building as a constructive process, the richness involved in human natural language communication, and the ambiguity of natural language as an asset. Johannsen and Rouse (1979) surveyed the whole range of mathematical models proposed for manual control monitoring and decision-making tasks in man-machine systems; many of the systems, but not all, are computer-based. While their focus is upon process control and related tasks, their survey proves relevant to the general question of modeling the user.

Conclusion

From the above review two things are clear: sufficient knowledge is not yet available, and it is not at all easy to describe and classify the user. The problem is similar to that which faced the Victorian entomologists until they had been able to gather and lay out their enormous assemblies of butterflies on the many-colored, very pretty collection trays which became fashionable wall hangings. This analogy shows the still greater complexity of pinning down the human user because he does not stay still. Any one user will not merely be different from others but will not stay the same over time because human learning causes significant change with experience.

So the concept of usability, when applied to any one user, must also be an evolutionary concept. It must be related not only to the tasks for which the user needs the aid of a tool, and to the state of his knowledge and experience at the start, but also to his learning capability and to his motivation and other factors which will cause a change with time.

Thus, to define adequately this first of the four principal components of usability, we must not merely be able to classify the user and specify the general characteristics of that group. We must also account for the extent of experience and learning and the changing level of sophistication. More work will need to be done to clarify the procedures and the degree of precision required to define the types of user and levels of sophistication. But the necessity is clear. As Miller (1978, pp. 6–7) comments: "Different groups of computer users have extensively different profiles of computer usage ... and also differ with respect to their needs and expectations, with the sophisticated user probably requiring much more function, performance, and flexibility than the unsophisticated group. This latter group, on the other hand, may be expected to require more assistance, more direction, and greater 'error-tolerance' than the former. In view of these expectations, we recommend testing of a facility which tailors the performance, function, and user-assistance levels of an interactive system to the use-profile of the user to achieve not only greater individualized user support but also more efficient overall computer system performance."

USABILITY COMPONENTS: 2. THE TASK

Basic Characteristics

The word 'task' is here used as a generic term. According to circumstances, it should be interpreted to mean anything from the total job down to the smallest detailed subtask. These different levels are discussed by Bennett (1971), who suggests that a "task taxonomy requires at least the following levels of units: a 'job', perhaps definable as a fulltime paid position; a 'function' a subdivision of a job, or a grouping of tasks (such as the research portion of a professor's job); a 'task', an undefined but fairly specific set of activities (for example, 'calibrate the equipment'), and a 'subtask', a subdivision of a task (e.g., 'adjust the knob')." These are now the standard terms used in human factors work. A job is the totality of a person's employed work, and the difference between one person's job and another depends essentially upon the different combinations of functions and tasks required of each person.

The Problem of Taxonomy

Again we find here the problem of classification. Very many different tasks may be performed by users during human-computer interaction, but there have been few attempts to develop taxonomies of these tasks. The only ones attempted have been in military contexts and, although useful, are too specific to be widely applied. More general studies of jobs and tasks in the psychological literature do not include the computer as a tool, and so are not relevant; moreover, most of this work has been at the job and function level rather than at the task and subtask level as defined by Bennett.

The Problem of Basic Units

When we consider the concept of task at the detailed level, clearly human jobs, functions, and tasks should be viewed as very complex, combinatorial iterations of a basic sequence: input-decision-output. Expressed in lay terms, the basic activities are, for example, reading or listening, thinking, deciding (and remembering), planning, and writing or speaking. These 'basic units' subserving the human conduct of a task are noted in Figure B-8. These activities are carried out iteratively many times, whether the task be that of a clerk inputting sales orders, a manager deciding a sales strategy, a controller

Basic Loop	Basic Activities
Input	Receiving/Interpreting (e.g., reading/listening/viewing)
Decision	Thinking ⎫ Deciding ⎬ Remembering Planning ⎭
Output	Communicating/Manipulating (e.g., writing/speaking/ operating the controls)

Figure B–8.   Basic units subserving human conduct of a task.

running a process plant, or a pilot flying an aircraft. But are these activities simple and stable enough to be considered as 'units'?

There is much debate among human scientists about the form, content, and characteristics of these basic units, discussed here in general rather than technical terms. Although the human sciences have now acquired a certain amount of basic knowledge about these human cognitive processes, we do not have comprehensive descriptions and theories that can be readily applied to the study of usability in human-computer interaction.

Consider reading as a basic activity. If it is to be useful as a simple unit from which tasks are compounded, then it should be unitary and invariant. But in human-computer interaction the user may be reading the text of a paper on a VDT for comprehension, or be reading a draft text to detect errors, or reading and answering a questionnaire form, or be reading a screen menu for the desired command, etc. In non-computer circumstances, these characteristics of the unit 'reading' have been shown to be different for such subtasks; indeed the last one might be given the name 'searching' to distinguish it. In a computer situation, as Ramsey and Atwood (1979) explain, "There is evidence that these specific tasks may vary in their requirements for minimum display resolution, line spacing, use of upper and lower case characters, and perhaps other variables."

Conclusion

Thus we have neither adequate task taxonomies nor suitable basic units as building blocks. This is probably the most significant gap in the field of human factors in relation to human-computer interaction. Much work is needed, focusing first upon very limited areas of application in order to lay the basic foundations so that eventually it will be possible to define and specify adequately the characteristics of the task in the equation of usability.

USABILITY COMPONENTS: 3. THE TOOL

Basic Characteristics

Some computer professionals may feel it vaguely insulting to call the fruits of their work, the computer system, a tool. No insult is intended, but that is what it is and should be for the user, however powerful a computer it may be. While the digital computer, and especially the VDT, are the subjects of this chapter, we should not overlook the analogue computer, the pocket calculator, and other related devices. Experience with related devices, particularly the pocket calculator, may considerably influence the attitudes and expectations of users towards the usability of computers.

Within one human generation, the digital computer has proliferated into many forms, such as large mainframes, local minicomputers, and single-user microcomputers. Even this generalization can be questioned because many minis are expanded to do the work of mainframes while others are single-user machines; microcomputers are also rapidly being developed as multi-user systems. But these distinctions are perhaps irrelevant for our purpose because the acknowledged aim of many computer designers is to give each user the feel of having the whole power of the machine to himself. If this is achieved, then it is seldom relevant to the user how the tool is configured unless he has special needs. For example, human factors specialists often need a stand-alone machine for their experiments so as to control absolutely and measure exactly the system response time to the user, or users with particular security requirements may need their own dedicated computer.

Many functions of the computer—such as capacity, speed, and reliability—are basic to its performance as a tool, and are amply provided by the industry. Other aspects, also inherent functions of the tool, should not be designed in isolation but with close attention to the needs and wants of the user (e.g., language facilities, security, and system response time). However, these and other characteristics of the computer as a tool (see Fig. B–9) are only experienced by the user through the medium of the interface.

The Interface

As Doherty (1979) explains, "What the user must input to the computer, and what the user sees in return, is the user's interface to the machine." The interface is any hardware or software feature with which the user may have to interact. So the interface comprises not only the obvious hardware elements affecting the user, but also the text and messages on the VDT screen, and such aspects as documentation to learn operating commands or interpret error messages.

The distinction between hardware and software interfaces must be made clear. The *hardware interface* comprises the displays, controls, terminals,

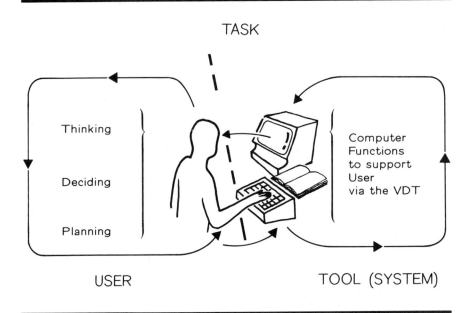

Figure B–9. The tool. (The computer and VDT parts of the user-machine system are often called 'the system' for convenience.) Bennett, *Building decision support systems,* © 1983. Reading, Mass.: Addison-Wesley. Reprinted with permission.

consoles, and similar equipment having a fixed physical form (Shackel, 1979b; cf. Appendix). The *software interface* comprises those parts of the communication medium which are not hardware, are often more transitory, and (if part of the message system between user and computer) are usually variable by program control. By definition the subject here is not the computer system aspects of the programming language in use, but the grammar, syntax, and other language aspects of the communication process between computer and user. These are manifested in the logical structure of content and procedures, and in the format, layout, verbosity, etc. of the sequences of human-computer messages. For instance, the layout of financial reports displayed on a terminal for a manager, and the messages he must key in to query other parts of the accounts, would be aspects of the software interface between the manager and the management information system. Questionnaires and order input forms are a software interface and must be designed to be filled in easily (by the public or by salespeople) and to be read easily by card punch or key-to-disc operators in the data preparation office.

This differentiation between hardware and software interfaces has been of some use in analysis and design, and clearly reflects the existing differentiation in the computer industry between hardware and software designers (engineers and programmers). However, many people recognize that this distinction between engineers and programmers may be counterproductive; current developments (e.g., firmware) are beginning to blur the divisions between hardware and software and the separation between the different types of designers. Moreover, this differentiation may not matter for the user because it depends upon the computer, not upon the usage.

We must also distinguish between the structural and cognitive interfaces. From the viewpoint of the user, the differentiation may simply be between structure and meaning. Although the medium, the message, and the meaning are all interwoven during successful human-computer communication, and the whole must be viewed as an integrated entity, this distinction between structure and meaning may be useful for our purposes. Based on this concept, the interface would consist of a structural component and a cognitive component. The *structural interface* would comprise all aspects concerned with the form of communication, and thus would include all the hardware and such items as the format and layout of the screen contents, etc. The *cognitive interface* would be concerned with the content and meaning of communication and thus would include the organization of information, its storage and retrieval, and ultimately the meaningfulness of the interaction between user and tool.

Language and Dialogue

The structural/cognitive and form/content dichotomies are reflected also in the distinction between language and dialogue. In everyday usage, because language is the necessary basis for dialogue, the terms dialogue and language tend to be used flexibly and with close if not overlapping meanings. Strictly, however, language is the underlying structure with various components and rules for linking them, whereas dialogue is the interactive usage of a mutually agreed language between communicators to exchange information. This formal distinction does not convey all the underlying meanings. Language may be the transfer medium, but dialogue has more dynamic implications of interactive construction and modification of mutual understanding—an 'effort after meaning' as Bertlett used to say—somewhat akin to the concept of a Socratic dialogue.

The rules and procedures of languages which computers can understand are usually very different from 'normal' human languages, so humans must learn the relevant computer language. At best it may take 3 to 6 months for the human to achieve reasonable facility, but at worst the human and computer may remain 'foreigners.' Designers gradually recognized that the computer would become usable for many, instead of only a few experts or specially trained operators, if more readily understandable communications could be implemented. Thus designers recognized the need to design interactive dialogue in a way which would be readily learned and understood by users. The classic book by Martin (1973a) was the first major foundation stone. The latest cornerstone has recently been added by Gaines (1981), who suggests that in programming man-computer interaction, the situation resembles that of 30 years ago for hardware design and 10 years ago for software design— still reliant upon unsystematized 'craft' skills passed on from master to apprentice. Gaines revises and develops the intuitive 'rules' for dialogue design originally proposed by Gaines and Facey (1975), discusses them in terms of user psychology, and suggests the eventual need to generate a technology of 'dialogue engineering.'

Conclusion

The distinctions of hardware/software, structural/cognitive, form/content, and language/dialogue are useful for exposition; however, they are not separate and independent entities. Inevitably, they interact together and with the task (at least) to influence the usability of the tool for the user.

USABILITY COMPONENTS: 4. THE ENVIRONMENT

Definition

This is a very broad category, comprising physical, psychological, and social aspects. The physical aspect includes the layout and spatial attributes of the desk, console or workstation involved and the wider factors of lighting, noise, and thermal environment. The psychological and social aspects include the influence of the working group, the job structure (e.g., shift working), the working system, the organizational climate (e.g., union relations), and even societal attitudes. In the last five years there has been particular attention to environmental issues. Concern for the quality of working life and for the potentiality of unemployment have focused the attention of management, unions, and workers alike upon problems of working with computers. As a result, some useful work, particularly upon physical aspects, has led to the publication of design guidelines for achieving usability and acceptability.

Physical Aspects

Most of the questions about workspace and physical environment in human-computer interaction are not specialized and involve only routine ergonomics. Therefore, the existing well-documented methods in ergonomics provide the necessary guidance (e.g. see Van Cott and Kincade, 1972; Shackel, 1974). However, field studies of current computer system usage show that there is typically a wide gap between what is known in ergonomics about physical environment factors, and what is actually applied in system design. Little ergonomics research is applied by manufacturers and employers.

For example, Stewart (1981) studied workplace environment issues at 320 workplaces in 20 applications, using the published criteria in the VDT Manual checklist (Cakir et al., 1980) as the basis for assessment. He points out that the environment may often serve as a convenient scapegoat for other complaints about VDTs or computers in general. Nevertheless, subjects reported that the thermal environment caused problems in almost 100% of the cases; heating and ventilation systems were seldom capable of controlling temperature, air flow, and humidity adequately even when operating perfectly. (Of course, Britain may not be typical of other parts of the world in this aspect.) Stewart made recommendations to change the environmental control system in 20% of cases, to change the lighting in 70% of cases, and to improve workplace aspects in 75% of cases. These questions of vision and lighting have received considerable attention; Ostberg (1976) among others has emphasized good workstation and environment design as well as attention to ophthalmic issues so as to minimize fatigue and visual strain.

The interaction of tool and task with environment aspects has been studied even more extensively. Duncan and Ferguson (1974) and Ferguson and Duncan (1974) were first to show how poor keyboard positioning and layout can adversely affect posture and cause severe discomfort and fatigue during the working day. Several studies reveal that many VDT users must adopt awkward postures to read the screen and printed material while operating the keyboard (see Grandjean and Vigliani, 1980). Even a good posture may still give problems if it has to be held for a prolonged period. Muscular fatigue resulting from posture problems is often experienced first as headaches and tired eyes—even though the eyes themselves are not being overworked. One solution is a well-designed workstation that the user can adjust, both to avoid awkward postures and to provide for shifts of posture to reduce fatigue. Another solution is to redesign the user's task; if VDT work is only part of the job, it will not have these adverse effects. Clearly the tool, task, and environment must be designed as an interactive whole to suit the user.

Two books have been published to provide designers with the human factors knowledge presently available. The book by Damodaran, Simpson, and Wilson (1980) concentrates mainly upon the user aspect of system issues in addition to workplace, environment and user support. The book by Cakir, Hart, and Stewart (1980) concentrates upon the visual display terminal, but also contains useful sections on workplace and environment (see Fig. B–10). Both contain checklists to help the designer, and the second is the first attempt at a design guide in the sequence of typical design procedures and process.

Psychological and Social Aspects

These aspects can perhaps best be conceived as widening circles of factors that may influence the user with his tool at his task. With each widening circle, the types of influence become more diffuse and also harder to discern (partly because the research is more wide-ranging and more difficult). Shackel (1979a, pp. 247–258) gives an eclectic summary of some occupational and social issues. A particular problem is that the terms—organizational, sociological, social—

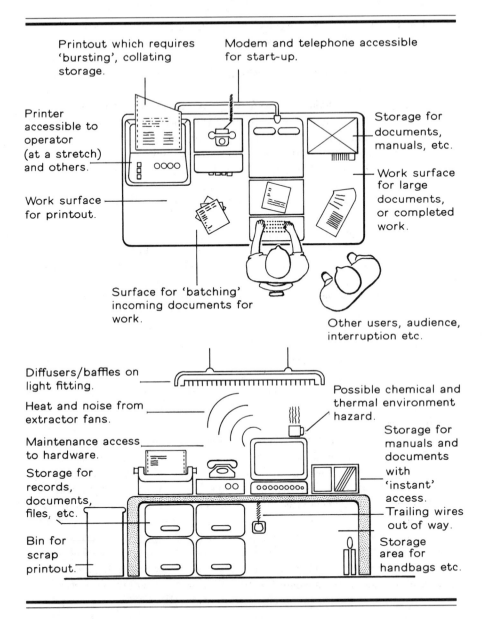

Figure B–10. Illustrations from the VDT Manual checklist section showing many of the workspace and environment factors requiring consideration. (Cakir et al., 1980).

are used with no consistency. We will arbitrarily identify the successive circles of influence as job design issues, occupational issues, organizational issues, and social/societal issues.

The importance of *job design and occupational issues* in relation to computer usage was revealed in the early 1970s by studies such as that by Eason et al. (1974) and some of those described by Parsons (1972), and even earlier in the formative study of Mumford and Banks (1968). Recent approaches to job design in the system context have been published in Andersen (1980); in particular, he describes the participative design approach developed by Mumford (1980) with two case studies. Eason and Sell (1981) also describe similar case studies.

Concerning *organizational issues*, Hedberg (1980) suggests that information system design is passing through a series of phases. In the present phase (at least in Sweden), attempts are being made to minimize social implications but, contradictorily, they can be followed by design deliberately intent on changing organizations. Hedberg hopes that a participative approach may develop although he presents two case studies illustrating how difficult it is to achieve this aim.

On the other side of this topic—the impact of computer systems upon organizations—Andersen and Rasmussen (1980) summarize the wide variety of research results and suggest that many effects may be less a product of the computer itself than of the procedures whereby design was conducted. They suggest that results can be very different when there is active participation in system design. A handbook detailing a methodology for specifying the system by a participative method is being developed at Cologne University (Kolf, 1980); the method aims to be comprehensive and quantified, requiring users to make rankings of the relative importance of up-to-date information, private information, detailed information, etc. I question whether complex organizational issues can be reduced to a formula—even with user participation—and still result in good usability, but undoubtedly such attempts and explorations are necessary if we are to quantify usability.

Concerning the wider *social and societal issues*, Gotlieb and Borodin (1973) presented a scholarly appraisal of the effects of computerization. In addition to chapters on the growth of computer applications in various fields, they provide chapters on each of the major kinds of societal effect such as privacy problems and legislation, artificial intelligence and its effect on the role of man, the changing nature of professionalism, the effects of computers on power distribution in the organization (i.e. centralization/decentralization), and the effects on employment. Admittedly this book was published before the age of the microcomputer, but many of the issues and factors discussed by the authors are relevant for both today and the future.

As a final speculation, we may consider for a moment the notions of the office of the future and the information society. What changes in work organization and in society might be appropriate for such very changed conditions? What consequences—such as new types of alienation—might arise? The June 17, 1976, editorial in *Computer Weekly* (quoted in Shackel, 1979a, p. 257) suggested the scenario which Toffler (1980) later explored in full. The energy shortage may make it unacceptable to transport executives and clerks each day to offices; instead, sophisticated communications devices with simulated three-dimensional displays may keep them working in an office in their own homes (the 'Electronic Cottage' of Toffler). Interestingly, the editorial then questions the implications of such a future: "This chilling possibility, that of being obliged to make do with the illusion for the reality when meeting people, seems to be the ultimate in the alienation of man from his fellows, which psychologists and sociologists already condemn. It may be questioned whether people will ever be content to shop or to enjoy their leisure in depersonalised non-tactile ways, however sophisticated the intervening gadgetry. One thing is certain, a lot of thinking and a lot of reorganisation has to be done between now and the year 2000." It was encouraging to see a computer trade journal develop such a broad recognition of the issues involved.

USABILITY COMPONENTS
COMBINED IN A WORKING UNIT

The Gaps in Our Knowledge

From the previous review of the four principal components, it is evident how limited it is to discuss them in isolation. For human-computer usage, the interaction between these four combined in a working unit must be the main concern. But here, above all, the gaps in our knowledge are most obvious.

Although the extent of our knowledge about each of them varies, there is still rather little in the form of a coordinated taxonomy about any of them. Consequently we know equally little in a taxonomic form about their interactive combinations. There have been only a few attempts at direct analysis (e.g., of user-task-tool interactions by Eason et al., 1974, 1975; and of this combination in relation specifically to managers' work by Eason, 1976, cf. also Fig. B–7). As a result, we have no real data to answer questions which may reasonably be posed by designers trying to implement human factors advice.

For example, in his perceptive review Bennett (1972) points out that there is "the important trade-off between perceived ease of use and flexibility to respond to individual demands," and suggests that "since this kind of perceived ease of use changes with user experience, the designer may want to plan his introduction of the conceptual framework in such a way that the user can match interface language features to his current level of sophistication." In order to follow this entirely valid precept, the designer may ask what level of flexibility of the system will correspond to the user's current level of sophistication, and still result in, say, 90% usability? At present we have no sound, experimentally derived bases for giving an answer in terms of one or two spot values, let alone for providing a comprehensive answer in terms of a graph or table of relationships.

Data input
Sales processing
Production planning and control
Process monitoring and control
Database query
Information storage and retrieval
   (e.g., non-military = libraries; M.I.S.
         military = tactical information
            system)
Management information system
Financial analysis
Financial modeling

(e.g., word processing,
  text editing,
  typesetting, run-off)
Message processing
  (e.g., voice processing,
  electronic mail)
Computer conferencing
Computer aided design
Computer aided learning
Games and gaming
Stimulation

Figure B–11. Some examples of User-Task-Tool-Environment combinations expressed in the language of computer applications.

On the other hand, if we look at some of the user-task-tool-environment combinations under a different name; i.e., as titles of computer applications, we recognize that considerable expertise already exists in the industry (see Fig. B–11). However, it is largely 'craft' knowledge, based upon pragmatic intuition and personal experience, often not published because proprietary, and by no means coordinated into scientific descriptions or paradigms. The beginnings of scientific studies analyzing consistently some of the variables certainly exist: for example, in text editing (Roberts, 1979; Card et al., 1980b; Embley and Nagy, 1981); in data base query (Gaines, 1979; Reisner, 1981), in process control (Johannsen and Rouse, 1978; Rouse,1981); in production planning and control (Sheridan and Johannsen, 1976; Gibson and Laios, 1978); and in computer conferencing (Hiltz and Turoff, 1978; Johansen et al., 1979). But because much of this work is oriented toward one particular computer application, it fails to examine the interactions of the four components in the analytical way suggested here.

The Approach Needed

What we need are major programs and studies that consistently vary several of the four component features against each other. To illustrate this point, let us briefly consider some results from Evans (1976) and Maguire (1981).

Evans describes his studies of a computer-based hospital patient interviewing system. He explains how he had expected the speed of the only available printer (110 baud—10 characters per second) to prove as unacceptable as it does to most of us because the silent reading speed of the average adult is about 20–30 cps (See Shackel, 1979b). To his great surprise, the patients found the speed entirely acceptable, and this was confirmed in subsequent studies. This result has attracted considerable attention because of its unexpectedness. In other words, many of us do not appreciate the wide variability between users, and subconsciously suppose that others will reflect our own reactions to any tool and task.

By contrast, Maguire found the reverse in apparently a similar situation. He installed an experimental public information system in the library in Leicester. He gathered both objective data and subjective comments from 316 visitors who used the system (which was unattended) and entered comments in a book. Maguire reports that one frequent criticism was that the printer was too slow. The speed was 300 baud (about 30 cps)! Maguire acknowledges the conflict with Evans' finding and suggests that the difference lies in the nature of the two systems. "The interrogative nature of computer screening requires the patient to read each question carefully, while the Leicester information system, which essentially displays pages of information, allows the user to omit certain parts at will. Another reason is that in recent years people have become conditioned to instant televisual displays as provided by the teletext services and computer games. In comparison the display rate of the information system would have seemed very sluggish." (Maguire, 1981). The hypothesized explanation for the faster display rate still being considered too slow by the users depends upon the different nature of the task involved and perhaps also upon the different environmental 'climate.' Although this explanation is convincing, it is not the same as proving the interrelationship between the component factors.

In another part of his thesis, Maguire (1981) describes an experiment which is a simple example of the type I advocate. He presented each person in two groups of 48 naive and 48 experienced users with two of four possible types of dialogue procedure, keeping the interactive description task and environment constant. The four dialogue procedures were:

1. tertiary input dialogue, consisting of questions from the computer and answers from the subject by pressing only one of three keys for 'yes,' 'no,' or 'don't know' (an exact equivalent of Evans hospital patient interview dialogue);
2. menu list, with the computer asking a question and then giving a number of alternatives in a menu;
3. restricted vocabulary, with the user again being presented with a question but with an array of 16 noun and adjective descriptors and some conjunctions from which to compose an answer;
4. unrestricted vocabulary, in which the user could respond with any words at all.

Afterwards the users expressed their preference regarding 'ease of use' and 'effectiveness' and compared the two dialogues by simply expressing a preference for one or the other. For 'ease of use,' the rankings by both naive and experienced subjects were the same: tertiary a clear first choice, followed by menu list, restricted, and unrestricted vocabulary. For 'effectiveness,' the rankings varied considerably. Naive subjects preferred unrestricted followed by tertiary. Experienced subjects preferred restricted followed by menu. However, the results matter less for my purpose than the organization of the study: two levels of the user component interacting with four types of tool arrangement on the same task and in the same environment.

Card provides another example of the required type of research program in Chapter 4 of this Section. We need many such experimental programs, and others even more comprehensive than these, before we can establish proper taxonomies of user-task-tool-environment combinations. Such comprehensive multidimensional studies are essential because, as Bennett (1979) says, "The application designer must consider the subrelationships between ... [the four principal components already specified in this chapter].... A shift in any one of the elements can alter the relative importance of the measures within the usability relationship."

Conclusion

This appraisal shows how far we still are from having the firm foundations for a science of usability, and from having at least an integrated ensemble of practical and specific facts from which to offer advice to designers. The knowledge that we do have is very fragmented, very specific, and based largely upon the skill and experience of human factors and computer specialists working in or very close to the industry. Perhaps this is only to be expected at the present stage of development, but much must be done before the relationship between usability and the four principal components can have an established basis more solid than that of intuition, hypothesis, and precept.

With that preliminary caution, perhaps some suggestions may be offered for how we may work toward achieving usability. I offer some suggestions on the one hand for research and on the other hand for design.

For research:

1. We need to gather as much data from case studies and experienced workers as possible to find generalizable results and deriving hypothesized taxonomies upon which to base proposals for empirical research programs.

2. We need to plan research programs to study the ranges of variables inherent in the four components in order to assemble the empirical findings upon which to develop first co-ordinating descriptions and later theories. For example, Johannsen and Rouse (1979) suggest a very useful hypothesis: "...human behaviour mainly reflects the task environment. Thus searching for a specific analytical model of general human behaviour may only be fruitful to the extent that all task environments are common. Perhaps then, one should first search

for commonality among environments rather than intrinsic human characteristics. In other words, a good model of the demands of the environment may allow a reasonable initial prediction of human performance. Thus, it is reasonable to assume initially that the human will adapt to the demands of the task and perform accordingly."

For design:

1. The computer system designer should understand that his mission is to create, and modify to suit, a highly sophisticated tool that above all will help the user with his tasks.
2. To adopt a user-oriented approach, the designer must attempt a comprehensive analysis, resulting in detailed specifications of
    (a) the characteristics, needs, and wants of the range of intended users;
    (b) the range of tasks and subtasks envisaged within all the user's job functions; and
    (c) the range of environments envisaged.
3. Because the users (or representatives of the users) probably know far more, intuitively and by experience, about the environment and tasks, the precept above all for the designer should be 'design interactively with the user.'

THE VDT: BEGINNING OR END OF USABILITY?

The Importance of the Terminal

The VDT is becoming the standard interface between the user and the computer. But it is more than this. As Doherty (1979) explains, "For the user of today's computing systems, the terminal is, pragmatically speaking, the computer." Therefore, the usability of the terminal will very much determine the usability of the whole computer system as a tool for the user. It can be the beginning or the end of usability.

Since the terminal is in effect the sole channel of communication to the computer, especially for the noncomputer-professional user, the terminal is of prime importance whether it is a VDT or any other type such as a teletypewriter. However, there is no doubt that the VDT is becoming the preferred medium for very many tasks and uses.

For example, Doherty (1979) reports the in-house experience at IBM: "...it is reasonable to expect a sharp increase in the demand for broad bandwidth display terminals in preference to typewriters. This has already manifested itself at Yorktown. In 1973 we had about 250 typewriterlike terminals and about 50 displays. Today there are about 120 typewriters and 550 displays, with another 250 displays needed by the end of 1979." From their substantial experience with computer conferencing, Turoff and Hiltz (1980) report that users often prefer to start with some type of printing terminal and then progress to a VDT with a nearby printer for occasional temporary hard copies—temporary because most are thrown away a day or two later like a daily newspaper (Price, Turoff, and Hiltz, 1980).

Terminal Development

It will not be sufficient for the VDT merely to maintain the characteristics which make it the preferred medium—primarily the speed with which text and similar material can be displayed. Already the marketplace is requiring VDT improvements in the stability and legibility of text characters, in the resolution and definition of graphics, and in the range of facilities provided as standard (from scrolling, blinking, and inverse video in the early days to the latest high-grade multi-color capability).

At present two major limitations must be solved: portability and screen size. For the VDT to substitute completely for paper, it must be reduced in size and weight (while increasing screen size and resolution) until it is no bigger than a large book. Extensive work on liquid crystal displays suggests that this breakthrough may occur within the next five years.

Regarding screen size, the two basic applications require two different approaches. For many text and word processing activities, usability demands more than the current standard 24 or 25 lines. A full page ($11 \times 8 \ 1/2$ or $11 \ 1/2 \times 8 \ 1/4$ inches) should be presented on the screen with good resolution. Some terminals and systems already have this capability; e.g., Xerox 8010 (see Fig. B–12), or Data Recall Diamond. The other application area is that of computer-aided design, requiring a large area display combined with high-resolution graphics. The present solution is to use the VDT as a scrolling window to achieve adequate resolution by displaying only a small part of the whole, combined with printed output on a plotting machine. The same problem exists when a VDT displays, for example, the mimic diagram of a chemical plant or electrical grid network for process control. The future demands the development of large screen displays and/or projection displays such as those explored in the 'dataland' work at MIT by Bolt (1977) and Negroponte (1981).

Thus, we see that the two major limitations of portability and screen size are well recognized and already in part solved. The next stage is to develop and produce usable solutions at a price inexpensive enough to make them widely available and acceptable.

There are, of course, other developments that would improve usability; for example, good voice output and voice recognition terminals. It is self-evident that substantial improvements in usefulness and usability are needed for the VDT to become a truly transparent window into the electronic workplace.

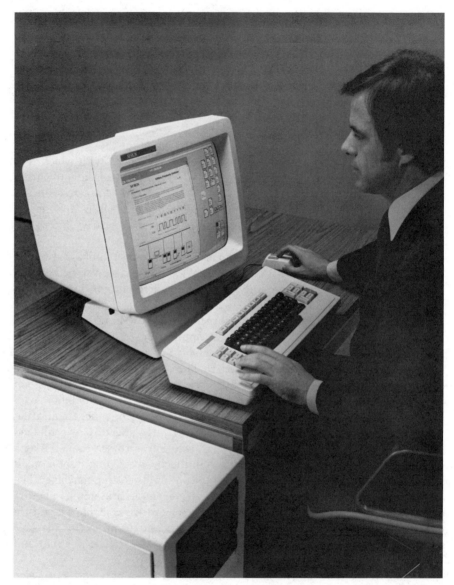

Figure B–12. The Xerox 8010 'Star' workstation which has a large screen and can display a full standard page of text.

Terminal Design

To achieve the high standard of usability needed for the VDT to intertwine the user happily with his computer tool. We must change our design approach, The word 'terminal' may mean the far end of a connecting link from the computer, but designed from that viewpoint it is unlikely to have high usability and to enhance user-computer communication. The designer must not perceive the terminal merely as an appendage to the computer; it must be regarded as an integrated workstation to fit the user like a craftman's hand tool. To do this the designer must start with the users and their tasks and must concentrate his thinking and his design around their capabilities and needs. The approach of workstation analysis and design in the ergonomics textbooks (cf. Shackel, 1974, Chapter 2) recommends that the design procedure start from the user as the center of the frame of reference. Thus, the analysis and the design reflect the situation as the user (operator, supervisor, manager, secretary , or whoever) actually perceives and experiences it.

When stated in this way, this concept is so simple and obvious that engineers and designers may question the reason for emphasizing it. But all we need do is ask how often they themselves actually achieve the mental reorientation needed to look at the situation in this way when making their design studies. Let me emphasize that no criticism is implied here. Designers must concentrate upon the aspects that are central to their professional roles as engineers, programmers, etc. However, to deal satisfactorily with ergonomic issues, the user-centered approach must be achieved at appropriate stages in the design process. This approach permits the analysis of the ergonomic features, and ensures a balanced viewpoint with which to reach the compromise decisions needed to harmonize ergonomic, engineering, cost, and other considerations.

There have been significant improvements in VDT design for usability in the last year or two. In general, technical quality is good, rapid introduction of technical innovation is widespread, and costs and prices are being reduced markedly. The design compromises, however, almost always favor the technical and economic factors. Yet, a few manufacturers are taking the lead in introducing ergonomics fully into their design procedures. We may therefore expect significant improvements, not merely in the marketing brochures, but also in the actual products in the next few years.

SUMMARY AND CONCLUSION

This chapter has introduced the concept of usability and illustrated the importance of this concept to the design and use of the VDT. Because the VDT is the principal interface between user and computer (indeed often *is* the computer for many users), I have presented the determinants of usability and suggested a framework for further research, development, and design for improved usability in computer systems and VDTs.

The idea that something may be potentially useful but actually not usable is of fairly recent origin. I have proposed an operational definition which, in shortened form, states that usability is the capability of a thing to be used by humans easily and effectively.

This essay reviewed the factors to be considered in making operational use of this definition. Usability depends upon good user-oriented design of hardware and software, and upon good user support (training, manuals, 'help' facilities, etc.). The range of users, tasks, and environments for which the system is intended must be specified and then achieved. Ease of use may be evaluated by subjective judgments and effectiveness of human use may be evaluated by objective measures of human performance. In these ways, I suggested, the potential usefulness (the functional utility) of a system may actually be harnessed, and the ability of the whole to be used successfully (the usability) may be measured.

I discussed at length the four principal components of usablility: the user, the task, the tool, and the environment. Each computing application involving humans is a system of these four components combined together in an interactive working unit. The importance of these interactions for usability, the gaps in our knowledge, and the type of research needed were considered. Finally, the place of the VDT in relation to the usability of the whole system was briefly reviewed and illustrated.

The visual display screen of today, especially if it is part of tomorrow's color terminal, is the modern Aladdin's magic lamp. In the story, only one simple rub of the lamp calls the Genie to the master's bidding. The procedures for using a VDT are seldom so simple. Indeed, a manager of a software/hardware supply house recently told me of an inexperienced user who telephoned to complain that the VDT screen had "frozen" for a whole day and there was no way he could draw a response from his computer. It turned out that the shift lock was locked on! This anecdote illustrates how the magic lamp of today needs the utmost simplicity and usability; one rub the wrong way may make it impossible for the Genie to obey any command.

The VDT is truly a potential window into an ingenious future. To unlock the shutters to that future, the user must be given the key of usability.

APPENDIX

Human Performance
    Basic characteristics and limitations: size, speed, skills, errors, flexibility
    Special aspects: selection, training, user support, modeling the user,
                decision-making, problem-solving

Computer System Performance
    Basic characteristics and limitations: capacity, speed, reliability
    Special aspects for HCI: language facilities, system response time, security

Hardware Interface
    Displays, Controls, Terminals and Consoles
    Applied ergonomics for good workstation design
    Human needs and new devices

Software Interface
    The nonhardware communication media
    Languages and linguistic systems (HCI aspects)
    Information organization and dialogue design:
        – logical structure of content and procedure
        – message structure and verbosity
        – display format and layout (including microfilm output,
        questionnaire, and other input forms)
    Human needs and new approaches

Environment
    Physical: workstation space and layout, lighting, noise, etc.
    Psychological influences:
        – the working group (motivation, stress)
        – job structure (working in shifts)
        – system structure (open/closed, rigid/flexible)
        – social climate
        – organization design
    Applied ergonomics and social science for good environment design

Specific Applications

Specialist users	Computer Assisted Learning
Business users	Computer Aided Design
Naive users	Computer Conferencing
Public systems	Computer Aided Process Control

Special Problems
    Evaluation:
        – especially criteria and methods
        – especially social implications versus cash costs
        – importance of real world studies (not in lab. only)
    Privacy of personal information
    Ergonomics of programming and the job of the programmer
    Documentation and related job aids
    Influence of HCI upon job design, organization design, and society.

Outline 1. Major factors in Human-Computer Interaction (HCI) (Figure 3 from Shackel, 1979a).

REFERENCES

Andersen, N. B., ed. 1980. *The human side of information processing.* Amsterdam: North-Holland.

Andersen, N. B., and Rasmussen, L. B. 1980. Sociological implications of computer systems. In *Human Interaction with Computers*, eds. H. T. Smith and T. R. G. Green, pp. 97–123. London: Academic Press.

Bennett, C. A. 1971. Towards empirical, practicable, comprehensive task taxonomy. *Human Factors* 13:229–35.

Bennett, J. L. 1972. The user interface in interactive systems. *Annual Review of Information Science and Technology* 7:159–96.

———. 1979. The commercial impact of usability in interactive systems. In *Man-Computer Communication*, ed. B. Shackel. *Infotech State of the Art Report Vol. 2*, pp. 1–17. Infotech International, Maidenhead, UK.

Bolt, R. A. 1977. Spatial data management-interim report. Architecture Machine Group, MIT, Cambridge, Mass.

British Computer Society. 1978. User requirements in data processing. Special report 29.11.78. The British Computer Society, London.

Brown, T., and Klerer, M. 1975. The effect of language design on time-sharing operational efficiency. *International Journal of Man-Machine Studies* 7:233–47.

Cakir, A.; Hart, D. J.; and Stewart, T. F. M. 1980. *Visual display terminals.* London: Wiley.

Card, S. K.; Moran, T. P.; and Newell, A. 1980a. The keystroke-level model for user performance time with interactive systems. *Communications of the ACM* 23:396–410.

———. 1980b. Computer text editing: an information processing analysis of a routine cognitive skill. *Cognitive Psychology* 12:32–74.

Card, W. I., et al. 1974. A comparison of doctor and computer interrogation of patients. *International Journal of Biomedical Computing* 5:175–87.

Cuff, R. N. 1980. On casual users. *International Journal of Man-Machine Studies* 12:163–87.

Damodaran, L. 1976. The role of user support. Paper to NATO ASI on Man-Computer Interaction. In Shackel (1981).

Damodaran, L.; Simpson, A.; and Wilson, P. 1980. Designing systems for people. NCC Publications. National Computing Centre, Manchester, UK.

De Greene, K. B. 1970. *Systems psychology.* New York: McGraw-Hill.

De Quincey, T. 1842. Ricardo and Adam Smith (Part III). *Blackwood's Magazine* 52:718–39.

Doherty, W. J. 1979. The commercial significance of man-computer interaction. In *Man-Computer Communication*, ed. B. Shackel, *Infotech State of the Art Report Vol. 2*, pp. 81–93. Infotech International, Maidenhead, UK.

Dolotta, T. A. 1976. *Data processing in 1980–85: a study of potential limits of progress.* New York: Wiley.

Duncan, J., and Ferguson, D. 1974. Keyboard operating posture and symptoms in operating. *Ergonomics* 17:651–62.

Eason, K. D.; Damodaran, L.; and Stewart, T. F. M. 1974. MICA survey: a report of a survey of man-computer interaction in commercial applications. Social Science Research Council Project Report on grant HR 1844/1, HVSAT Research Group, Dept. of Human Sciences, University of Technology, Loughborough, UK.

——. 1975. Interface problems in man-computer interaction. In *Human Choice and Computers*, ed. E. Mumford and H. Sackman, pp. 91–105. Amsterdam: North-Holland.

Eason, K. D. 1976. A task-tool analysis of manager-computer interaction. Paper to NATO ASI on Man-Computer Interaction. In Shackel (1981).

——. 1979. Man-computer communication in public and private computing. *Proceedings of the Infotech Conference on User-Friendly Systems*, pp. 10/1–10/13. Infotech International, Maidenhead, UK.

——. 1980. The potential of computing for the public. *Proceedings of the Infotech Conference on The Non-Expert User.* Infotech International, Maidenhead, UK.

Eason, K. D., and Sell, R. G. 1981. Case studies in job design for information processing tasks. In *Stress, Work Design and Productivity*, ed. E. N. Corlett and J. Richardson, pp. 195–208. London: Wiley.

Edwards, E., and Lees, F. P. 1972. *Man and computer in process control.* London: Institute of Chemical Engineers.

——. 1974. *The human operator in process control.* London: Taylor and Francis.

Embley, D. W.; Lan, M. T.; Leinbaugh, D. W.; and Nagy, G. 1978. A procedure for predicting program editor performance from the user's point of view. *International Journal of Man-Machine Studies* 10:639–50.

Embley, D. W., and Nagy, G. 1981. Behavioral aspects of text editors. *Computing Surveys* 13.1:33–70.

Evans, C. R. 1976. Improving the communication between people and computers. Paper to NATO ASI on Man-Computer Interaction. In Shackel (1981).

Ferguson, D., and Duncan, J. 1974. Keyboard design and operating posture. *Ergonomics* 17:731–44.

Gaines, B. R. 1979. Logical foundations for data base systems. *International Journal of Man-Machine Studies* 11:481–500.

——. 1981. The technology of interaction—dialogue programming rules. *International Journal of Man-Machine Studies* 14:133–50.

Gaines, B. R., and Facey, P. V. 1975. Some experience in interactive system development and application. *Proceedings of the IEEE* 63.6:894–911.

Gartner, G. 1981. The light at the end of the economic tunnel. *Computing* 30 April, 1981, p. 12.

Gibson, R., and Laios, L. 1978. The presentation of information to the job-shop scheduler. *Human Factors* 20:725–32.

Gilb, T. 1980. Humanized computers: the need for them and the substantial pay-off. *Computers and People* May–June, pp. 7–12, 19.

Gotlieb, C. C., and Borodin, A. 1973. *Social issues in computing.* London: Academic Press.

Grandjean, E., and Vigliani, E., eds. 1980. *Ergonomic aspects of visual display terminals.* London: Taylor and Francis.

Harris, L. 1977. User oriented data base query with the ROBOT natural language query system. *International Journal of Man-Machine Studies* 9:697–713.

Hays, M. L.; O'Connor, M. F.; and Petersen, C. R. 1975. An application of multi-attribute utility theory: design-to-cost evaluation of the US Navy's electronic warfare system. Tech. Rept. DT/TR 75–3. Decisions and Designs Inc., McLean, Vir. 22101.

Hedberg, B. 1980. Using computerised information systems to design better organisations and jobs. In Andersen (1980).

Hiltz, S. R., and Turoff, M. 1978. *The network nation.* Reading, Mass.: Addison-Wesley.

Igersheim, R. H. 1976. Managerial response to an information system. *AFIPS Conference Proceedings* 45:877–82.

Ivergard, T. B. K. 1976. Man-computer interaction in public systems. Paper to NATO ASI on Man-Computer Interaction. In Shackel (1981).

Johannsen, G., and Rouse, W. B. 1979. Mathematical concepts for modeling behaviour in complex man-machine systems. *Human Factors* 21:733-47.

Johansen, R.; Vallee, J.; and Spangler, K. 1979. *Electronic meetings.* Reading, Mass.: Addison-Wesley.

Kay, A., and Goldberg, A. 1977. Personal dynamic media. *Computer* 10.3:31–41.

Kennedy, T. C. S. 1975. Some behavioural factors affecting the training of naive users of an interactive computer system. *International Journal of Man-Machine Studies* 7:817–34.

Klemmer, E. T., and Lockhead, G. R. 1962. Productivity and errors in two keying tasks: a field study. *Journal of Applied Psychology* 46:401–8.

Kolf, F. 1980. Guidelines for the organisational implementation of information systems: concepts and experiences with the PORGI implementation handbook. In Andersen (1980).

Licklider, J. C. R. 1960. Man-computer symbiosis. *IRE Transactions on Human Factors in Electronics.* HFE1, March, pp. 4–11

Lucas, R. W. 1977. A study of patients' attitudes to computer interrogation. *International Journal of Man-Machine Studies* 9:69–86.

Maguire, M. G. 1981. A study of the problems of man-computer dialogues for naive users. Ph.D. thesis, Dept. of Maths., Computing and Statistics, Leicester Polytechnic, Leicester, UK.

Malde, B. 1977. The human intermediary in the use of computers. *Computers and People* 26.2:22–3.

———. 1978. Further research in double interaction: the simultaneous conduct of man-man and man-computer interaction. Ph.D. thesis, Loughborough University, Loughborough, UK.

Martin, J. 1973a. *Design of man-computer dialogues.* Englewood Cliffs, N.J.: Prentice-Hall.

Martin, T. H. 1973b. The user interface in interactive systems. *Annual Review of Information Science and Technology* 8:203–19.

Martin, T. H., and Parker, E. B. 1971. Designing for user acceptance of an interactive bibliographic search facility. In *Interactive Bibliographic Search: The User/Computer Interface*, ed. D. E. Walker, pp. 45–52. Montrale, N.J.: AFIPS Press.

Melnyk, V. 1972. Man-machine interface: frustration. *Journal of the American Society for Information Science* 26.6:392–401.

Miller, L. A. 1978. Behavioral studies of the programming process. IBM Report RC7367, 23 Oct. 1978. IBM T. J. Watson Research Labs., Yorktown Heights, N.Y.

Miller, L. A., and Thomas, J. C. 1977. Behavioral issues in the use of interactive systems. *International Journal of Man-Machine Studies* 9:509–36.

Miller, R. B. 1971. Human ease of use criteria and their tradeoffs. TR 00.2185, 12 April 1971. IBM Corporation, Poughkeepsie, N.Y.

Mumford, E. 1980. The participative design of clerical information systems— two case studies. In Andersen (1980).

Mumford, E., and Banks, O. 1968. *The computer and the clerk.* London: Routledge and Kegan Paul.

Mumford, E., and Sackman, H. 1975. *Human choice and computers.* Amsterdam: North-Holland.

Negroponte, N. 1981. Media Room. *Proceedings S.I.D.* 22–2:109–13.

Nicholls, J. E. 1979. Programming the end user. In *Man-Computer Communication*, ed. B. Shackel. *Infotech State of the Art Report Vol. 2*, pp. 263–72. Infotech International, Maidenhead, UK.

Ostberg, O. 1976. Office computerisation in Sweden: worker participation, workplace design considerations and the reduction of visual strain. Paper to NATO ASI on Man-Computer Interaction. In Shackel (1981).

Palme, J. 1977. A man-computer interface encouraging user growth. FAO Rept. C10073-Ms (E5, H9), Stockholm: Forsvarets Forskningsanstalt.

Parsons, H. M. 1972. *Man-machine system experiments.* Baltimore: Johns Hopkins Press.

Pearce, B. G. ed. 1983. Health hazards of VDUs? Conference Proceedings. London: Wiley, forthcoming.

Phister, M. 1976. *Data processing technology and economics*. Santa Monica, Calif.: Santa Monica Pub. Co.

Price, C. R.; Turoff, M.; and Hiltz, S. R. 1980. Electronic mail and teleconferencing: 'information' or communication? March 1980. EURIM 4 Conference, Brussels.

Ramsey, H. R., and Atwood, M. E. 1979. Human factors in computer systems: a review of the literature. Tech. Rept. SAI-79-111-DEN (NTIS No. ADA075679) Englewood, Colo.: Science Applications.

Ramsey, H. R.; Atwood, M. E.; and Kirshbaum, P. J. 1978. A critically annotated bibliography of the literature of human factors in systems. Tech. Rept. SAI-78-070-DEN (NTIS No. ADA058081) Englewood, Colo.: Science Applications.

Reisner, P. 1981. Human factors studies of data base query languages: a survey and assessment. *Computing Surveys* 13.1:13–31.

Roberts, T. L. 1979. Evaluation of computer text-editors. Xerox Report SSL-79-9, Xerox Palo Alto Research Center, Palo Alto, Calif.

Rouse, W. B. 1975. Design of man-computer interfaces for online interactive systems. *Proceedings of the IEEE* 63.6:847–57.

————. 1977. Human-computer interaction in multitask situations. *IEEE Transactions on Systems, Man, and Cybernetics* SMC7.5:384–92.

————. 1981. Human-computer interaction in the control of dynamic systems. *Computing Surveys* 13.1:71–99.

Sackman, H. 1970. *Man/computer problem solving*. Philadelphia: Auerbach.

Shackel, B. 1969. Man-computer interaction: the contribution of the human sciences. *Ergonomics* 12:485–99.

————. ed. 1974. *Applied ergonomics handbook*. Guildford, UK: IPC Science and Technology Press.

————. 1979a. Man-computer communication. *Infotech State of the Art Report Vol. 1*. Infotech International, Maidenhead, UK.

————. 1979b. The ergonomics of the man-computer interface. In *Man-Computer Communication*, ed. B. Shackel. *Infotech State of the Art Report Vol. 2*, pp. 299-324. Infotech International, Maidenhead, UK.

————. 1981. *Man-computer interaction*. Alphen-aan-den Rijn, Netherlands: Sijthoff and Noordhoff.

Shackel, B., and Shipley, P. 1969. Man-computer interaction: a review of ergonomics literature and related research. EMI Electronics Report DMP 3472. EMI, Hayes, Middlesex, UK.

Sheridan, T. B., and Johannsen, G., eds. 1976. *Monitoring behaviour and supervisory control*. London: Plenum.

Stewart, T. F. M. 1974. Ergonomic aspects of man-computer problem solving. *Applied Ergonomics* 5:209–12.

————. 1976a. Displays and the software interface. *Applied Ergonomics* 7:137–46.

————. 1976b. The specialist user. Paper to NATO ASI on Man-Computer Interaction. In Shackel (1981).

————. 1981. More practical experiences in solving VDU ergonomics problems. In Pearce (1983).

Thomas, J. C. 1977. Psychological issues in data base management. In *Proceedings of the 3rd International Conference on Very Large Data Bases* pp. 169–84. New York: IEEE.

————. 1978. A design-interpretation analysis of natural English with applications to man-computer interaction. *International Journal of Man-Machine Studies* 10:651–68.

Ting, T. C., and Badre, A. N. 1976. A dynamic model of man-machine interactions: design and application with an audiographic learning facility. *International Journal of Man-Machine Studies* 8:75–88.

Toffler, A. 1980. *The third wave.* London: Collins.

Turoff, M., and Hiltz, S. R. 1980. Personal communication to the Author. April, 1980.

Van Cott, H. P., and Kincade, R. G., eds. 1972. *Human engineering guide to equipment design.* Wash., D.C.: U.S. Govt. Printing Office.

Zoltan, E., and Chapanis, A. 1982. What do professional persons think about computers? *Behavior and Information Technology* 1.1:55–68.

DESIGNING THE VDT INTERFACE FOR HUMAN-COMPUTER PRODUCTIVITY

James H. Bair

INTRODUCTION

Computers are intended to provide some payback for their direct use by individuals. This simple statement has been the implicit basis for the acquisition of billions of dollars worth of computer-based office equipment in the past few years. It has been a generally accepted premise for the data processing industry. However, I observed a typical case recently which caused me to question that premise. It was the last day before a critical report had to be printed and shipped to a client. Some years of experience had reinforced the policy of providing backup when such deadlines are imminent. Report production continued using the advanced text processing system, and, just in case, work proceeded manually, using typewriters, "whiteout", and all the other conventional methods of document production.*

To the surprise and consternation of all involved, the manual process required less effort than the computer-based process, and both resulted in the same quality. It even seemed to involve less frustration and stress, a not

---

*The views expressed in this article are those of the author and not necessarily those of Bell-Northern Research.

uncommon phenomenon with computers (Zuboff, 1982). When the lease of the computer system was also considered, there was a general cry of disbelief at the overall cost. Something had gone awry in this use of computers in the office, contrary to expectations based on the current fad. Perhaps the productive use of computers might be a far more complex challenge than the "bandwagon crier" led prospective users to believe. This example will be analyzed in more detail in the sections that follow.

The problem lies in the fact that the *functionality* of a computer system has in itself a low relationship to improving productivity. A product with the advertised function "word processing" may or may not yield the productivity improvements claimed for word processing in general. It is the *design* of computers that will determine profitable use. This appears to be more the case with the recently popularized functions intended for office automation such as computer messaging, records management, teleconferencing, calendaring, spreadsheet calculations, and personal administration. These have been offered together as "integrated office systems" (IOS) or as unifunctional products such as word processors. There are over 100 office automation products now available and that presents a major problem: product selection generally precedes the direct experience necessary to evaluate design. This first step is like the supermarket phase of preparing a gourmet dinner. The selection of the ingredients will limit the outcome, no matter how excellent the cooking.

This chapter presents design factors that can greatly assist in product selection as well as development. These same design factors that can improve productivity can also affect the salability of products, thus providing the basis of a potential competitive edge in the highly diverse marketplace. However, little is known about the impact of superior design on marketability. There may be little relationship between design and perceived value unless the buyers' perspective can be broadened to include ideas such as those presented here. The different perspectives of design will be discussed later. First, we begin with brief definitions of "productivity" and "design." Then the problem of design, a framework for understanding and measuring design effects on productivity, and recommendations for improving designs are offered.

DEFINITIONS

Productivity

People often disagree about the meaning of some of the major concepts important to this discussion. First, we do not construe the concept of productivity in a Tayloristic sense as the term was applied to manufacturing assembly lines. Some economists have derided this "ethos of efficiency" because it is constraining and inhumane. For this discussion, production implies quantification of both effort and return, but there is allowance for the gray area of difficult-to-quantify returns for knowledge-worker effort.

Traditionally, productivity is the ratio of the number of units of output to the number of units of input ($P = O/I$). Productivity rises when the number of units of output increases and the number of units of input holds constant; or, conversely, when the number of units of output remains fixed and the number of units of input is decreased. In manufacturing, output is generally measured by counting the units of production, e.g., the number of toothbrushes rolling off an assembly line, or the number of flatirons. Input consists of such factors as labor, direct expenses, and overhead. Productivity can be measured by converting the input and output units to their respective dollar equivalents. This is relatively easy to do where input and output units are readily identifiable and countable.

However, it is much more difficult to measure the productivity of knowledge workers (KW) because input and output are not straightforward to quantify. The production of knowledge workers is varied and largely intangible; more qualitative elements are involved than quantitative, and output results may not be immediately apparent. By its very nature, the information which knowledge workers process is amorphous, renewable, and dynamically changing in relevance and value as a function of time (Cuadra, 1982). Consequently, productivity will be viewed as the looser relationship between effort expended and results returned.

Design

The concept of design can imply everything from computer hardware architecture to software modularity. However, from the user's perspective, design can be understood as the process that produces what the user sees, touches, and interacts with on several levels. The levels include the keyboard, pointing devices, and other controls; a presentation language that delivers information to the user; an action language that commands the computer; a knowledge of specific actions and sequences of actions that are necessary to accomplish office tasks; and the support system that encourages the necessary learning and usage. Essentially, design results in a system which represents one instance of a "window" into the digital information world.

For this discussion, we focus on those aspects of design of an IOS (Integrated Office System) product that affect its usage by an individual operator. This consists primarily of the *action language* whereby the user controls the computer, and secondarily, the *presentation language* for providing feedback to the user. This focus is necessary to narrow the scope of this paper sufficiently to permit specific and concrete recommendations that will have the most impact on user productivity.

SETTING THE SCOPE OF
PRODUCTIVITY DISCUSSION

Having narrowed our scope in terms of design, we will further narrow it in terms of productivity. The overall system affecting productivity includes the computer, the user interacting with a machine, the organization, and the economy—far too much for a single discussion. It is necessary to limit the large number of variables that must be taken into account in order to study productivity change. Identifying levels of productivity change facilitates realistic investigation and provides a conceptual framework. Performance at each level is dependent upon the performance of the constituent subsystems. The choice of a level will limit the variables that must be taken into account thus defining the productivity measurement scope. Four levels of productivity change and the respective variables have been identified (Bair, 1982):

1. Computer. The computer's actual performance measured against its technical specifications.
2. Human-Computer Dyad. The human and computer system, working as a unit, where the cost equals computer cost plus human effort (labor). See Figure C–1.
3. Organization. Many humans or human-computer dyads connected formally and informally in a communication system that has definable input and output.
4. Economic. The business context of an organization such as the marketplace, the national economy, and the labor pool.

Level 1: Computer

Computer performance can be determined in an isolated laboratory setting. Such a determination includes the performance of the computer that is testable using laboratory equipment, and it does not take into account operator factors such as usability, ease of learning, or the management of the installation. It does include reliability (failure rate), equipment error rate, maximum execution speed, required maintenance, and equipment capabilities or features. Concerns about human factors at this level include ergonomics (display resolution, keyboard layout, etc.), and operation effort such as the keystrokes per transaction. Operation effort may be determined by time and motion studies.

Level 2: Human-Computer Dyad

Human-computer performance depends upon equipment performance and is measured in the larger context of user performance. Thus, individual differences between users, workflow control, operating methods, learning rates, and the variations in input and output have to be considered. At this level,

**NON-SPECIALIST
END-USER**

**VDT: WINDOW INTO
THE COMPUTER WORLD**

Knowledge and skills

software design

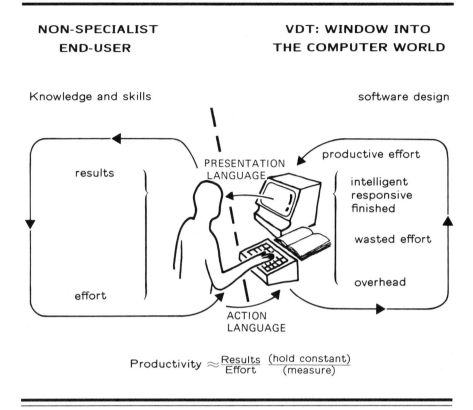

results

PRESENTATION
LANGUAGE

productive effort

intelligent
responsive
finished

wasted effort

overhead

effort

ACTION
LANGUAGE

$$\text{Productivity} \approx \frac{\text{Results}}{\text{Effort}} \quad \frac{\text{(hold constant)}}{\text{(measure)}}$$

Figure C–1.   Human-computer dyad.

productivity is most commonly measured by the production rate; for example, the number of lines typed per day for a word processing function. Human factors are indirectly measured by error rate and increases in errors due to fatigue. Cost factors involve the complex trade-off between the output per unit labor and the utilization rate. Utilization is a function of usability and the number of functions available. The effect of different features, such as character display versus bit-mapped display, can be measured at this level.

Level 3: Organization

Organizational performance depends on the equipment performance, user performance, and office work unit performance. Production typically is measured by counting the products that are completed on schedule. However, numerous factors affect user performance beyond the human-computer dyad, making organizational performance much more difficult to quantify (Bullen, Bennett, and Carlson, 1982). Factors such as attitudes, morale, management style, organizational climate, and office operating procedures must be taken into account. Performance indicators include personnel absenteeism, turnover, overtime, and labor costs. Labor costs may be for output units or for units of time. Identified goals and functions of the organization must be translated into performance criteria.

Organizational performance also has a qualitative dimension that is more difficult to measure. However, the ultimate judge of quality is the recipient of the end products of the organizational unit. In offices where the primary product is textual (reports, plans, papers, etc.), the management is likely to be the recipient. To measure quality, we can obtain subjective judgments from the product recipients by using well-developed measurement instruments from the social sciences (Bair, 1974). Similar instruments can also be used to rate the quality of services and processes where specific products are difficult to define.

Level 4: Economic

The economic level refers to the impacts of the economic environment on organizational behavior (Strassmann, 1977). For example, an austerity program due to the state of the economy may decrease morale and provide inadequate resources to meet organizational goals. Lack of personnel or support services could cancel any advantages of increased human-computer performance. Conversely, economic conditions can place high demand and workload on the organization, resulting in temporarily increased performance. The general state of the economy affects the availability of labor, materials and services, support costs, and so on. Government policies, current sales, seasonal variations, and earnings all place different pressures on an organization that ultimately affect the performance of individuals. Separating these effects from those of the computer system itself is necessary in order to determine the system's impact on productivity.

The discussion in this chapter focuses on Level 2, although the measurement or understanding of productivity must ultimately take into consideration all four levels. Historically, it has been very misleading to focus only on the human-computer dyad level without understanding the overall context as described above. Most word processing equipment has been justified by measuring changes in typing performance of an operator-machine dyad. Results at this level showed as much as 300% productivity improvement (Konkel and Peck, 1976), or more specifically, three times more lines of typewritten text per hour. However, these results overlooked the relationship at an organizational level between the word processing service and the service users. For example, typing tasks were queued for weeks, and when finally returned, contained numerous errors that the author had to mark for correction. Authors, on the other hand, considered word processing an invitation to increase the number of revisions tenfold, thus canceling any potential productivity increase for the organization.

THE HUMAN-COMPUTER DYAD

The Problem

A major criterion used in the buyer community for selecting one system over another is the functionality of the product, i.e., teleconferencing, messaging, word processing, filing, spreadsheet calculations, or data base management. Buyers tend to not discriminate among products having the same functions, and thus place insufficient emphasis on design. In some cases, the criterion is a new technological development or easy-to-identify, "gee-whiz" novelty. Numerous "soft" factors enter into the selection, including vendor loyalty and the personality of the salesperson.

This widespread practice is leading to IOS implementations that do not improve productivity. They are too inefficient at the human-computer level, as in the document production example described in the introduction and below in more detail. Since the *status quo* is difficult to challenge under any circumstances, and particularly difficult here because of a low awareness of the problem, we will present the problem as three hypotheses and follow with an example.

1. The human effort required to accomplish a task may often be greater with the computer than without.
2. Given typical designs, it is difficult to provide concrete evidence for sufficient benefits to justify the extra effort of using an IOS.
3. Functionality may be present, but efficiency of use may not.

Evidence to support these negative hypotheses is not widely available in the literature. Comparisons have been made between different system text editors (Roberts, 1979), but few have been made between an IOS and a manual approach to accomplish an office task. An unpublished comparison was made by the author at the Stanford Research Institute and is summarized in Figure C–2. The observation constitutes only one data-point, but informal discussion indicates that it is representative of a significant proportion of the outcomes in document production applications. The study found that it would have required the same amount of labor to prepare a document manually as it did using an expensive computer system (approximately $15 per hour).

Why did it require similar time and effort using the document production function of an IOS compared to manual typing? At a detailed level, the answer would be tedious (one of the reasons buyers are not aware of it). It involves the execution of numerous procedures by the system in response to even more numerous actions by the user. User actions take *time*, as is shown in detail by Card, Moran, and Newell (1980) and in the chapter by Card. For example, the system files must be located and retrieved each time the user logs onto the system. The logon procedure itself consumes time and often is thwarted by modems that do not respond and computers that are "full." The entry of text requires an additional effort to define the format of the text, in this example

Work product: 100 page final report, mostly text
Proportion of Change required: 35% of the text

Using an IOS

System: A screen editor operating under UNIX
Labor required: Approximately 11 hours over 2 days
New Errors: Approximately 1 every 2 pages

Manual Typing Alternative

Labor required: 11 hours at 60 wpm
Errors: 1 every 3 pages

Figure C–2. Unproductive use of an IOS.

by typing in three or four character directives, or "macros," for every format change except the end of a line. Often the effect of the macros on the format is uncertain, so time must be spent printing drafts periodically to "see what happened."

Perhaps the most important consumption of time in the IOS editing process is the identification of the changes to be made in the text. In each case, a cursor must be stepped along characters and lines (rows of characters) to the beginning and the end of the change. In the case of "moves" and "copies," the beginning and end of the text must be identified and then the destination of text must be found. Additionally, for each change the user must search a paper copy of the text and then translate that paper search to the computer search. Often it is easier to type in some characters that identify the necessary locations ("literal string") than to move the cursor. Whatever the unique editing operation, these actions require time, and much of that time is overhead necessitated only by the limited IOS design. A set of recommended features will be presented in later sections that minimize the overhead of system usage and operation, and at the same time give the user more control and consequent satisfaction.

Is this an isolated instance unrepresentative of integrated office systems in general? A few years ago, the Comptroller General of the United States published a blue paper asking the question more generally for the federal government (1979). The study showed that the millions of dollars expended on word processors had not observably reduced operating cost. Instead, operating costs had increased due to the acquisition of word processors. More recently, a large soft-drink manufacturer purchased $17 million dollars worth of word processing equipment from one of the most popular vendors. Within six months they returned the order because productivity had dropped 50%. Of course, this latter example is not documented and is subject to challenge. However, it should serve as a serious warning of the consequences to buyers and vendors if user performance is not given increased attention.

Why is there not a more general awareness of these problems with the productive use of current IOS systems, at least for the editing/document production function? Why do people continue to buy systems that apparently have high user overhead and result in unproductive performance? One major reason is the perspective of the opposing forces affecting system design and acquisition.

FOUR PERSPECTIVES

Perhaps design problems would be readily solvable if the agreed-upon solution were to meet user needs for improved performance. However, there are four very different perceptions of the required solution that confound even the most user-oriented design approach: (1) what the system-chooser will buy, (2) what the user says he needs, (3) what industry can develop, and (4) what will actually increase human-computer productivity. Each perspective brings a fundamentally different question:

1. Buyers in the marketplace: "What can I afford?"
2. End-user subjective perception: "What do I like?"
3. Vendor/technologist: "What can I make?"
4. User-science empirical measurement: "What enables optimum performance?"

Perspective 1: Chooser

The system chooser is the decision maker in an institution acquiring a service. His criteria are primarily economic, including a limited investment per person, a desired rate of return, and a defined amortization period. Very often, up-front economic constraints prohibit sufficient investment in well-designed equipment and user support needed to achieve critical mass (e.g., having enough users) and long-range viability.

Perspective 2: End User

A frequent misconception is that the user can tell designers what he needs. However, the process of self-diagnosis is woefully inadequate as the sole determinant of needs. Certainly, users must be polled and seriously regarded when selecting a system, but super-human powers of prediction should not be expected of them. A user cannot evaluate a technology he or she has not used. Effort is much better spent determining the user's values and criteria for success in the context of his current work environment. Design can then be refined based on how the user needs to perform, independent of a particular technology.

Perspective 3:   Vendor

Even if the user could anticipate the optimum design of useful technology, industry currently would have difficulty delivering that design at a competitive price. In numerous consulting studies, the author has found that currently available systems could not meet the chooser's or the user's criteria. Perhaps we are seeing industry's reaction to user self-diagnosis, resulting in a situation where neither the user's actual needs or industry's sales requirements capability are met—almost a "catch-22" effect. Industry perceives users' needs in light of the popular capabilities of mass-produced technology. For example, if the user wants an integrated telecommunications system for voice and data, he most likely will receive a telephone PBX switch that requires duplicate wiring for any digital transmission, in other words, a local area network and a separate voice network. Or, for office automation, he will likely receive a word processor which uses special purpose hardware for mechanized typing and disregards other office functions; in other words, a mass-produced non-solution. The limitation is not the potential of industry, but industry's perception of system design, an idea vividly presented by Morton, et al. (1979).

Perspective 4:   User-Science

The convergence of the foregoing three perspectives does not yet address the most important question: what will increase user effectiveness? Plagued with two problems—how to measure changes in effectiveness and how to determine the relationship of these changes to design variables—this perspective remains a frontier for design-related research. In an overview of a measurement methodology for automated offices (Bair, 1982), the author proposed a conceptual model of the variables that must be measured, methods of measurement, and the measurement controls that must be followed. Some of the results of measurement, particularly the relationship if design changes to improve efficiency, are reported in other publications (Bair, 1979). A conclusion from this work is that users often cannot judge what will improve their effectiveness. The effect of design factors must be measured indirectly, regardless of whether the factors are cursor control or the capabilities of an electronic message function.

There are two notable examples of the need for the user-science approach. First, I have found that users resist buying or using the "mouse" cursor control device. However, user-scientists at SRI International (Engelbart, 1973) and elsewhere (Card, 1978) have shown significant improvements in the efficiency of editing and other interactive VDT tasks using the mouse. The improvement is so great that it appears worth the effort to add a mouse to present work stations. More than ten years after the original research, adding a mouse is now possible for personal computers through the use of software (VisiOn^{TM} from Visicorp and others). The mouse is also included as part of the Lisa^{TM} from Apple Computer. The second example results from the difference between initial user desires for functional capabilities of electronic message systems and their perceptions after several months of experience. Invariably, the user's desire for a simple system with few commands for sending short messages gives way to dissatisfaction with the limited functions and results in a demand for the additional functions identified by user-science.

In these examples, users could not define the interface design or the capabilities and functions required to increase their effectiveness. Thus, users' perceptions, only one of four perspectives of system design, are not appropriate as the sole basis of design decisions. However, the user's perspective is a very important component in implementation success. The user's perceptions can aid designers in understanding user expectations of system characteristics, and can provide the basis of user participation in implementation.

MEASUREMENT OF
HUMAN-COMPUTER PERFORMANCE

Three assumptions about human-computer performance and productivity are made for this discussion. The first assumption is that an isolated subsystem's performance can be meaningfully measured, even though it is affected by numerous external variables. While the isolation is artificial, measurement is possible because the variables from the other subsystems can be held constant while computer design is varied. We have completed successful measurements at Bell-Northern Research (BNR) enabling us to compare IOS designs (unpublished).

Secondly, the optimization of performance does not require a statistical understanding of the design factors that lead to differences in performance. When measurements show a significant difference in performance using different computers, the computer system increasing the performance of the dyad can be selected for production or implementation, all other factors being equal.

Thirdly, productivity improvement at the higher, organizational level is not guaranteed by optimizing the individual subsystems. But there is a high probability of a strong effect. The focus here is on the dyad as a building block, supposedly the most important constituent of organizational productivity change when an IOS is implemented.

We also assume that the design factors that are responsible for different measurement outcomes can be treated as aggregates. Isolating the degree to which each design factor affects productivity is difficult. Any single factor may have an unmeasurable influence on performance, but collectively the influence of groups of factors is indentifiable through the measures or analysis discussed here.

Although the discussion of quantitative versus qualitative measurement is being sidestepped here, important measures of quality are described. In this context, quality refers to the user's expectations for computer performance. The user's performance will be negatively affected if his actions lead to results different from those he expected. The hesitancy that results from a computer response inconsistent with user expectations will obviously result in slower task accomplishment. Conversely, the appeal of a design may enhance performance by increasing motivation and concentration. Given these assumptions, the measures of human-computer performance which can provide quantitative as well as qualitative data are listed in Figure C–3.

An example of a typical task will illustrate the less straightforward measures beginning with *mental workload*. Online composition is one of the longest tasks when IOSs are fully utilized. It includes some initial editing, although additional editing is likely to be done by the author from a marked-up printout of a draft. During composition the user's concentration should be entirely on the content of the document. The mental workload imposed by the system will interfere with that composition process, adding what is essentially an overhead burden. The measurement involves counting the number of times the user must divert his attention from the content to the use of the system. He may need to merely command, "Insert," and point to the location on the screen. Or he may have to enter directives that differentiate paragraphs, headings, bullets, etc. An unnecessary decision must be made for each directive, and additional mental effort may be required to select or remember the needed directive.

A test of interference effect, common in psychological research, can serve to measure the relative *mental workload* of designs. Subjects are asked an

---

Quantitive Measures: Efficiency
1.   Total job time
2.   Task time (several tasks make up a job)
3.   Mental workload
     a. number and difficulty of decisions
     b. effect of cognitive interference
4.   Number of keystrokes
5.   Number of errors in command-control input
6.   Learning time (for comparative capability)

Qualitative Measures: Value
1.   Consistency
2.   Complexity
3.   Appearance and appeal
4.   Comparability of output
5.   Predictability of system behavior

Figure C–3.   Measures of human-computer performance.

unrelated question which interferes with an editing task. A longer response time to this question indicates more mental effort is required by the editing task. Similarly, the effect of the question on the editing task completion time indicates how much mental effort is required by the editor. Roberts (1979) used this method to show that the design of some editor systems requires more mental workload than others. In general, the greater the effect of interference, the poorer the design.

The *number of keystrokes* required by different designs varies considerably. Card et al. (1980) have measured the time for each keystroke. The number of keystrokes is counted during an actual task performance, or they are estimated through analysis of the interaction sequences required by different system designs. The keystrokes required for system control are differentiated from those required for entering text during composition. The total number of control keystrokes multiplied by the standard time for each is a measure of the added effort required for system operation. A system that requires significantly fewer keystrokes, and thus less overhead time, results in improved user performance.

The keystroke-level measurement is useful but insufficient to determine the optimal design. Often an increased number of keystrokes may result in a reduced *number of errors*. This trade-off can be measured by counting the number of errors the user makes. With some designs, such as the Augment system (Tymshare, Inc.), extra keystrokes are necessary in order to provide a consistent action language. The trade-off is justified if it results in fewer errors, or decreased learning or relearning time.

Learning time is one of the most touted judgments of design in the IOS marketplace. Though it is important and can be easily observed and measured, it may be misleading. It must be evaluated based on the capability attained when a user is considered to have "learned the system." A longer learning time is warranted if the user can access more needed functions. The learning effort to accomplish certain tasks must also be weighed against the other tasks the user can accomplish using the same skills.

The qualitative concept of *consistency* can offset *complexity*. It is generally assumed that an exceptionally complex design will require significantly more time to accomplish the tasks. However, a system that is complex need not reduce performance if it is relatively consistent. For example, the spelling check function varies considerably in consistency and complexity, and its operation is usually indicative of overall design. In one exemplary system, the spelling check is both inconsistent and complex. First, the user must run the spell program against a file of text, generating another file with the list of candidate misspelled words. The two files must be loaded simultaneously, so that the user can switch between them. Then he must find the candidate misspelling in the text file, and replace it with the correct word from the word list file. The process of re-finding the misspelled word repeats what the program already did in its run over the file. In addition, this procedure is inconsistent with all other editing tasks. The process is even more complex than this description of it, yet it is part of a "successful" IOS currently on the market. A contrasting system presents each candidate word by highlighting it on the screen, and simultaneously presents the candidate correct spellings in a different window on the screen. The user merely points with a mouse to the appropriate correct spelling, which can then be automatically corrected throughout the remainder of the file. This procedure is consistent with other editing tasks.

The foregoing example illustrates the kind of situation where the overhead effort for using a function, i.e. the former spelling check, is greater than the benefit. In the document production example, the user may elect to compose offline for similar reasons. These examples focus exclusively on designs where usage overhead is the deciding factor. However, if the spelling check or the document production function provide sufficiently valuable results, the usage cost may be accommodated. Thus, a *comparison of results* should be included in qualitative evaluations. For example, the opportunity to produce typeset results in document production may trade off against other factors such as usage complexity.

Similarly, the use of a product will be affected by its *appearance*. If it is appealing and the user does not feel demeaned while using it, it will probably promote performance. Online keyboarding that makes a manager appear to be doing clerical work is likely to be demotivating. However, the same task accomplished on a flashy, portable terminal that looks like a high-powered analytical tool (e.g., the Compass from Grid Systems Inc.) may motivate the user to perform more efficiently.

Perhaps the most important measure of overall design adequacy is the degree to which a user's commands lead to results he expects. With sufficient learning, the user will build a mental model of the *system's behavior,* a process becoming understood by cognitive psychologists such as Moran (1981). During composition, the user expects that the entry of text is captured and retained unless he commands otherwise. His model does not include potential loss of his recorded thoughts due to memory errors, disk crashes, or noise in the communication lines. If a user composes a long paragraph and suddenly it disappears because of a phone line disconnection that aborts the program, he will loose motivation to use the system. Similarly, if a user enters a formatting command during keyboarding and on the printed version observes a result contrary to his expectations, the wasted effort can lead to demotivation. As we will discuss in the next section, users' expectations shift as they obtain more experience and as they evolve as system users.

TWO MEASUREMENT CHALLENGES

The use of the quantitative and qualitative measures discussed in the foregoing section must take into account at least the two measurement challenges presented below.

Challenge 1:   User Experience Confounds Measurement[*]

Generalizing from a laboratory situation to the "real world" is more difficult when studying users of IOS than other users of technology. Measurement must take into account that first, the user's skill development improves performance; second, there are different user roles in the daily office environment; and third, users continually change and evolve as they gain experience. The challenge of generalizing results from users who are continually undergoing change is greater than might be initially expected.

The development of a skill we can refer to as intuition is likely to be a key confounding variable. In this context, intuition is not taken as innate, but as an intellectual skill. The effect is analogous to that observed in learning natural language, such as English. A small child cannot even conceive of the abstract system of symbols we call language. His conception is initially restricted to a physical world within the reach of his senses. The child's learning of language depends on developing intuition, or what Piaget (1955) calls "a subliminal syntax generator," not acquiring a set of explicit rules. Just as the child's experience is the basis for knowing how to construct utterances as meaningful sequences of words, the user learns the language of digital technology. As experience grows, so does the subliminal understanding, or Gestalt, of how and what to do next in the complex interaction with a computer. Future performance may be guided by this learned intuition and thus may not be easily projected from current measurements.

The intuitive skills of communicating with computers may have less influence than the development of motor skills. Studies done at BNR (unpublished) found that motor skills were a major factor in determining performance. Cursor positioning and use of the 96-plus ASCII keys and function buttons requires skills beyond typing. The longer and more intense (in terms of hours per day) the usage, the more likely a user is to gain facility with the typical VDT/keyboard interface. Heavy users tend to be clerical staff, who also seem to have the patience to cope with awkward motor actions. Since managers and professionals are not likely to have "longtensity" (defined as "longevity plus intensity of use" by Bair, 1974), they will never develop the motor skill level of clerical persons.

The role of individuals in the office, ranging from clerical to executive, has a strong effect on the development of both intellectual and motor skills. In my research, it is becoming clear that the interface design which promotes high performance for the clerical user may be dangerously inadequate for the professional. Thus, we cannot generalize to all users from the unskilled user who will never master the dexterity required by typical designs. In addition, the unskilled user may develop the intellectual understanding that generates greater need for features and functions. In other words, the user may have the

---

[*]The examples presented as part of this account are based on repeated experiences with actual systems.

need but not the opportunity to develop the requisite skill. The office situation promotes this because managers rarely have periods of uninterrupted time to interact with the computer.

Changes over time in intellectual and motor skills result in major user differences which can be described as *evolutionary*. Users progress through several stages as they acquire skills and understanding (Palme, 1982). Any measurement must be adjusted to accommodate the user's present stage. For example, we cannot compare new users (up to one month) and long-term users. Neither may have progressed beyond a "hunt and peck" approach to the keyboard, but the long-term user will be much more in need of consistent and predictable performance on the part of the system. All too often, a system designed to be simple for the beginner will not perform well for the long-term user who has evolved in his understanding of the features and functions he needs.

Challenge 2: New Users are Not Specialists

Office uses of computers tend to be much more casual than in previous data processing applications of interactive computer technology, such as point-of-sale systems. Casual usage of a wide variety of functions, such as electronic mail, results in a new breed of users—the nonspecialists. Figure C–4 summarizes the differences between specialists and nonspecialists. The specialist user is essentially hired to operate a terminal to complete required tasks; for example, order entry clerks, airline reservation attendants, programmers, and MIS data base operators. The special nuances of terminals, log-in protocols, network connections, and communication modalities are dealt with as part of the job. In a recent study of information processing at a large bank, BNR found surprising tolerance by these specialists for suboptimal performance and design. For example, they tolerated interactive response times of two to five minutes and the need for several actions to move a block of text. Specialists accepted poor system performance because they were accustomed to it and system usage was required as part of their job.

The nonspecialist user does not need computer technology for successful completion of his job. He already has adequate tools to accomplish what he was hired for, tools taken for granted such as paper, telephones, and view-graphs. The motivation to use new tools requires perceiving them to be easy to use, reliable, and as responsive as the old tools. While perception of increased capability can be traded off against poor design, the user's awareness of decreased efficiency may eventually erode the tolerance. Consider that the 1985 integrated office system is targeted at professionals, managers, and executives, who are results-oriented and ambitious. It is highly improbable that a product could penetrate much of this market with current computer interfaces and the users' lower tolerance for design shortcomings.

Another way to describe the differences between new office users and specialists is in terms of compliance. Compliance results from the pressure

Specialist:

1. System use is part of employment
2. Job cannot be done without system
3. Willing to invest whatever effort necessary
   for operation
4. Very often has technical background
5. High compliance
6. Uni-task and uni-function worker

Nonspecialist:

1. System use not necessary
2. Job can be adequately done without system
3. Ideally would not invest any extra effort
4. Often not interested in technical details
5. Low compliance
6. Multi-function, knowledge worker

Figure C–4. Differences between specialist and nonspecialist users of computer systems.

placed on the individual by his organization to use the system and this has been documented as one of the most important predictors of system acceptance and amount of subsequent usage (Hiltz and Kerr, 1981). Hiltz's extensive research focuses on the causes of system acceptance. However, acceptance implies a choice about system usage. The specialist user essentially has no choice and will tolerate poor design, whereas the nonspecialist user has a different psychological perspective. This has long been implicitly recognized, as indicated by commonplace statements such as "managers will not type." But it remains a problem insufficiently addressed by designers of office systems. Ways in which IOSs can be designed to encourage voluntary use are discussed in the next section.

RECOMMENDATIONS FOR DESIGN

Many recommendations in the literature on interface design appear inconsistent and abstract, such as "systems should be user friendly." But the existence of platitudes does not preclude the need for general recommendations to significantly increase the users' performance through interface design. The three recommendations presented here are distilled from the literature and the author's research and experience. Specific features that would optimize performance are listed under each recommendation.

Recommendation I: Maximize
The Routine Intelligence of the System

Most IOSs do not "understand" the simplest elements of the user's information environment, such as required output formats and components of language (Nickerson, 1981). This recommendation is intended to be a simple idea of how to enhance user performance, and not an excursion into the futuristic world of artificial intelligence. Understanding the user's information environment implies some intelligence, but it can be differentiated from heuristic processes by referring to it as "routine." Some examples of routine intelligence applications are listed in Figure C–5.

Routine "intelligence" has two widely differing components: first, the accomplishment of structured, repetitive tasks by the computer, and second, the ability to manipulate information components such as words and paragraphs. In the earlier example of document production, the user spent a great deal of time finding the text to be edited, manipulating the text character by character, and then inserting formatting instructions, as well as retrieving files and logging on and off the system. We do not need to know the exact time required by these different actions; if they are minimized, we have saved time. Both components of routine intelligence can increase efficiency as shown by the author's studies and experience. Without going into a detailed comparison, the following suggests an alternative to the dumb interface used in our example.

Logging on must be done numerous times unless the computer connection can be maintained through breaks, lunch, etc. It would be trivial for a computer terminal to accept a credit card or user command to "connect me" and then handle the details, including dial-up, data rate selection, and program call. For example, in order to connect to a foreign host the GRID Compass personal computer requires only switching the power on, typing a password, and selecting a menu item. The GRID Compass will dial all calls and make all connections with needed remote resources.

Users will readily agree with the need for automatic connection and logon. By contrast, the "understanding" of basic language components is a bit

Logon logistics
File writing actions
Language components; e.g., words, sentences, paragraphs
Structural relationships between headings, sections, tables, figures, etc.
Formats for printing
Spelling, to check and learn user's words

Figure C–5.   Examples of what an IOS should understand.

more difficult to visualize. Its most basic form is simply word wrap, where a user does not have to end lines with a carriage return—the system uses spaces and punctuation to "understand" word bounds and fits the words to lines without user effort.

Although most people structure text into paragraphs and sections, only one system on the market permits manipulation of these language components and maintains the relationship between them (Tymshare's Augment, described in Uhlig et al., 1979). Other systems come close by enabling the user to mark the start and end of paragraphs, but the relationship between paragraphs and headings is not "known" to the computer. In our example, the user spent a lot of time "cutting and pasting" sections and paragraphs. Each editing action required that the user find the beginning and ending of each block of text on the screen that was on a paper draft. This is time consuming, and the cursor control requires stressful precision motor coordination. With the recommended computer "understanding" of language structure, the user would see a representation of paragraphs and headings, with each paragraph tied to its heading or preceding paragraph. The user can point to any part of the representation of paragraphs and headings to move, copy, or delete it. In this case the user is editing structure rather than words. This method of seeing the structure of a document on the screen contrasts sharply with most editors which force the user to address text as a long, monotonous list of characters and lines. Tables and figures should also be addressable as units, as on Apple Computer's new Lisa (for graphics only), rather than marked explicitly at the beginning and ending by the user.

There has long been a general awareness that "what you see is what you get" should apply to the format of text on a screen. Unfortunately, the limits of current VDT technology which, for historical reasons, are usually 80 columns by 24 lines of characters, prevents the display of typeset text. Ideally, the user should see a page format that is automatically determined by a comfortable default (e.g., page width of 8.5 inches) on the screen. Any changes would be made by pointing to the new location of margins, footers, and type font changes. But the current VDTs do not readily permit this, especially since 24 lines do not begin to approximate a page. Alternatively, the more conventional method of formatting, inserting directives as in our example, should be done automatically. Some systems do have a program that inserts all the necessary, predetermined format directives into the file. This "intelligence" about formats can save a large amount of time, and it also renders the system more appealing to nonspecialist users like managers.

Spelling-checking is an obvious contributor to improved performance, but it is still unavailable in many systems, probably because of the storage resource required for the dictionary. A speller is a good example of IOS intelligence because it can "learn" misspellings that recur and can automatically replace recurrences throughout a file. Technologically, this is accomplished through a simple search of the file and comparison to the dictionary. Spelling checkers, just one component of support for writing, have become a major selling point of products such as the IBM Displaywriter. The Writers' Workbench developed by Bell Labs (MacDonald et al., 1982) offers a broader range of support. IBM is researching a similar system which proofreads, comments on style, and analyzes sentence construction, particularly length. The semantic and syntactic rules for language are much too complex for an automatic, stylistic rewrite, but suggestions can be made; for example, "there are too many long words". Although the full Workbench package is not commercially available, subsets have been in common use for some time, such as the program "Read" which judges the reading difficulty by reporting the average number of syllables per word.

Recommendation II: Maximize Responsiveness

The second most important aspect of the human-computer interaction is responsiveness, but not merely that which is due to computer response time. Response time (the lag between a user's action and computer presentation) is so critical and fundamental to any office usage that its minimization is taken as essential in this discussion (Shneiderman, 1982a). Four other characteristics of responsiveness that strongly affect user performance are listed in Figure C–6. These are important far beyond the technical implementation difficulty.

Interrupt control should enable the user to instantly interrupt or abort any user-initiated process. Perhaps this is a subtle feature and, because of its seeming triviality, it is overlooked in many IOSs. In fact, it is built into some operating systems (e.g., DEC TENEX and TOPS 20). Interrupt control includes two commands executable by the user at all times: abort and interrupt. In the maxi-machines from DEC, typing a "Control O" aborts the user's current processing of application or utility programs; the operating system is not stopped. A "Control C" interrupts any process and leaves the user in the last highest level of the operating system from which he can run another program or restart the same program. For architectural reasons, the widely touted operating system, UNIX ^{TM} (Bell Laboratories) does not permit either command. UNIX does respond to the ASCII key "BREAK" sometimes, but it appears that only a programmer can reliably determine when. (UNIX will be discussed more later.)

Interrupt control
Immediate status information
Error recovery
Immediate acknowledgment of input

Figure C–6.   Examples of responsiveness features.

In the user's environment, the need for interrupt control seems obvious, but some examples may avoid the confusion encountered during other discussions. Consider the initiation of an output processor operation where a 100-page document is formatted according to imbedded formatting directives. The user may find early in the formatting process that a missing right margin directive will completely change the format. The capability to abort this process will avoid the overhead of waiting for the undesired output. Or, a manager may complete and initiate the "send" command for a computer message only to realize that a critical recipient is not on the original distribution list; he aborts and saves embarrassment. Examples are countless, but the availability of these features is woefully inadequate, especially with the use of the UNIX operating system in office products (Norman, 1981).

The whole notion of operating systems and control keys seems unfriendly and is probably not conducive to performance. A large "STOP" key on the Xerox Star (8010), however, is an example of an IOS product which incorporates the needed control in a friendly way. The Star also provides friendly feedback about its status: an image of an hourglass appears on the screen while the computer is processing a command.

Providing *immediate status information* upon user demand is necessary whenever delays in response are encountered (e.g., by typing a "Control T" to the TENEX operating system). Although continuing advances in computer technology will result in faster responses, there will be situations where the processing takes a noticeably longer than expected time, leaving the user in an uncertain and uncomfortable position. Imaginative programmers have added to the feedback from an exemplary system (DEC's TOPS 20), "running" if everything is OK, "walking" if a little slow, and "limping" if there is a high load with slow response time.

The third responsiveness feature, *error recovery*, enables the user to recover from an erroneous command by backing up to an earlier state. Infrequently needed but of major importance when it is, the most common example is the deletion of large quantities of information by mistake. The technical difficulty and cost of building the necessary recording and process-tracking software is enormous. It is possible, however, as demonstrated by the Xerox Star and the Lexar Axxa which have "oops" keys. Vendors may not be disposed toward providing this feature unless there is sufficient user demand.

The method a system uses to acknowledge or *"echo" a user's input* is usually subtle, but it can have a strong influence on performance. It would be difficult to play a musical instrument if the notes were audible several seconds after played. If the notes were heard in clusters after several had been played, it would be as frustrating as the echo of user key strokes from the typical timeshared main-frame computer. Frustration would be the symptom and reduced performance the effect. Yet many computer systems, especially the largest vendors', are built with exactly this kind of interaction. The user may type a full line of instructions and only upon typing a return at the end of the line will there be any interaction with the computer. If the command line has an error in the first character position, the entire line may be rejected. Instead, the system should "listen" the entire time and inform the user immediately upon detecting an error. Immediate interaction with the computer upon each keystroke enables the user to proceed much faster, building up a rhythm that significantly improves performance. In situations where the computer is remote from the user and a "dumb" terminal is used, immediate echo and continuous monitoring of user input allow the system to support the pace and tempo of the user.

Office system vendors are rapidly taking advantage of personal computers, where the interactive resources are local, thus removing sources of delay. But the user commands described above for instant control still may not be included by designers because of the short development cycle and the limited memory (RAM) capacity of earlier personal computers. Availabilty of these features can be determined during any equipment demonstration.

Recommendation III: Relate the Value Of the Function to the Level of User Effort

The level of effort invested in the use of any technological tool should, of course, yield a proportionate return on the investment. This is consistent with the observation that perceived cost-benefits are the best predictor of system usage (Hiltz, 1980). Cost-benefits, or return on effort invested, vary considerably across computer applications such as programming and word processing. In the case of programming, a good return on the investment needed to learn, operate, and perform overhead tasks is likely because computer operation is as much an end as it is a means. The computer and associated software environment are analogous to raw materials that are shaped into the functioning product through programming. In the case of word processing, additional effort to operate the system is difficult to justify because the end is to produce documents. A word processing application uses the computer for tasks which can be accomplished using conventional tools with little sacrifice in quality. Word processing is a service, not a development process; the applications software is justifiable only as a more efficient and capable means of processing words.

Most office systems are not finished tools. Many tasks are left to the user who is forced to invest effort in operating the machine which does not add directly to the product, such as a report. There are numerous examples that vary across systems, and filing is one of the more common. Stand-alone products that use floppy disks (increasingly prevalent due to the rapid acquisition of personal computers) introduce additional work for handling and storage of the disks. The user may have to find and load the application software disks as well as the text/data disks. Retrieving the correct software and loading it is an extra, overhead task.

Using floppy disks essentially transfers the problems of information storage and retrieval in the paper office system to the computer based system. Floppies were not developed with data bases in mind, but because of shortsighted emphasis on reduced hardware costs, they are used for office filing. The most common way to find an office record when the specific floppy is not known is to load each disk separately and list or search through its contents. The office information system based on floppies is an expensive mistake, not only because the shelves full of disks will eventually have to be read into online data bases for searching, but also because the usage overhead is high. It is easy to forget that the reason for capturing information in digital form is ostensibly to permit online search and retrieval.

Large scale computers that provide centralized file systems also have overhead requirements. For example, users may have to continually monitor their file space allocation and take action to release space when limits are reached. Each file should be periodically evaluated to determine if it should be retained or archived to an offline storage medium. These kinds of actions may seem consistent with information management in all media, including paper. However, it is particularly dangerous to neglect file space maintenance when using computer media. If file space is exceeded, the user is not stopped from doing further work, but he may lose the information which represents his most valued efforts. This author lost several hours of effort on this paper when the maxi-timesharing system used all disk space within a few seconds because of a run-away program. As a result, the system was unable to properly record text edits (disk writes) and thus lost the entire document because the file was rendered unreadable. Of course, the author was suitably informed of the condition: "Fatal system error—restart the program."

Situations abound where users are confronted with system operations that require special knowledge (Vallee, 1982). The process of connecting to a remote resource can involve complicated terminal settings, frustrating noise in the communication line, and dropped connections. Perhaps most aggravating is the lack of information about the current situation. The feedback about the foregoing "fatal error" was cryptic and too late. But how about, "Illegal instruction at 1010101011"? Perhaps the error message could read, "I've just come to an impasse and can't proceed; please take the following action." A program that can generate "illegal instruction" can surely say something that nonprogrammers can understand.

A major source of the usage overhead is the timesharing operating system. Operating systems are a general purpose resource, and are not intended specifically for office or other nontechnical applications. The most widely known operating system is UNIX mentioned above, which runs primarily on DEC minicomputers. Norman (1981) gives a vivid account of the nonsensical vagaries of this "programmer's delight." It is further criticized by several experts who state that "UNIX's user interface is poor" (Lettieri, 1982). Since the operating system must manage multitask and multiuser environments, the solution may not be to rewrite it with a friendly interface, or to add program modules to manage filing and archiving for the user, but to hide UNIX from the user altogether. This appears to have been done by Fortune Systems with the "32/16" personal computer-based office system. Observations to date have identified some performance difficulties, which appear to be associated with the demands UNIX places on the hardware (which can become slow) and with the danger of the user being unwittingly removed from the office applications software into UNIX, not a good place for the unschooled to be. This is just one example of design concerns that arise because of the new class of nonspecialist user discussed earlier. The ideas presented here are summarized in Figure C–7.

During the past fifteen years, there have been many requests in the literature for the provision of error messages that are meaningful to non-technical users, and research has been done to support the need (Shneiderman, 1982b). The implications of cryptic, meaningless messages and other hang-overs from programming usage should be considered. Each non-task-oriented requirement generated by programmer-oriented designs detracts from user productivity. A system that requires a number of irrelevant tasks may not be able to improve the user's performance. Thus, a major justification for integrated office systems may be lost.

Perhaps it is too early in the evolution of computer technology to expect reasonable conversations with machines. Since a computer is a discrete, bi-nary, and deterministic device, it can only simulate the tolerance of ambiguity that is natural for humans. Processing ambiguous input will be increasingly one of the contributions of artificial intelligence. The temporary inhumanity of computers is wisely explored by Rauziano (1982) who aptly describes the state-of-the-art as "Conversations with Intelligent Chaos."

SUMMARY

The claim that the use of computers automatically enables individuals to enhance their performance in the nonspecialist applications available through integrated office systems is challenged. Observations, often anecdotal, raise

---

Minimum system operation overhead
Avoid programming decisions or conventions
Avoid non–task related work (e.g., managing floppy disks)
No programming responses (e.g., "illegal instruction")
Prevent user contact with operating systems

Figure C–7.   Summary of user effort requirements.

questions that can only be answered by an analysis of the effort expended to use computers in the new applications. Clearly, designs once adequate for specialist uses, such as programming, are not adequate for integrated office systems.

Office systems usage introduces a concrete criterion for computer system design: the improvement of productivity. Productivity has been a mysterious and undefinable quantity in the unstructured office, but the levels and methods of measurement permit a quantitative as well as subjective evaluation of design. Before computers can increase productivity, the interaction between user and computer must be at least as efficient as the conventional processing of information.

There are four major points presented in this chapter:

1. The second level of the productivity measurement framework, the human-computer dyad, is the current bottleneck to productivity improvement. Organizations cannot expect computer-based office systems to improve operational performance until usage is straightforward and efficient. It may not be meaningful to measure productivity impacts of integrated office systems at the organizational level with the current state-of-the-art in office systems.

2. A plausible reason for the proliferation of design problems in office systems is that there are four divergent perspectives of the solution: Buyers are driven by affordability; vendors by profitability; users by appearance; and researchers by detailed analyses. Understanding all the perspectives and the blind spots of each can enhance the probability of a solution.

3. Researchers can bring concrete measures to bear on user performance, perhaps stimulating a second look by those who are trapped in the convenient myopia of the other perspectives. Buyers might have to realize that the least expensive product costs more in the long run. Vendors could even be shocked by the realization that if their products do not measure up, they may lose to a competitor who does not hedge design in order to lower cost. Users might realize that working with an efficient system is as much fun and productive as working with one buried in overhead tasks. Researchers might generalize from those results which are consistent with organizations' need for improved productivity.

4. A general indictment of computers for office use would merely accompany the hundreds of similar papers to "write-only files" unless some recommendations could alleviate the problem. One short treatise cannot bring about a solution to unconscious design. It is hoped that the recommendations in this chapter will influence both the selection and design of systems intended for nonspecialist, office users. The recommendations are to (1) maximize routine intelligence, (2) maximize responsiveness, and (3) minimize overhead effort. These are

but a small set of the design requirements that will inevitably be addressed as computers and telecommunications systems become more congenial and productive to use.

REFERENCES

Bair, J. H. 1974. *Evaluation and analysis of an augmented knowledge workshop.* Final Report for Phase I, Rome Air Development Center, DC–TR–74–79, NTIS No. AD 778 835/9.

————. 1979. Avoiding working nonsolutions to electronic office design. *Proceedings of the IEEE Computer Society Conference–COMPCON* San Francisco.

————. 1982. *Productivity assessment of office information systems technology.* In *Emerging Office Systems,* ed. R. Landau et al. Norwood, N.J.: Ablex Pub.

Bullen, C. V.; Bennett, J. L.; and Carlson, E. D. 1982. A case study in office workstation use. *IBM Systems Journal* 21:351–69.

Card, S. K.; English, W. K.; and Burr, B. J. 1978. Evaluation of mouse, rate-controlled isometric joystick, step keys, and text keys for text selection on a CRT. *Ergonomics* 21:601–12.

Card, S. K.; Moran, T. P.; Newell, A. 1980. The keystroke-level model of user performance time with interactive systems. *Communications of the ACM* 23:396–410.

Comptroller General. 1979. *Federal productivity suffers because word processing is not well managed.* Report to the Congress of the United States. April, 1979. Wash., D.C.

Cuadra, C. 1982. Personal communication at University of California, Los Angeles, May, 1982.

Engelbart, D. C.; Norton, J. C.; and Watson, R. W. 1973. The augmented knowledge workshop. In *AFIPS Conference Proceedings, National Computer Conference 21* 42:9–21.

Hiltz, S. R.; and Kerr, E. B. 1981. *Studies of computer mediated communications systems; a synthesis of findings.* Final report. Wash., D.C.: Division of Information Science and Technology, National Science Foundation.

Hiltz, S. R., and Turoff, M. 1980. *The network nation.* New York: Addison-Wesley.

Konkel, G. J., and Peck, P. J. 1976. Traditional secretarial cost compared to word processing. *The office* Feb., pp. 67–8.

Lettieri, L. 1982. Can UNIX cut it in the commercial world? *Mini-Micro Systems* June, pp. 155–58.

MacDonald, N. H.; Frase, L. T.; Gingrith, P. S.; and Keenan, S. A. 1982. The Writers Workbench Computer aids for text analysis. *IEEE Transactions on Communication* Com-30:105–10.

Moran, T. P. 1981. An applied psychology of the user. *Computing Surveys* 13:1–11.

Morton, J. et al. 1979. Interaction with a computer: a framework. In *Teleinfomatics 1979—IFIP International Conference,* pp. 201–8. Amsterdam: North-Holland.

Nickerson, R. S. 1981. Why interactive computer systems are sometimes not used by people who might benefit from them. *International Journal of Man-machine Studies* 15:469–83.

Norman, D. 1981. The trouble with UNIX. *Datamation* November, pp. 139–50.

Palme, J. 1982. A man-computer interface encouraging user growth. In *Emerging Office Systems*, ed. R. Landau; J. H. Bair; and J. H. Siegman, pp. 103–24. Norwood, N.J.: Ablex.

Piaget, J. 1955. *The Language and Thought of the Child.* Trans. M. Gabain. New York: World.

Rauziano, V. 1982. Conversations with intelligent chaos. *Datamation* May, pp. 122–36.

Roberts, T. L. 1979. Evaluation of computer text editors. Xerox Applied Information-Processing Psychology Project. Report SSL–79–9. Palo Alto, Calif.

Shneiderman, B. 1982a. The future of interactive systems and the emergence of direct manipulation. In *NYU Symposium on User Interfaces* May 26–28. TR–1156 available from author, Dept. of Computer Science, University of Maryland, College Park, MD.

————. 1982b. System message design: guidelines and experimental results. In *Directions in Human-Computer Interaction*, ed. A. Badre, and B. Shneiderman, pp. 55–78. Norwood, N.J.: Ablex.

Strassmann, P. A. 1977. Organization productivity—the role of information technology. In *Information Processing 77*, ed. B. Gilchrist, pp. 503–8. New York: North–Holland.

Uhlig, R.; Farber, D.; and Bair, J. H. 1979. *The office of the future: communications and computers.* New York: North–Holland.

Vallee, J. 1982. *The network revolution: confessions of a computer scientist.* Berkeley, Calif.: AND/OR Press.

Zuboff, S. 1982. New worlds of computer–mediated work. *Harvard Business Review* Sept.–Oct., pp. 142–52.

HUMAN LIMITS AND THE VDT COMPUTER INTERFACE

Stuart K. Card

INTRODUCTION

If users could be provided with four arms, perhaps after the manner of grafted fruit trees, the design of computer interfaces using Visual Display Terminals could be simplified greatly. One hand would point with pen or finger or mouse to the object of interest on the VDT screen; another would press a key indicating what function to perform. The remaining two hands would be used to type text on the typewriter keyboard. Since the majority of computer systems require these four functional hands, whereas the majority of users come supplied with but two, the designer must either accept the inefficiencies of having the user's two hands switch back and forth among devices, or he must combine the work of two or more functional hands on a single device (for example, command menus selected with a pointing device or a command mode on the keyboard). Whatever the solution, it will be just one of the ways in which the physical and cognitive limits of the human user express themselves in the design of a computer interface.

The argument of the inadequacy of the human factors science base derives partly from work on a National Research Council report "Automation in Combat Aircraft" (NRC, 1982). The central ideas for how to address this inadequacy were developed in collaboration with Thomas Moran and Allen Newell (see Card, Moran, and Newell, 1983).

It is the common desire of most computer interface designers to recognize and design for the characteristics of their users, but it is also commonly agreed that this is not an easy matter. Not only is there no recognized methodology of interface design, there also is little systematic knowledge relating designs to expected user performance. The purpose of this chapter is to sketch how progress might be made in this area. I shall proceed by identifying some of the limitations on human performance, and by showing how these are reflected in characteristics of the human-computer interface. Finally, I will suggest a means for calculating, or at least predicting, at design time the human performance that may be expected in the use of the system. But first, it is important to begin with an appreciation of the particular kind of interface with which we are concerned.

THE VDT-BASED COMPUTER INTERFACE

The development of personal computers with wide bandwidth linkages to a VDT, especially systems with bitmapped raster graphics, has greatly increased the potential power of human-computer interaction. Yet there is presently an inadequate science base for understanding how this power can be used. A few examples will show some current techniques in VDT use and how they result in powerful human-computer interfaces.

Examples of Current VDT-Based Interfaces

A variety of devices used with a VDT are displayed in Figure D–1*. Visible in the figure are a vector display, a lightpen, a tablet and stylus, a joystick, a keyboard, an array of buttons, and even a panel of control dials. Many other devices, such as high-resolution touch panels, linear potentiometers, and pens of various sorts are becoming available. The point of the figure is to emphasize the variety of devices available and how different they are from the simple keyboard-display combination so common in the past.

Figure D–2 illustrates some novel techniques of interaction—this time emphasizing software. Here the user employs a keyboard with special keys and a mouse pointing device. One way in which the mouse is used is to move small pictures around on the screen. For example, if the user wants to print a document, he moves a picture of a piece of paper over to the picture of the printer; if he has received a message, a small picture of an envelope appears in his in-basket and he can use the mouse to reach for the message and open it. This style of interaction reduces the number of explicit commands and thereby simplifies system operation.

---

*A full caption and credits for each figure are given at the end of this chapter.

Figure D–1.   VDT with common input devices.

Figure D–3 illustrates another VDT interfacing technique: windows (also called viewports). The overlapping windows allow the user to control a larger amount of information on his VDT screen than would otherwise be the case. If the user selects one of the overlapped windows with the mouse, that window instantly appears on top, overlapping the others under it. This figure also shows the ease with which text and graphics can be intermixed.

Figure D–4 illustrates the use of soft fonts. Unlike the older VDTs, in which fonts were generated by a hardware character generator, many systems now use software-defined fonts. In this figure, the user is editing the software character generator, which is simultaneously being used to generate the characters for the display used for editing. The character being edited is

Figure D–2.   Xerox 8010 Star professional workstation.

displayed in enlarged format so that the user may easily manipulate individual bits, but the small versions of the letters are also affected.

Finally, Figure D–5 shows a VDT with soft push-buttons. The user touches a picture of a button displayed on the screen, and a touch panel senses the position of his finger. The button changes color or gives some other indication of being "pushed." Soft push-buttons allow very rapid mockup of control panels before they are built, or allow the system to display configurations of buttons appropriate to a particular state of the machine.

The examples make two points. First, the day of the 24 by 80 character VDT has long since passed. While such terminals will continue to be built for some time because of cost and technological and organizational inertia, the number of possibilities for applications and graceful user dialogues that arise with graphical VDTs means that the graphical VDT can be expected to become the industry standard. Second, techniques such as those used in the afore-described interfaces give the designer leverage for making powerful interfaces. But leverage works two ways: while it is possible to make interfaces

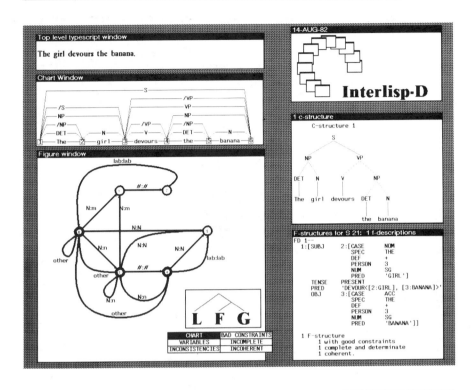

Figure D–3. The use of multiple windows in the Xerox 1100 Interlisp-D programming environment.

much better than before, it is also possible to make them much worse. Hence the importance of understanding what is good and bad in interface design.

Inadequacy of the Science Base

How can we develop an engineering discipline of VDT interface design, a methodology for finding the good interface designs and avoiding the bad ones? One paradigm often used is to measure System A and to compare its performance to that of System B. There are at least four difficulties with such a paradigm. First, it is inefficient. There are many instances of A and B, and generalization can be treacherous. Second, if it is known only that A is better than B, but not the cause of the difference, then the results may not be true for similar systems. A′ might be worse than B′ because of a change in type font or key locations, for example. Third, experiments to measure A and B cannot be done very well at design time. Human experiments on a system prototype

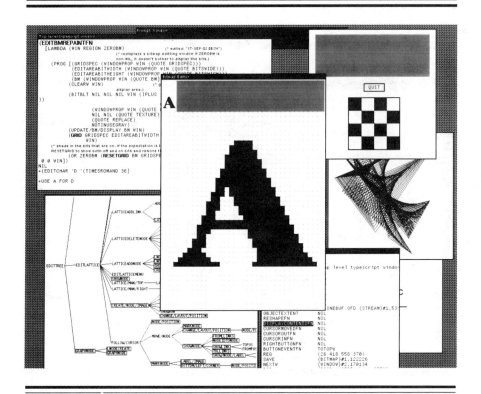

Figure D–4.   The Bitmap Editor of the Xerox Interlisp-D system.

require waiting until there is a running prototype. But by the time there is
a prototype, a system is often over budget or over time, or there have been
so many political compromises made that major changes are impossible. The
system improvements possible under such circumstances are details, like the
operating instructions, that are not the machine features responsible for great
system performance leverage. Finally, rarely during system development is
there the necessary time to do experiments right. Because of time and budget
pressures, the number of subjects may be too small, important controls may
be missing, important alternatives may not be explored—all of which means
that similar experiments must be repeated for different systems because the
designers lack confidence in the results.

The real problem in designing interfaces is the inadequate science base
upon which to ground the human engineering of the systems. Generic research
must be done to put intellectual capital on the shelf for the design of future
systems. Three distinct sorts of studies are required:

1. studies of actual systems,

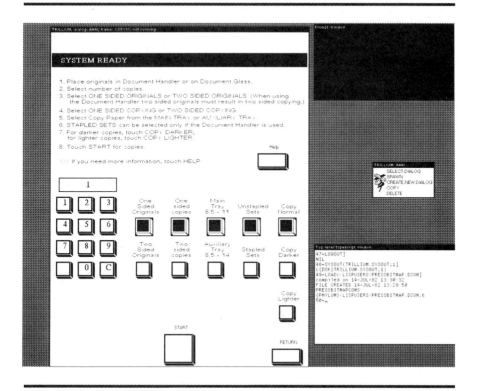

Figure D–5.   Soft push buttons of the TRILLIUM system.

2. studies of system components, and

3. studies of applied human information-processing generally.

Studies of actual systems are needed because they directly address what we are trying to understand, and all laboratory abstractions contain the danger that they may be not be generalizable back to the full system. Studies of system components are needed because while there are a very large number of potential interfaces, these interfaces are actually, and surprisingly, designed from the same relatively small number of components combined repeatedly. With an understanding of these components, we can understand the design of the systems themselves. Finally, studies of general human information-processing mechanisms are needed in order to understand the way in which human characteristics interact with system designs. Since this last is not compelling in the absence of a concrete proposal, I shall take it up first. Then I shall show how limitations of the human identified in the model of human processing are reflected in characteristics of his performance with computer interfaces.

USER INFORMATION-PROCESSING MECHANISMS

Anyone who has ever tried to improve his design effort by perusing the experimental psychology literature knows what a frustrating experience that can be. Four main difficulties stand out:

1. Relevant results are widely scattered.
2. They often apply with confidence only to certain narrow experimental paradigms.
3. The worth of a model is often assessed only by fitting it with parameters derived from the data itself.
4. Models are assessed in terms of statistically significant differences between theory and data.

On the contrary, for application in computer science:

1. We need a unified model of the human.
2. The model should be applicable across various tasks.
3. It should allow the calculation of new results using tables of parameters already in hand.
4. We want to know how good an approximation the model is to the observable behavior.

It is especially important to understand that "statistical significance" has only a limited, secondary role in evaluating system designs and theories. After all, if the number of trials or the number of subjects is but increased sufficiently, a significant difference between one thing and another will almost always ensue. On the other hand, a difference between two systems significant at $p < 0.0001$ might only be a matter of 1% and might easily be irrelevant; a matter (and here is the important part) to be decided on the basis of the content of a problem rather than on the statistics alone. The proper role of statistics is to make sure that a certain magnitude of effect, interesting itself in the context of a particular problem, is not an artifact due to chance variation. Statistics cannot tell us mechanically, without regard to content, what is interesting and what is not. For example, a theory that could predict within $\pm 50\%$ at design time the number of hours required to learn a new computer system, for some appropriate technical specification of the system and intended class of users, would be a great scientific advance of considerable practical use. Yet the theory would surely fail all devisable statistical tests for being "significantly different from the data."

It is in this spirit of task analysis, calculation, and approximation that the following model of human information processing is presented. The model is not intended as a detailed model of what is really "in the head" so much as an engineering approximation from which constraints and properties of human-computer interfaces can be derived. For these reasons, accuracy has purposefully been traded for simplicity and wider coverage.

The Model Human Processor

Consider the human processor from the point of view of a computer scientist understanding a complicated computer system. The computer scientist often finds it helpful to suppress the details of computer systems in order to be able to understand how the larger system fits together. One way to do this is to employ a technique such as the PMS notation (Siewiorek, Bell, and Newell, 1981) that conceives the system in terms of processors, memories, and switches. In a similar spirit, we can give a description, which we shall call the Model Human Processor, in terms of processors, memories, and principles of operations. The processors and memories, Figure D–6(a), summarize properties of the human functional information-processing architecture. The principles of operation, Figure D–6(b), give some additional principles for predicting human performance that are not easily expressible architecturally.

In, this view, the human contains three processors—a Perceptual Processor, a Cognitive Processor and a Motor Processor—all operating in "pipelined parallel." That is, a person can read one word while saying the previously read word, both at the same time but only under the right circumstances. We can also distinguish four memories. Two of the memories are sensory buffers for the eyes and ears. To continue the computer metaphor, they are the sample-and-hold circuits and the analogue-to-digital converters for the eyes and ears. Another memory is the Working Memory, a sort of cache memory—the place where recently experienced and currently active information is quickly accessible. And finally there is Long-Term Memory, in which the user holds his general store of knowledge. We should not think of Working Memory and Long-Term Memory as separate sets of storage registers; it is closer to current opinion in psychology to consider Long-Term Memory as a directed graph of semantically linked nodes and of Working Memory as a small subset of those which are "activated" at any given moment.

To illustrate the model, the boxes in Figure D–7 trace how a user is supposed to do the simple task of pressing a button whenever a certain letter appears on his VDT: a letter appears on the screen. One Perceptual Processor cycle later, the letter has been transmitted to the Visual Image Store, in which it is represented as some physical code (that is, in some form affected by the intensity of the light and other physical variables) and very quickly thereafter (at a rate below the time grain of the model) a symbolic (not affected by physical intensity) version of the letter appears in Working Memory. It requires one Cognitive Processor cycle for the user to make the decision to push the Yes button and one Motor Processor cycle actually to push it.

Processor Parameters

In addition to the qualitative description of the human processor we have just given, the Model Human Processor includes a few quantitative parameters. We can characterize the processors by their cycle time, and the

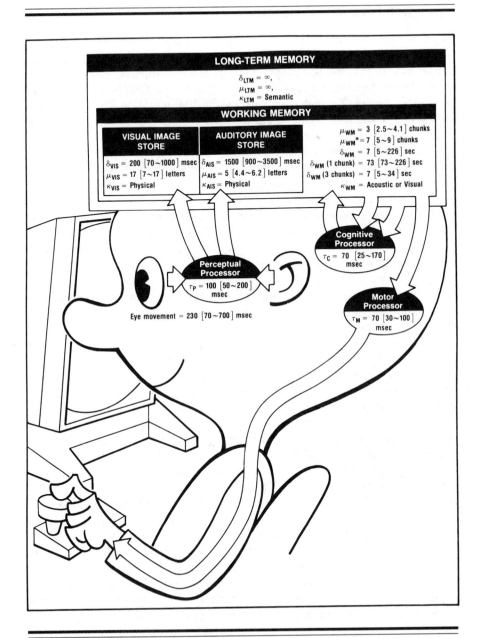

Figure D–6(a). The Model Human Processor.

memories by their decay rates, their capacities, and the codings they use. All of these parameters, summarized in Figure D–6 (a), arise from a review and

P1. Variable Perceptual Processor Rate Principle. The Perceptual Processor cycle time τ_P varies inversely with stimulus intensity.

P2. Encoding Specificity Principle. Specific encoding operations performed on what is perceived determine what is stored, and what is stored determines what retrieval cues are effective in providing access to what is stored.

P3. Discrimination Principle. The difficulty of memory retrieval is determined by the candidates that exist in the memory, relative to the retrieval clues.

P4. Variable Cognitive Processor Rate Principle. The Cognitive Processor cycle time τ_C is shorter when greater effort is induced by increased task demands or information loads; it also diminishes with practice.

P5. Fitts's Law. The time T_{pos} to move the hand to a target of size S which lies a distance D away is given by

$$T_{pos} = I_M \log_2(D/S + .5), \text{ where } I_M = 100 \, [70 \sim 120] \text{ msec/bit}.$$

P6. Power Law of Practice. The time T_n on perform a task to the nth trial follows a power law:

$$T_n = T_1 n^{-\alpha}, \text{ where } \alpha = .4 \, [.2 \sim .6].$$

P7. The Uncertainty Principle. Decision time T increases with uncertainty about the judgment or decision to be made,

$$T = I_C H,$$

where H is the information-theoretic entropy of the decision and $I_C = 150 \, [0 \sim 157]$ msec/bit. For n equally probably alternatives (Hick's Law),

$$H = \log_2(n + 1).$$

For n alternatives with different probabilities of occurring p_i,

$$H = \sum_i p_i \log_2(1/p_i + 1).$$

P8. Rationality Principle. A person acts so as to attain his goals through rational action, given the structure of the task and his inputs of information and bounded by limitations on his knowledge and processing ability:

Goals + Task + Operators + Inputs + Knowledge + Process-Limits $\rightarrow$ Behavior.

P9. The Problem Space Principle. The rational activity in which people engage to solve a problem can be described in terms of (1) a set of states of knowledge, (2) operators for changing one state into another, (3) constraints on applying operators, and (4) control knowledge for deciding which operator to apply next.

Figure D–6(b). The Model Human Processor.

simplification of the psychological literature. The full review is contained in Card, Moran, and Newell (1983). Here I will simply summarize the major points.

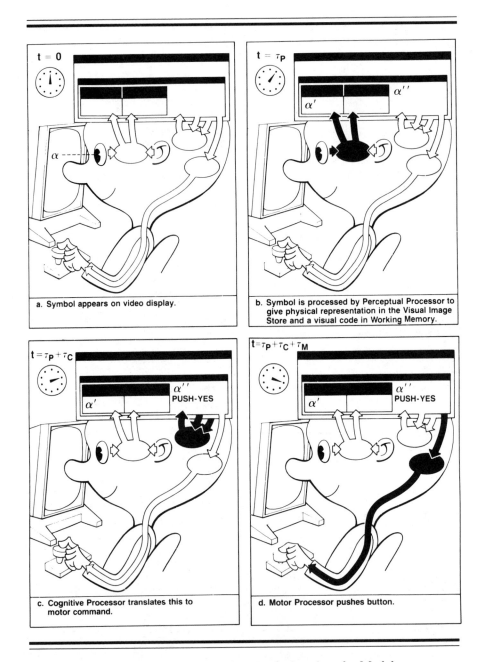

Figure D–7. Simple reaction time analysis using the Model Human Processor.

Let us start with the cycle time of the Perceptual Processor. There are a number of experiments which have established Bloch's Law (1885): as long as the duration of a flashed light is less than about 100 milliseconds (msec), in our terms one Perceptual Processor cycle, one light will look the same as another light twice as intense but only one half as long. This is a special case of the more general observation that two perceptual events occurring within about 100 msec of each other will under most conditions be combined into a single perceptual event. Another line of evidence concerns what is known as perceptual masking. A person shown a briefly flashed letter and then 100 msec later shown a circle surrounding the letter will not register the letter. Intriguingly, the alpha rhythm of the brain, varying between 77 ∼ 125 msec (Harter, 1967), is also in this range.

These experiments, and others, lead us to two conclusions. First, a number of quite different techniques converge to produce numbers which tend to be a little less than 0.1 sec per cycle. Second, various ways of estimating these numbers give somewhat different values as a result of second-order effects ignored by the Model Human Processor, or as a result of individual differences among subjects, or even because the experiments measure slightly different things. The values we shall give our parameters will reflect both of these facts. On the one hand, we shall give our best estimate for the parameter. In this case the Perceptual Processor cycle time will be set at $\tau_P = 100$ msec, approximately the average of the values from a number of experiments reviewed. On the other hand, we will also include a range in rounded numbers, in this case 50 ∼ 200 msec, of the reasonable experimental values reported. In compact form, we shall write these two together as

$$\tau_P = 100 \ [50 \sim 200] \ \text{msec.}$$

We should also note that a user must move the 1 ∼ 2 degree high-resolution center of his visual field so that it covers what he wishes to examine. The visual system is organized so that this high-resolution part moves quickly to some location and then remains fixed for a while before moving to some new location. Each of these fixations (including movement time) lasts

$$230 \ [70 \sim 700] \ \text{msec.}$$

The Cognitive Processor also gives values on the order of 0.1 sec/cycle. One set of relevant experiments derives from a paradigm called memory scanning invented by Sternberg (1966) at Bell Laboratories. A user read a set of items, such as the letters B, A, C, G, is asked if some letter, say A, is in the list. The response time has been found to be a linear function of the number of items in the list. In our terms, the user must scan down the list using one Cognitive Processor cycle for each item. The time per item, hence the time per cycle, varies in these experiments from as low as 27 msec for numbers to as much as 93 msec for random forms.

In another task, first measured by Jevons (1871), the experimenter shows the subject some number of objects and ask him how many there are. Again the time required for the subject to answer is linearly proportional to the number of items with time/item of around 40 msec for four or fewer dots (Chi and Klahr, 1975) to 94 msec (individuals ranged from 40 to 172 msec) for four or fewer 3-dimensional objects (Akin and Chase 1978). Yet another task has the subject count silently to himself as fast as possible, producing times on the order of 167 msec/digit (Landauer, 1962). From these studies and others, we can derive the cycle time of the Cognitive Processor to be

$$\tau_C = 70\,[25 \sim 170]\ \text{msec}.$$

Finally, experiments on the rate at which people can move their hand or foot or tongue also give numbers around 0.1 sec/movement. For example, tapping takes $35 \sim 65$ msec/movement. Repeating a key in typing for a good typist takes about 90 msec. So the Motor Processor cycle time is

$$\tau_M = 70\,[30 \sim 100]\ \text{msec}.$$

Now we can return to our example in Figure D–7 and ask how long should the response take. As the figures shows, the task requires one cycle each of the Perceptual Processor, the Cognitive Processor, and the Motor Processor for a total time of $\tau_P + \tau_C + \tau_M$, or

Perceive stimulus	$\tau_P =$	$100\ [50 \sim 200]$ msec
Decide to respond	$\tau_C =$	$70\ [25 \sim 170]$ msec
Respond	$\tau_M =$	$70\ [30 \sim 100]$ msec
Total		$240\ [105 \sim 470]$ msec.

As another example, consider the task of scribbling as fast as possible between two parallel lines. Figure D–8 shows a typical result. Two kinds of periodicity are evident in this scribble: one very rapid and another shown by the slower adjustments made by the user attempting to stay between the lines. In terms of the Model Human Processor, these periodicities correspond to two processing routes through Figure D–6(a): The fast scribbles are the maximum output rate of the Motor Processor. According to our model, there should be a direction change every $70\ [30 \sim 100]$ msec. In fact there are 68 corrections in 5 sec or $5/68 = 74$ msec/correction. The slower adjustments require the scribbler to notice that his scribbles are the wrong size (one Perceptual Processor Cycle), to decide which way to adjust them (one Cognitive Processor Cycle), and to respond with an adjustment (one Motor Process or Cycle)—all of which should take $240\ [105 \sim 470]$ msec as computed above. In Figure D–8 there are 20 such corrections in 5 sec, or $5/20 = 250$ msec/correction.

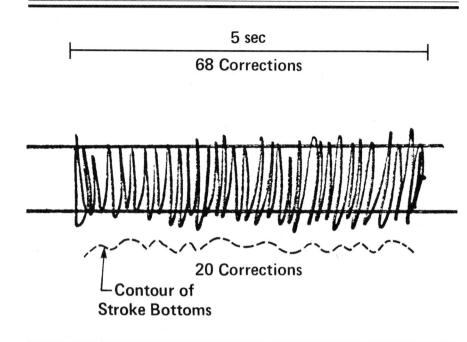

Figure D–8.   Scribbling as rapidly as possible for 5 sec while trying
to stay between two lines.

Memory Parameters

Now let us consider the memory parameters of the Model Human
Processor as illustrated in Figure D–1(a). There are three such parameters of
interest: memory capacity, code type, and decay rate.

Capacity

The most important memory capacity, that for Working Memory, seems
to be about $3 \sim 4$ items:

$$\mu_{WM} = 3\,[2.5 \sim 4.1]\ \text{msec.}$$

Of course, if one were to give a subject a seven digit telephone number and ask
him to repeat it, he probably could. The reason is that he is using not only
Working Memory, but also some Long-Term Memory in the process. Since
these two are closely packaged together as a system, the number of items that
can be repeated back is the famous 7 ± 2 number. To distinguish this number
from the capacity of Working Memory proper, we say that the user has an
effective Working Memory size of

$$\mu_{WM}^* = 7 \, [5 \sim 9] \text{ msec.}$$

But if one were to read a long string of digits to a subject, then unexpectedly in the middle ask him to repeat as many back as possible, the number of digits he could repeat would be closer to $3 \sim 4$ than to 7.

The capacity of Long-Term Memory is indefinitely high, so while there must be some limit, we can express the fact that Long-Term Memory capacity does not seem to play a practical role in limited user performance by

$$\mu_{LTM} = \infty.$$

Code type

The type of coding used to store information in memory is a complicated topic, but for our purposes it is only necessary to distinguish a few major types of codes. The sensory buffers, that is the Visual Image Store (VIS) and the Auditory Image Store (AIS), use some sort of physical code. If a light is brighter, it takes longer to decay (Fig. D–9):

$$\kappa_{VIS} = \text{Physical};$$
$$\kappa_{AIS} = \text{Physical}.$$

This is not the case for Working Memory. If a subject is given a set of letters to remember, one of the mistakes he is likely to make when repeating it is to give a wrong letter that sounds similar to the correct letter. This is a clue that the code in Working Memory for the letter is acoustic; in other cases it is possible to demonstrate that the user employs visual codes. But the codes are not physical, and therefore:

$$\kappa_{WM} = \text{Acoustic or Visual}.$$

For Long-Term Memory the confusions are likely to be semantic, not between two things which look or sound alike, but between two things which have similar meanings:

$$\kappa_{LTM} = \text{Semantic}.$$

Decay rate

The decay rate of an item in Working Memory or the sensory memories seems to depend on the number of items in memory. One way of measuring the decay rate, developed by Sperling (1960) and Averbach and Coriell (1961) at Bell Laboratories, is to flash subjects a set of letters in some sort of array where the number of letters in the array is larger than the effective Working

Memory capacity, μ^*_{WM}. The subjects are only able to report back μ^*_{WM} of them, although they claim to have seen them all. To get around this Working Memory limit for reporting, subjects are given some cue shortly after the letters have been presented that tells them which part of the display to report. For example, a tone might indicate which row to report. If there are four rows of four letters each, and if the subject could report correctly three of the four letters of the row on which he was cued, then he is supposed to have $3/4 \times 16 = 12$ letters available in the Visual Image Store at that time, or $12 - 7 = 5$ letters available in excess of Working Memory capacity. By varying the time between the flash and the reporting cue, it is possible to trace the decay of the Visual Image Store. Figure D–9 plots log letters available in excess of Working Memory capacity as a function of time for three experiments on the Visual Information Store and one experiment on the Auditory Image Store. The curves show that the decay plotted this way is exponential (a straight line in semi-log coordinates) and that it depends on the number of items. From the slope of these lines, we can compute the half-life, δ, and use this to define the decay. From these and other experiments we derive:

$$\delta_{VIS} = 200 \, [70 \sim 1000] \text{ msec, and}$$
$$\delta_{AIS} = 1500 \, [900 \sim 3500] \text{ msec.}$$

One method to measure Working Memory decay, is to give the subject some items to remember and then to prevent him in some way from rehearsing them. After a certain period of time, he is asked for the item. Figure D–10 gives the results from this sort of experiment. Again, the decay rate depends on the number of items to be remembered. More technically, it depends on the number of "chunks" to be remembered, that is, the number of meaningful units:

$$\delta_{WM}(1 \text{ chunk}) = 200 \, [70 \sim 1000] \text{ msec, and}$$
$$\delta_{WM}(3 \text{ chunks}) = 1500 \, [900 \sim 3500] \text{ msec.}$$

Notice that the decay rate is about the same for three consonants or for three words. Here I add a caveat. The most serious cause of forgetting in Working Memory is thought to be interference between new items and items already in memory. However, it is difficult, even in the laboratory, to differentiate cleanly this kind of decay from the decay that would be obtained if pure time was the variable. Even though this is a difficult problem for experimental psychology, the very fact of the difficulty means it is possible, for engineering purposes, to simplify the analysis by acting as though time were the independent variable.

Sample calculations

Now let us perform some sample calculations to give further illustration of the Model Human Processor's application.

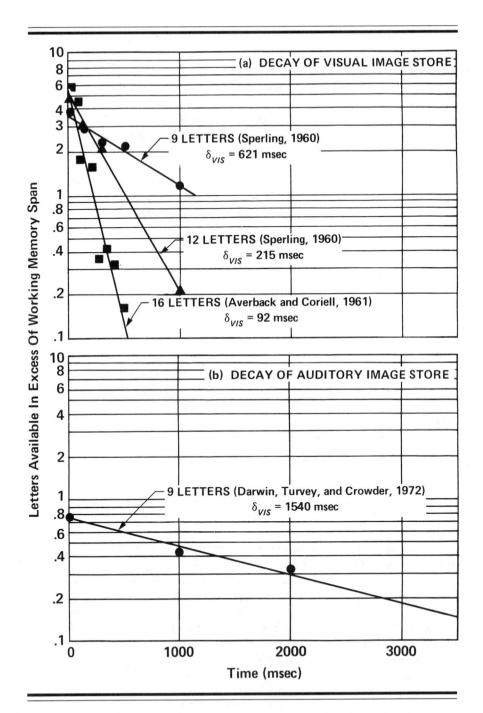

Figure D–9. Time decay of Visual and Auditory Image Stores.
(a) Decay of Visual Image Store. **(b)** Decay of Auditory Image
Store.

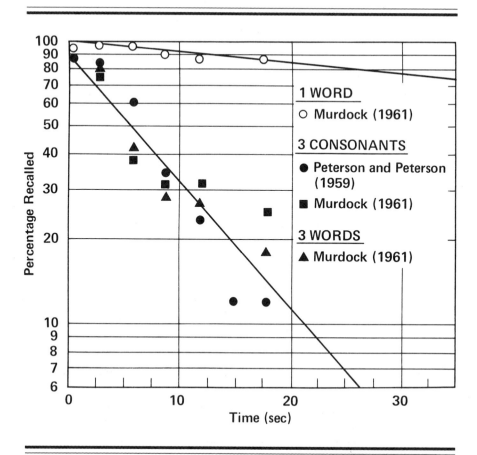

Figure D–10. Working Memory decay rate.

Example 1. In a graphic computer simulation of a pool game, there are many occasions upon which one ball appears to bump into another ball, causing the second one to move. What is the time available, after the collision, to compute the initial move of the second ball, before the illusion of causality breaks down?

We have said that events which occur within one cycle of the Perceptual Processor will tend to be perceived as a single percept. So if the second ball begins moving within $\tau_P = 100$ msec of the collision, it will appear the first ball caused the second to move. If we want to be very sure, since 100 msec is the time at which the causality will break down, we should use the lower bound of $\tau_P = 50$ msec. Figure D–11 shows the results of an experiment in which one ball appeared to collide with a second ball that moved after various delays. Subjects were asked to judge whether they perceived a single causal

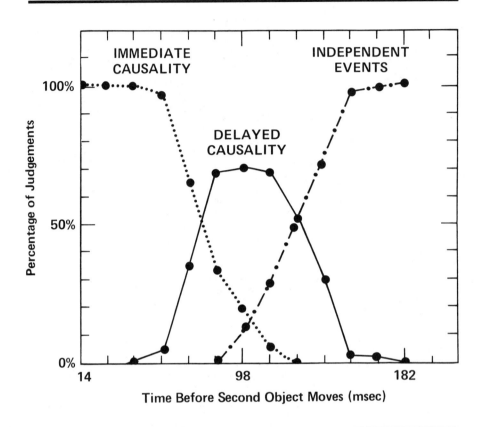

Figure D–11. Perceived causality as a function of inter-event time.

event, two independent events, or a third category called delayed causation. The figure shows that the dividing point between causation and independent events was near the 100 msec predicted; furthermore, events which occurred with a delay of less than 50 msec were almost always perceived as causal.

Example 2. How fast can a person read text?

Suppose that when people read they need to use one eye movement for every letter. If, as in Figure D–6(a), the fixation time could be taken as 230 msec/fixation, that would imply a reading rate of

$$(5 \text{ saccade/word})(230 \text{ msec/saccade}) = 52 \text{ words/minute}.$$

On the other hand, suppose people on the average require only one eye-movement per word. That would give

$$(1\text{ saccade/word})(230\text{ msec/saccade}) = 261\text{ words/minute},$$

a rate, incidentally, closer to being typical. Finally, it has been found that 13 characters is about the most people can perceive within a fixation. If by some means the reader could read so that he saw 13 new characters ($= 2.5$ words) each time, his reading rate would be

$$(1/2.5\text{ saccade/word})(230\text{ msec/saccade}) = 652\text{ words/minute}.$$

In other words, speed readers who claim to read 2000 or 5000 words/minute are actually skimming.

> **Example 3.** Show that a user will probably remember the meaningful file name CAT longer than the arbitrary name TXD.

The solution to this problem can be approached using the Working Memory decay-rate parameter. The user will probably remember a meaningful file name like "CAT" as one chunk, whereas a meaningless name like "TXD" will require 3 chunks, one for each letter. As we have noted (Figs. D–6(a) and 10), a single chunk decays much more slowly (half-life $\delta_{WM} = 73$ [73 $\sim$ 226] msec) than three chunks ($\delta_{WM} = 7$ [5 $\sim$ 34] msec). In fact, there should be an order of magnitude, $73/7 \simeq 10$ difference in the decay time.

INTERFACE COMPONENTS

Now that we have discussed human information-processing generally, let us turn to an examination of several computer interface components. Here we can see characteristics of the human processor reflected in system user performance. As examples, I shall discuss the design of keyboards, pointing devices, and expert dialogues.

Keyboards

Keystroking Rate

Good typists can type 60 $\sim$ 100 words/minute. This imposes a substantial limitation on the rate a user can communicate with a computer system. From whence does it arise? Could people type at infinite speed with enough practice? A simple calculation based on the Model Human Processor shows approximately where the upper bound in human keying performance lies.

> **Example 4.** How fast can a person type?

A keystroke consists of two actions: raising the finger and lowering the finger. According to our model, each should take about one Motor Processor

Cycle or 2×70 msec $= 140$ msec, about 78 words/minute. Actually, the user can at least partially overlap one keystroke with the next. If he could completely overlap the downward part of one stroke with the upward part of the next, then the typing rate would be twice this, or 156 words/minute. The actual performance of fast typists, where some but not all keystrokes overlap, would be expected to be in this region. Indeed $90 \sim 110$ words per minute is considered excellent typing performance and 130 words/minute is typing speed-competition performance.

Speed of Keyboards

Now let us consider the performance consequences of the arrangement of the keys on the keyboard for expert performance. While this might, at first glance, seem a simple matter for experiment, in fact convincing experimental demonstrations of key arrangements are difficult and expensive due to the large amount of learning required of the subject. Subjects must be recruited and trained for months until they reach expert speed, during which time they must not use the standard Sholes arrangement so that they are not already contaminated by standard keyboard experience. The designer cannot, practically speaking, fiddle with experiments on 16 different key arrangements and choose the best. With the help of some additional keystroking data such as the digraph times in Figure D–12 from Kinkead (1975), however, it is possible to make rapid calculations in the spirit of the Model Human Processor that approximate the results to be expected. Figure D–12 gives data for the times to type some key, for example, the letter g, if the previous key was from the alternate hand (example: k), the same hand (example: a), the same finger (example: r), or the same key (the letter: g). Let us consider an example.

Example 5. A manufacturer is considering whether to use an alphabetic keyboard (see Fig. D–13) on his small business com-

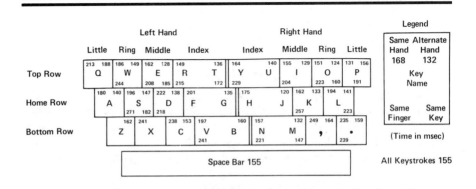

Figure D–12. Inter-keystroke times.

puter system. Among several factors influencing his decision is the question of whether experienced users will find the keyboard slower for touch typing than the standard Sholes (QWERTY) keyboard arrangement. What is the relative typing speed for expert users on the two keyboards?

We can compute the nominal typing rate with the proposed keyboard by using a table of all the digraphs in English (such as Underwood and Schulz, 1960) and multiplying the frequency of occurrence of each digraph by the time from Figure D–12 required for that digraph. When we do this for the alphabetic keyboard in Figure D–13, we get 164 msec/keystroke = 66 words/min. When we do the same exercise with a standard Sholes keyboard, we get 152 msec/keystroke = 72 words/min. In other words, the alphabetic keyboard is calculated to be about 8% slower than the standard keyboard. Depending on one's purpose, this may or may not be a reasonable penalty to pay for an alphabetic keyboard.

The design of keyboard arrangements is of some current interest. The argument usually goes that there are so many keyboards out in the world that it is impractical to change from the standard Sholes arrangement once the enormous expense of retraining is considered. Hence, consideration of new keyboard designs is a waste of time. But there is a counterargument (for which I am indebted to David Thornburg) that runs like this: At just this point there is a technology window that is about to open, during which it is practical to consider new keyboards. In consequence of the mass proliferation of computer devices now just beginning, the number of keyboards in the world is expected to increase by an order of magnitude greater than what exists today. Furthermore, these keyboards will go especially to people

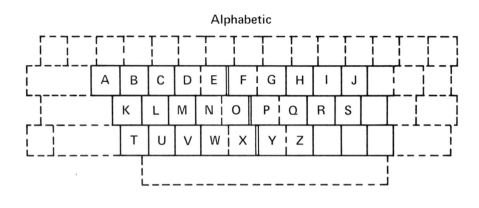

Figure D–13. Proposed arrangement of letters on typewriter.

without touch-typing skills, for example, business executives and grade-school children. In a few years, of course, the expansion will have occurred; these people will be accustomed to typing on whatever keyboards were available and the technology window will close. So there is a limited time during which a new keyboard arrangement could emerge and have a reasonable opportunity for technological diffusion. Calculations like this are the simplest way of exploring the performance consequences of different arrangements since answers are available within seconds instead of months.

Pointing Devices

The trend for the future is clearly for the graphics interface to dominate in human-computer interaction. An important component of this interface is the device the user employs to select some object on the VDT screen. Again, the characteristics of the human information processor set constraints on the design and use of such devices. As examples of these constraints, we can examine the minimum time required to point to an object on the screen and how this varies with alternative pointing devices.

Minimum pointing time

Let us consider the task of pointing to some target with a pencil or a finger (Fig. D–14). A little experimentation shows that the time to point to a target decreases if the target is located closer or if it is larger.

Example 6. What is the minimum time for pointing to a target S cm wide that is D cm distant?

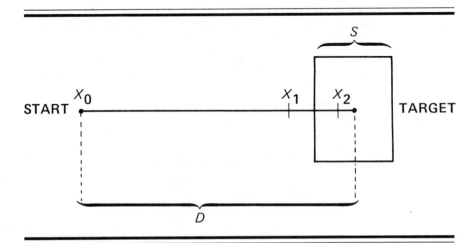

Figure D–14. Analysis of the movement of a user's hand to a target.

According to the Model Human Processor, the user makes such a movement through a series of discrete micromovements. The user moves his hand (one Motor Processor Cycle), observes how well it is moving as it moves (one Perceptual Processor Cycle), and decides how to correct the motion (one Cognitive Processor Cycle). Let us assume that each micromovement of the hand brings the hand towards the target subject to a certain constant error, say 7%. The user keeps going around this cycle until finally he perceives that the hand is within the target area and so stops. As we have seen previously, each of these cycles ought to take nominally $\tau_P + \tau_C + \tau_M = 240$ msec. If this is so, then the time to point to the target is just $240n$ msec, where n is the number of cycles. The question of how long it takes to point to a target reduces to the question of how many cycles it takes to get within the target. We can compute this number by referring to Figure D–14 and by assuming a constant error. Suppose the user starts X_0 cm from the target. After the first cycle he will be

$$X_1 = \epsilon X_0 = \epsilon D$$

away from the target, where ϵ is the error. After the next cycle he will be

$$X_2 = \epsilon X_1 = \epsilon(\epsilon D) = \epsilon^2 D$$

away. After the nth cycle, he will be

$$X_n = \epsilon^n D$$

away. The hand will stop when

$$\epsilon^n D \leq S/2,$$

that is, when the finger is somewhere within the target. Solving for n, we get

$$n = \frac{\log_2\left(\frac{2D}{S}\right)}{\log_2 \epsilon}.$$

Thus the minimum movement time is:

$$
\begin{aligned}
\text{Movement time} &= (\tau_P + \tau_C + \tau_M)n \\
&= (\tau_P + \tau_C + \tau_M)\frac{-\log_2\left(\frac{2D}{S}\right)}{\log_2 \epsilon} \\
&= -\left[\frac{\tau_P + \tau_C + \tau_M}{\log_2 \epsilon}\right]\log_2\left(\frac{2D}{S}\right).
\end{aligned}
$$

Substituting for the cycle times of the processors and taking the $\epsilon = .07$ from the literature, gives

$$\text{Movement time} = .1 \log_2 \left(\frac{2D}{S} \right).$$

This result is known as Fitts's Law. Welford (1968) has shown that it can be improved slightly by the addition of a constant within the log, so the version we shall use for movement time (see Figure D–1(b)) is

$$\text{Movement time} = .1 \log_2 \left(\frac{2D}{S} + .5 \right). \qquad \text{Eq. (1)}$$

We can now proceed to use this result, together with our results on keystroking, to consider the speed of different pointing devices.

Speed of pointing devices

Figure D–15 contains examples of several pointing devices. The device in Figure D–15(a) is a mouse. Figure D–15(b) shows a sort of joystick designed to be mounted as a key on a keyboard. When the knob on the top of the device is pushed in some direction, the knob itself moves very little, but a strain gauge senses the force and moves the cursor with a rate proportional to the square of the force. Figure D–15(c) shows a standard set of step keys. Figure D–15(d) shows a set of text keys with keys to advance the cursor by a character, a word, a line, or a paragraph and a shift key, which when depressed, reverses the direction of the cursor.

Experiments on the speed with which users can use each of these devices to point to a text target show that the mouse is superior to the other devices in speed (and accuracy, too) and that the step keys are particularly deficient (Figs. D–16(a) and (b)). The differences in the times for the devices can can be accounted for by the Model Human Processor. Pointing time for the step keys and text keys is proportional to the number of keystrokes required, as seen in Figure D–17(a). The constants of proportionality—74 msec/keystroke for the step keys and 209 msec/keystroke for the text keys—are in the general range of keystroke times discussed earlier. The step key rate is faster partially because it had a high-speed automatic repetition feature and partially because the sequence of keystrokes is simpler. But while the step keys are faster, keystroke per keystroke, many more keystrokes are required than for the text keys; hence the step keys are slower.

Both the mouse and the joystick have pointing times given by Fitts's Law (Fig. D–17(b)). In the case of this particular joystick, apparently the fact that the control was nonlinear made the device suboptimal. The mouse is able to achieve the .1 sec/bit expected from our derivation from the Model Human Processor in Eq. (1). This fact has important implications. The limitation

Figure D–15. Some devices used in pointing to a place on
the VDT screen.

on pointing time with the mouse is not the design of the device itself, but
the information-processing rate of the user's eye-hand coordination system.
This in turn means that, using the same set of muscles at least, it is probably
impossible to build a pointing device which does pointing substantially faster
than the mouse, although there may be a number of devices equally as good.

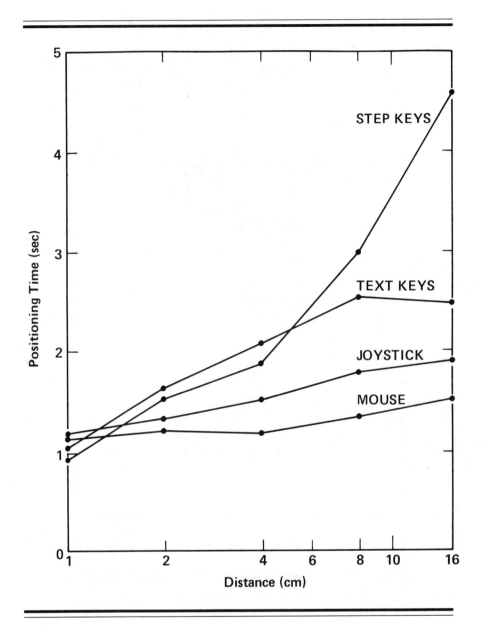

Figure D–16(a).   The effects of distance on time to select a text target.

EXPERT DIALOGUES

Our results on keystroking and pointing can be taken as part of a more general analysis of expert computer interaction (that is, for computer dialogues where what to do is not itself problematic). Keystroking and pointing are some of

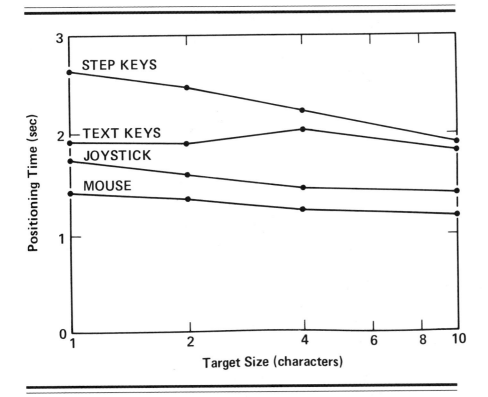

Figure D–16(b).   The effects of target size on time to select a text
  target.

the operations performed by a user. These and others are listed in Table 1
together with typical times for each. The keystroking rate is listed for touch-
typing. This rate depends upon the particular user group, but .2 sec/keystroke
is a good nominal number for reasonable typists. Pointing time is based on
the mouse and in this table is simplified to an average time. Of course a
more precise estimate could be obtained by using the equations in Figures
D–16(a) and (b), but this single value is often sufficient. "Homing" refers to
the reaching and adjusting of the hand position preparatory to using a device.
The time of .4 sec is based on the mouse, but times do not greatly differ for
the other devices in Figure D–15.

In addition to these physical times, there is, of course, a certain amount
of mental preparation time required by the user at different points in his task.
From previous experiments, we have estimated this at 1.35 sec, although it
can be quite variable. Finally there is the response time of the system, by
which I mean the nonoverlapped system time the user has to wait for the
computer to respond to a user action. These values for elemental operations
can be used to estimate user task performance time as follows.

TABLE 1

Operator	Description		Time(s)	Ref.
K[*text*]	KEY IN *text*			
		(Best typist, 135 wpm)	$t_K = 0.08$	[a]
		(Good typist, 90 wpm)	$= 0.12$	[a]
		(Average typist, 55 wpm)	$= 0.20$	[a]
		(Nonsecretary, 40 wpm)	$= 0.28$	[a]
		(Typing random letters)	$= 0.50$	[a]
		(Typing complex codes)	$= 0.75$	[a]
		(Nontypist)	$= 1.20$	[a]
	Examples of notation:			
	K[SHIFT i SP a m]	(Type the phrase "I am")		
	5K[*word*]	(Type a 5-letter word)		
	K[CTRL r]	(Type CTRL-R)		
	K[M2]	(Push button 2 on mouse)		
P[*object*]	POINT WITH MOUSE TO *object*		$t_P = 1.10$	[b]
	Example of notation:			
	P[*word*]	(Point to a word)		
H[*device*]	HOME HAND(S) ONTO *device*		$t_H = 0.40$	[c]
	Examples of notation:			
	H[MOUSE]	(Reach to mouse and grasp)		
	H[KEYBOARD]	(Move fingers to home row on keyboard)		
M	MENTALLY PREPARE		$t_M = 1.35$	[d]
	Use (1) before first letter of a command name, (2) before first terminator of a variable argument string, or (3) before pointing to a command.			
	Examples of notation:			
	MK[r]	(Before command name)		
	K[*word*]MK[ESC]	(Before ESC terminator)		
	MK[ESC]	(Only before first terminator)		
	MP[QUIT]K[M1]	(Before pointing to command)		
	P[*word*]K[M2]	(Not before selection of argument)		
R(*t*)	WAIT *t* SEC FOR RESPONSE		t	

REFERENCES: [a] Devoe (1967), [b] Card, English, and Burr (1978), [c] Card, Moran, and Newell (1980a), [d] Card, Moran, and Newell (1980b).

Table 1. Operations for Keystroke-Level Model. For a more complete description, see Card, Moran, and Newell (1980b, 1983).

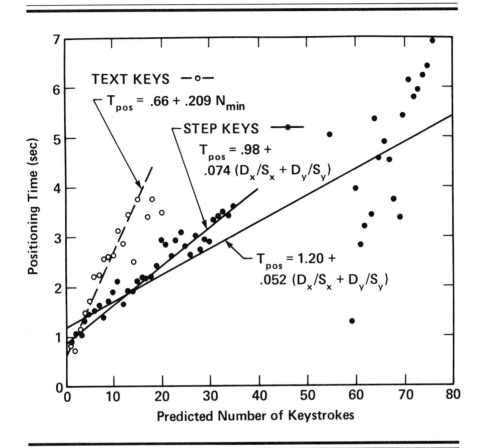

Figure D–17(a). Positioning time key-operated devices as a function of the number of keystrokes required.

Example 7. Suppose we have a VDT-based text editor with a mouse and that the task is to replace one five letter word with another five letter word located a line below it. The sequence of actions required by the user and their time analysis can be given as follows:

	Action	Operator	Time
1.	Home hand on mouse	H[MOUSE]	t_H
2.	Point to word	P[*word*]	t_P
3.	Select word	K[M2]	t_K
4.	Home hand on keyboard	H[KEYBOARD]	t_H
5.	Give Replace command	M K[r]	$t_M + t_K$

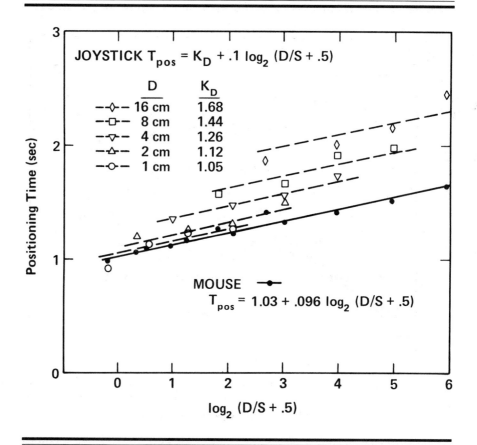

Figure D–17(b). Positioning time analogue devices as a function of Fitts's Index of Difficulty.

| 6. | Type new word | 5K [*word*] | $5t_K$ |
| 7. | Terminate word | M K [ESCAPE] | $t_M + t_K$ |

The total time for the user to do the task (excluding the amount of time he spent formulating the actions or the system response time) is calculated to be

$$T_{execute} = 2t_M + 8t_K + 2t_H + t_P$$
$$= 2(1.35) + 8(.2) + 2(.40) + 1.10$$
$$= 6.2 \text{ sec.}$$

How accurate is such an analysis? Figure D–18 shows the result of an experiment in which 28 users exercised 3 text editors, 3 graphics programs, and

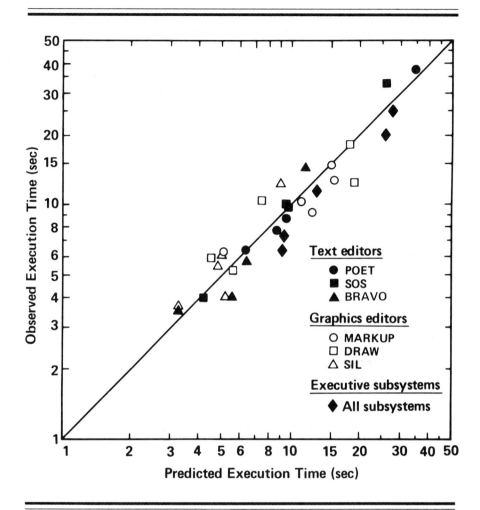

Figure D–18.   Observed user performance time for executing commands.

5 systems programs on a variety of tasks. The plot can be characterized by saying that under laboratory conditions, and when the sequence of operations performed by the user is known, the model is accurate to within a standard error of 20 ~ 30%, significantly different from the observations, but easily accurate enough to do various kinds of calculations useful in design.

Example 8.   A user is typing a text and he detects a misspelled word n words back. How long will it take him to correct and resume typing?

In this editor, the user has available to him two methods, let us call them Method W and Method R. Method W required typing CTRL-W for each word to be erased, making his correction, then retyping all the text. Our analysis for this method is:

Method W:

1.	Press and hold CTRL key	MK[CTRL]
2.	Invoke BACKWARD n times	$n((1/4)$MK[w]$)$
3.	Type new word	5.5K[*word*]
4.	Retype destroyed text	$5.5(n-1)$K

The result is that the time to perform this method is proportional to the number of words back.

$$T_{execute} = (1 + n/4)t_M + (1 + 6.5n)t_K \qquad \text{Eq. (2)}$$
$$= 1.6 + 2.16n \text{ sec.}$$

In Method R, the user goes into command mode, selects the offending word with the mouse, issues a replace command to retype the word, then gets back into command mode, points to where he left off typing, and issues an insert command. Our analysis for this method is:

Method R:

1.	Terminate type-in	MK[ESC]
	REPLACE BAD WORD	
2.	Home hand on mouse	H[MOUSE]
3.	Point to target word	P[*word*]
4.	Select it	K[M2]
5.	Home hand on keyboard	H[KEYBOARD]
6.	Invoke Replace command	MK[r]
7.	Type new word	4.5K[*word*]
8.	Terminate Replace command	MK[ESC]
	RESUME TYPING	
9.	Home hand on mouse	H[MOUSE]
10.	Point to last input word	P[*word*]
11.	Select it	K[M2]
	RE-ENTER TYPE-IN MODE	
12.	Home hand on keyboard	H[KEYBOARD]
13.	Invoke insert command	MK[i]

$$T_{execute} = 4t_M + 10.5t_K + 4t_H + 2t_P \qquad \text{Eq. (3)}$$
$$= 12.1 \text{ sec.}$$

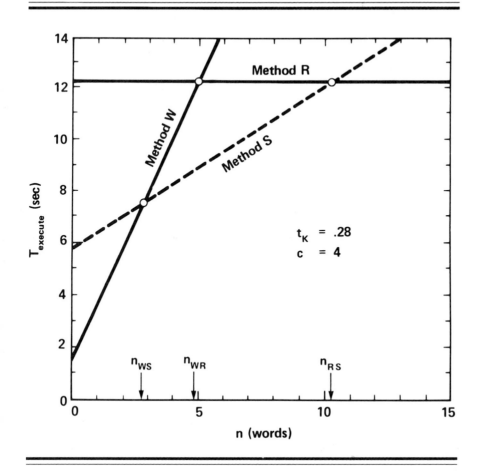

Figure D–19. Execution time for three methods.

This method takes a constant 12 sec regardless of the number of words back the error occurs (assuming it is on the same page). If we now plot the time required for these two methods as a function of the number of words back the error is, we obtain Figure D–19. The plot shows that Method W is faster for small n, but that after a point Method R is faster.

Example 9. Suppose that a systems programmer proposes a new command for help in this task. In the proposed system modification, call it Method S, the user proceeds similarly to Method W, except this time he uses a command, CTRL-S, that skips backward one word at a time without deleting the word as CTRL-W had done. When he gets to the target word, he uses CTRL-W to delete it and types in the replacement word. Then he uses another new command, CTRL-R, to move the cursor back to where he was before he started backing up. Does the new method improve user performance on the system?

At least in a research environment, the time between (some) systems programmers getting an idea for a new command and already losing themselves in implementing code can be on the order of 20 minutes. To persuade the programmer whether or not the command is useful, we need a practical tool that can be used quickly, like in 20 minutes. Thus the speed with which our analysis can be done is a valuable property. Our analysis of the proposed system enhancements is:

Method S (New Method):

1. Setup Backskip command   MK[CTRL]
2. Execute Backskip $n-1$ times $(n-1)(1/4)$MK[s]
3. Call Backword command   MK[w]
4. Type new word 4.5K[$word$]
5. Call Resume command   MK[CTRL r]

$$T_{execute} = (3 + (n-1))t_M + (n + 7.5)t_K$$
$$= 5.8 + .62n \text{ sec.}$$

The dependence of the time for the new method on n is graphed as the dotted line in Figure D–19. As the figure shows, there is a range in which Method S is superior to the other two methods because it takes the least time. Unless there are other reasons to the contrary, this might be a reasonable system enhancement. There are three qualifications to this statement, however. First, the analysis has been simplified by ignoring the probability distribution on n (which can be added easily, but only complicates this presentation). Second, we have only discussed minimizing time. Certainly, there are other indexes of merit in design such as time to learn, frequency of user errors, or even amount of machine memory required. It might be that this idea for improving speed of use makes the system more difficult to learn and that the increased difficulty of learning is more important than the speedup in use. System design always involves the trade-offs of contending goals, but to do the trade-off one must be able to understand what one is trading. Hence the use of the foregoing analysis.

The third qualification is interesting itself to discuss in terms of the model. In the previous analysis, we assumed a certain typing rate for the user. Suppose the actual users type at a different rate. Do our conclusions still hold? This is a typical question when we design systems that are to be used by both novices and experts. The question can be answered through further manipulations of the previous results. In Figure D–19 there are a number of crossover points, places where one method changes from being inferior to

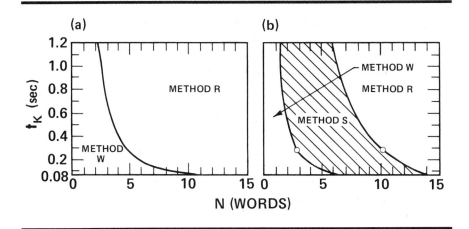

Figure D–20.   Regions in the $\tau_K \times n$ abstract parameter space for which each of the three methods is fastest. **(a)** The situation when only Method W and Method R exist. **(b)** The situation after Method S is added.

another method to being superior. By combining Eq. (2) and Eq. (3), we can solve for n_{WR} as a function of typing rate and plot the crossover point in Figure D–20(a). This diagram gives us something reminiscent of a phase space in chemistry. Given the number of words back and the user typing rate, we can identify whether Method W or Method R is faster according to which region the point determined by the two variables falls. If we now add the new Method S and perform the same analysis, we see that Method S is the fastest method for a considerable proportion of the likely typing rates and words back values (crosshatched region of Figure D–20(b)). For this reason, we can conclude that our previous conclusion that the new Method S might be useful is not very sensitive to user typing rate.

CONCLUSION

In this chapter, I have tried to sketch one way in which progress might be made in building a science base to support interface design. The central theme was the development of a model of human information-processing limits, robust and simple enough to be applied in practical calculations. To make this theme concrete, I have presented the details of one such model, the Model Human Processor. A practical model of human processing can serve as an organizing force helping to relate studies of interface components (keyboards, pointing devices, command menu schemes, and many others) that otherwise would form a collective jumble. It can help us analyze intact systems, as does the

Keystroke-Level Model outlined above. Thus we can trace the processing limits of the user through their various implications for the components of the interface and finally to the consequences of human limits for the design of whole systems.

To do this, we must analyze the task the user is to do and the operations available in the system he is to use. In Shackel's terms (Chapter 2), we must analyze the user, the task, and the tool. The account we have given has concentrated mostly on expert users and mostly on the prediction of time-based phenomena. That is appropriate because considerations of time must be addressed by any device that is to become a true tool for repeated work (text editors, for example.) Our account has, therefore, led from the basic information-processing psychology of the user to the motion-and-time-study industrial engineering of the interface.

But there is another class of VDT interface design problems centered around the usability of computers by novice users, casual users, or users with difficult problems to solve. In this case, the user is engaged in problem solving and time is no longer the dominant consideration. Such design problems can also be handled within the framework of a unified model of human processing such as the Model Human Processor. But here a different set of concepts is called for: the principle of bounded rationality, problem spaces, mental models, and chunking.

According to the principle of bounded rationality, people act rationally to solve a problem subject to limitations on their knowledge, memory, and other abilities. User behavior can, therefore, be understood by analysis of the rational actions available at any point in a system and an analysis of user limitations. The set of all these rational user actions is called a problem space (Newell and Simon, 1972) and user behavior often takes the form of heuristic search through the problem space. Also, a user's rational course of action is often highly dependent on his mental model of how the system works. He builds up this mental model and other information he uses, such as specific learned procedures, in units called chunks, that reflect the basic way in which mental knowledge is organized. The user's mental models and the user's way of chunking his knowledge are reflected in the structure of his problem space. But for expert behavior, this more general description of the user has a simplified form: There is little puzzlement about which course of action to pursue and user performance is determined by the time required to do various actions. Whereas the novice exhibits problem solving behavior, the behavior of the expert is better described as cognitive skill.

The aim of the Model Human Processor is to abet work toward a set of techniques for aiding the practicing interface designer. These techniques must be grounded in the theory and empirical facts of human information processing. I have tried to sketch here how computer interface techniques might be brought within a common theoretical framework; further suggestions on extensions to problem solving tasks can be found in Card, Moran, and Newell (1983, Chapters 2 and 11). Considerable work remains to be done, however, on all levels of computer interfaces before there is an engineering discipline of user interface design.

REFERENCES

Akin, O., and Chase, W. 1978. Quantification of three-dimensional structures. *Journal of Experimental Psychology* 4:397–410.

Averbach, E., and Coriell, A. S. 1961. Short-term memory in vision. *Bell System Technical Journal* 40:309–28.

Bloch, A.M. 1885. Expérience sur la vision. *Comptes Rendus de Seances de la Société de Biologie* (Paris) 34:493–95.

Card, S. K. 1979. A method for calculating performance times for users of interactive computing systems. In *International Conference on Cybernetics and Society*, pp. 653–58.

Card, S. K.; English, W. K.; and Burr, B. J. 1978. Evaluation of mouse, rate-controlled isometric joystick, step keys, and text keys for text selection on a CRT. *Ergonomics* 21:601–13.

Card, S. K.; Moran, T. P.; and Newell, A. 1980a. Computer text-editing: an information-processing analysis of a routine cognitive skill. *Cognitive Psychology* 12:32–74.

———. 1980b. The Keystroke-Level Model for user performance time with interactive systems. *Communications of the ACM* 23:396–410.

———. 1983. *The psychology of human-computer interaction.* Hillsdale, N.J.: Lawrence Erlbaum Associates.

Chi, M. T., and Klahr, D. 1975. Span and rate of apprehension in children and adults. *Journal of Experimental Child Psychology* 19:434–39.

Darwin, C. J.; Turvey, M. T.; and Crowder, R. G. 1972. An auditory analaogue of the Sperling partial report procedure: evidence for brief auditory storage. *Cognitive Psychology* 3:255–67.

Devoe, D. B. 1967. Alternatives to handprinting in the manual entry of data. *IEEE Transactions on Human Factors in Electronics* HFE–8:21–31.

Harter, M. R. 1967. Excitability and cortical scanning: a review of two hypotheses of central intermittency in perception. *Psychological Bulletin* 68:47–58.

Jevons, W. S. 1871. The power of numerical discrimination. *Nature* 3: 281–2.

Interlisp-D Group. 1981. Papers on Interlisp-D, report CIS–5. Xerox Palo Alto Research Center, Palo Alto, Calif.

Kaplan, R. M., and Bresnan, J. W. 1982. Lexical-functional grammar: a formal system for grammatical representation. In *The mental representation of grammatical relations*, ed. J. W. Bresnan, pp. 173–281. Cambridge, Mass.: MIT Press.

Kinkead, R. 1975. Typing speed, keying rates, and optimal keyboard layouts. *Proceedings of the 19th Annual Meeting of the Human Factors Society*, pp. 159–61.

Landauer, T. K. 1962. Rate of implicit speech. *Perception and Psychophysics* 15:646.

Michotte, A. 1946/1963. *The perception of causality.* English translation, Basic Books, 1963. Originally published as *La Perception de la Causalité.* Louvain: Publications Universitaires de Louvain, 1946.

Murdock, B.B., Jr. 1961. Short-term retention of single paired-associates. *Psychological Reports* 8:280.

National Research Council. 1982. *Automation in combat aircraft.* Washington, D.C.: National Academy Press.

Newell, A., and Simon, H. A. 1972. *Human problem solving.* Englewood Cliffs, N.J.: Prentice-Hall.

Peterson, L. R., and Peterson, M. J. 1959. Short-term retention of individual verbal items. *Journal of Experimental Psychology* 58:193–8.

Siewiorek, D.; Bell, G.; and Newell, A. 1981. *Computer structures.* New York: McGraw-Hill.

Sperling, G. 1960. The information available in brief visual presentations. *Psychological Monographs* 74 (11, Whole No. 498).

Sternberg, S. 1966. High-speed scanning in human memory. *Science* 153:652–54.

Underwood, B. J., and Schulz, R. W. 1960. *Meaningfulness and verbal learning.* Philadelphia: Lippincott.

Welford, A. T. 1968. *Fundamentals of skill.* London: Methuen.

CAPTIONS

Figure D–1. VDT with common input devices. Revised version of Foley and Van Dam (1982), Figure 1.14. The figure on the raster display is from a familiar Smalltalk bitmap, originally drawn by Alan Kay.

Figure D–2. Xerox 8010 Star professional workstation showing the use of command keys, mouse, and icons for representing reports, files, in-basket, printer, and other objects. Photo by K. O. Beckman, courtesy Xerox Corporation.

Figure D–3. The use of multiple windows in the Xerox 1100 Interlisp-D programming environment (Interlisp-D Group, 1981). Windows can hold text or any sort of graphic material and windows can even overlap other windows. The figure shows the use of windows by a linguistic analysis program LFT (Kaplan and Bresnan, 1982) written in Interlisp-D. As the program parses an English sentence, various linguistic structures displayed textually and graphically in the windows are dynamically updated.

Figure D–4. The Bitmap Editor of the Xerox Interlisp-D system. In the picture, individual pixels of the letter A are being edited by using the mouse to point to squares on an enlarged grid that represent individual raster pixels making up the letter. An unenlarged version of the letter is also displayed to aid the user. The checkerboard pattern at the upper right is the pattern of pixels used to generate the gray tone above it.

Figure D–5. Soft pushbuttons of the TRILLIUM system for laying out control panels, programmed by Austin Henderson, Xerox Palo Alto Research Center, in the Interlisp-D system of the Xerox 1100.

Figure D–6(a). The Model Human Processor—memories, processes, and basic principle of operation. Sensory information flows into Working Memory through the Perceptual Processor; motor programs are set in motion through activation of chunks in Working Memory. The basic principle of operation of the Model Human Processor is the Recognize-Act cycle of the Cognitive Processor: On each cycle, the contents of Working Memory activate actions associatively linked to them in Long-Term Memory, which, in turn, modify the contents of Working Memory. Reprinted, with permission from Card, Moran, and Newell (1983), © Lawrence Erlbaum Associates.

Figure D–7. Simple reaction time analysis using the Model Human Processor. Reprinted, with permission from Card, Moran, and Newell (1983), © Lawrence Erlbaum Associates.

Figure D–8. Scribbling as rapidly as possible for 5 sec while trying to stay between two lines. Reprinted, with permission from Card, Moran, and Newell (1983), © Lawrence Erlbaum Associates.

Figure D–9. Time decay of Visual and Auditory Image Stores.

(a) Decay of Visual Image Store. In each experiment, a matrix of letters was made observable tachistoscopically for 50 msec. In the case of the Sperling experiments, a tone sounded after the offset of the letters to indicate which row should be recalled. In the case of the Averbach and Coriell experiment, a bar appeared after the offset of the letters next to the letter to be identified. The percentage of indicated letters that could could be recalled eventually reaches an asymptote at μ_{WM}. The graph plots the percentage of letters reported correctly in excess of μ_{WM} as a function of time before the indicator.

(b) Decay of Auditory Image Store. Nine letters were played to the observers over stereo earphones arranged so that three sequences of letters appeared to come from each of three directions. A light lit after the offset of the letters to indicate which sequence should be recalled. The graph plots the percentage of the relevant 3-letter sequences in excess of μ_{WM} reported correctly as a function of time before the light was lit. Reprinted, with permission from Card, Moran, and Newell (1983), © Lawrence Erlbaum Associates.

Figure D–10. Working Memory decay rate. The subject is given either 1 or 3 words or consonants to remember. He counts backwards (preventing rehearsal) for a time and then recalls the stimulus. The graph plots the proportion of items correctly recalled as a function of the time elapsed until recall began. Reprinted, with permission, from Card, Moran, and Newell (1983), © Lawrence Erlbaum Associates.

Figure D–11. Perceived causality as a function of inter-event time. Type of perceived causality as judged by observers is plotted as a function of the interval separating the end of Object A's motion with the beginning of B's motion. Average of three subjects. From *The Perception of Causality* by A. Michotte (Fig. 5, p. 94). English translation © 1963 by Methuen and Co., Ltd. Reprinted by permission of Basic Books, Inc.

Figure D–12. Inter-keystroke times based on 155,000 keystrokes from 22 typists. After Kinkead (1975). Reprinted, with permission, from Card, Moran, and Newell (1983), © Lawrence Erlbaum Associates.

Figure D–13. Proposed alphabetic arrangement of letters on typewriter for Example 5. Reprinted, with permission, from Card, Moran, and Newell (1983), © Lawrence Erlbaum Associates.

Figure D–14. Analysis of the movement of a user's hand to a target. The hand starts from the point labeled START and is to move to anywhere inside the TARGET as fast as possible. D is the distance to the target and S is its width. Reprinted, with permission, from Card, Moran, and Newell (1983), © Lawrence Erlbaum Associates.

Figure D–15. Some devices used in pointing to a place on the VDT screen. Reprinted, with permission, from Card, English, and Burr (1978), © Taylor and Francis, Ltd..

Figure D–16. The effects of distance and target size on time to select a text target using the devices in Figure 10. Reprinted, with permission, from Card, English, and Burr (1978), © Taylor and Francis, Ltd..

Figure D–17. Positioning time **(a)** key-operated devices as a function of the number of keystrokes required and of **(b)** analogue devices as a function of Fitts's Index of Difficulty $\log_2(D/S+0.5)$. Reprinted, with permission, from Card, English, and Burr (1978), © Taylor and Francis, Ltd..

Figure D–18. Observed user performance time for executing commands as a function of predictions of the Keystroke-Level Model. Reprinted, with permission, from Card, Moran, and Newell (1980b), © Association for Computing Machinery.

Figure D–19. Execution time for three methods used in Example 8. Reprinted, with permission, from Card, Moran, and Newell (1980b), © Association for Computing Machinery.

Figure D–20. Regions in the $\tau_K \times n$ abstract parameter space for which each of the three methods is fastest. **(a)** The situation when only Method W and Method R exist. **(b)** The situation after Method S is added. Reprinted, with permission, from Card (1979), © Institute for Electrical and Electronics Engineering, Inc.

MANAGING TO MEET USABILITY REQUIREMENTS
Establishing and Meeting Software Development Goals

John L. Bennett

INTRODUCTION

The other authors in this section have outlined both the system qualities important to people and the processing skills of those people as they use computers accessed through Visual Display Terminals (VDTs) to carry out their work. Themes in the preceding chapters progressed from an explicit focus on the user in a customer environment toward a focus on the information needed by the vendor in a development environment.

In this chapter I turn attention to the process of building systems that are responsive to the needs of users in the customer environment. I discuss issues from the perspective of the design and development groups charged

This chapter is expanded from the paper "Managing to Meet Usability Goals in the Development of Office Systems," J. Bennett, *Office Automation Conference '82 Digest*, AFIPS Press, Arlington, VA, 1982. I thank Eric Carlson, Phyllis Reisner, and Steve Zilles, colleagues at IBM Research, San Jose, for their interactions with me to help clarify my language and distinctions. I developed many of the ideas while working with marketing people, and I particularly acknowledge assistance from Gene O'Rourke and Jack Pugliesie.

161

with building systems. Given that customer requirements and constraints have been outlined, the problem becomes one of managing vendor resources so that a system matched to customer requirements and user constraints emerges from the development process.

Developers are concerned with the basis for making the trade-offs that affect usability. An example of a development trade-off is taking time to design an online user aid and allocating computer storage space for its use versus expecting the user to find assistance in a printed manual. Trade-offs may be technical ("How does the development team exploit the available technology?"), or economic ("How does the development team produce a system that it can afford to build, that customers can afford to buy, and that users will spend time using?"), or trade-offs may relate to schedule ("How does the development team cope, on the one hand, with the need to test the usability of the system through the use of prototypes, and, on the other hand, with the need to meet development deadlines required for a timely offering of a product to customers?").

Defining Usability

I adopt the term and concept of "usability" (from Shackel), first distinguishing it from "function." Function is concerned with the technical capabilities of the system: *what* the system can do. Usability is concerned with the process of use, the steps the user must take: *how* the user achieves results.

In the first part of the chapter I review, interpret, adapt, and apply what the preceding authors have said about usability. I address those points that are of particular interest to system planners, designers, and developers. This is the kind of synthesis that each development team must make.

I then further define usability within a relationship among elements. The elements include specific TASKS carried out in the work ENVIRONMENT, the characteristics of the USER carrying out the tasks, and the characteristics of the SYSTEM (hardware, software, and supporting documentation) with which the user interacts. This definition helps us understand factors influencing user acceptance criteria, such as learning, throughput performance, flexibility, and attitude toward continued system use. I will develop sample measures as indicators for each of these criteria. The quality of the system as defined will influence the training process and the kind and extent of user support (through information centers, consultants) needed in the customer environment described by Keen and Bair.

We must understand clearly and define objectively the usability goals if we are to meet them during development. While I focus on usability, keep in mind that goals in this category are only one aspect of system quality that should be managed while making technical, cost, and schedule trade-offs during the system development cycle.

Providing a Framework for
Communication of Usability Goals

The central purpose of this chapter is to outline a framework for communication about usability between market-oriented people and technology-oriented people during the development process. I focus on the steps end users must follow to access a system's various functions. These steps are in effect established for the user when the system is first designed, but often without explicit consideration on the part of the design team. Design of the details affecting the process of use is sometimes left by default to the programming team. The result can be a system with important functional capabilities obscured inadvertently by tedious steps which users must follow. If the intended users have the same experience and expectations as members of the development team, then this may not be a problem. However, Bair gives numerous examples of steps and procedures (e.g., finding disk space, a tedious logon process) that systems often require, but that are not related to the work results that the user seeks to achieve, and are not part of the user's expectation.

In the second part of the chapter, I have adapted the work of Tom Gilb to present a "design by objectives" matrix as one way to communicate measurable goals. Requirements personnel in the vendor organization, the people most familiar with the customer environment and its needs, are often not well versed in the details and implications of the latest hardware and software technology. At the same time, development personnel, the technology-oriented people who build the system, are often unaware as to how the system will be learned and used by the intended end users. The statements of goals can serve as a bridge throughout the development cycle between the language and culture of requirements personnel and the different language and culture of development personnel.

Management can use the goal matrix to provide effective input on development priorities as the team iterates on design decisions. Higher management needs to have a top level (broadest goals) overview. Development management needs to understand detailed trade-offs. I will show sample target goals and measures, and how those goals can be expanded to resolve development issues.

USABILITY: DEFINED WITHIN A
RELATIONSHIP AMONG ELEMENTS

The user's interaction with a system takes place across an interface to the system (Fig. E–1). The interface, typically a VDT, provides a means for showing information to the user and a means for the user to give directions to the system. Displayed information can simultaneously give cues for immediate user action and can serve as a model to educate the user in longer-term

Analysis of Usability:

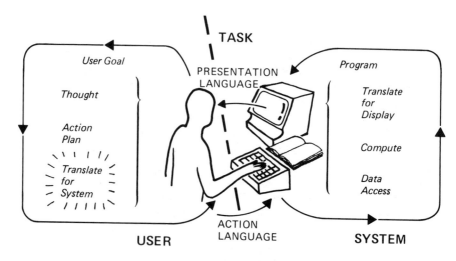

PURPOSE
- For each individual interaction
- For a series of steps to achieve a task result

Figure E–1. The Presentation Language and the Action Language support the USER carrying out a TASK through interaction with the SYSTEM. The goal of managing usability is to make it easy for the user to translate from goals into a series of actions leading to results that meet user and system PURPOSE in the user's ENVIRONMENT. Bennett, *Building decision support systems,* © 1983. Reading, Mass.: Addison-Wesley. Reprinted with permission.

effective system use. To meet usability goals, the entire development team working on the system must be conscious of the effect created at this user interface.

Usability is related to ease of learning and to ease of use. It becomes defined within a relationship among TASK, USER, and SYSTEM as the system is used for a PURPOSE within an ENVIRONMENT.

According to Shackel, for user acceptance a system must meet the following goals:

1. **Learnability.** A specified level of user performance is obtained by some required percentage of a sample of intended users with some specified time from beginning of user training.

2. **Throughput.** The tasks required of users can be accomplished by some required percentage of a sample of intended users with the required speed and with fewer than the specified number of errors.

3. **Flexibility.** For a range of environments, users can adapt the system to a new style of interaction as they change in skill or as the environment changes.

The human performance measures related to learnability, throughput, and flexibility must be met within an acceptable human cost in terms of comfort, satisfaction, fatigue, ease, and personal effort. The net result will appear in a fourth goal:

4. **Attitude.** Users want to continue to use the system, and they find ways to expand their personal productivity through system use.

In short, usability goals will be achieved if a system's *potential* is *actually used* both effectively (to a specified level of human performance) and willingly (to a specified level of subjective assessment). The specified range of users (given stated training and user support) must be served for the range of tasks within the specified range of environments. Managing to meet usability goals during development is essentially complex because people and judgments are involved from start to finish.

In adapting Shackel's definition of usability, I look at the elements in a slightly different order. My focus is on function, the physical and logical capability of the system to achieve results. I anticipate the TASKS that the function will support. For example, if the system does not support audio input and output, then the system is unlikely to be used in tasks requiring telephone conversation. Given that the system does provide useful function, then the nature of the TASK supported (e.g., clerical, managerial) will determine the kind of USER (e.g. typist, administrative, principal) likely to be working at the VDT that provides access to the SYSTEM (hardware, software, documentation). TASK completion requires a sequence of system displays and user actions. The user's perceptions of the design of the presentation language and the action language (Fig. E–1) will be a major determinant of usability.

The user's productivity (the kind of work supported and the speed with which it can be accomplished, as discussed by Bair) is affected by both the functions available to carry out the job (e.g., the user can manipulate a spread sheet on the display, the user can send messages to other users) and the required process that must be followed to benefit from the function (i.e., series of user steps, sequence of user actions).

From the perspective of the behavioral scientist, the user is the central focus and the system is viewed as one tool among many. From the perspective of the development team, the system is the central focus and the team makes design decisions affecting the system's use in a way intended to be acceptable to the user.

The PURPOSE of system use may be measured objectively. For example, one could measure the speed with which an assigned task, such as the production of a form letter, can be completed. Or the PURPOSE of system use may be measured less objectively. For example, a self-motivated worker may use the system to answer a client's ad hoc questions in depth. This latter quality is harder to evaluate because it is highly sensitive to the commitment of the user. The development team can incorporate system use experience by reviewing current user communities. The development team can also study basic human capabilities as documented in experimental psychology literature to produce systems that support such users in achievement of intended results (see Card's chapter).

Scenarios as an Aid in Specifying Usability Goals

A particular system design usually implies a particular process of use. However, we cannot expect to know in advance all the ways in which a system will be used in practice. Even if each step is relatively structured, the user can connect together many sequences of interactions. As observed by Shackel, Bair, and Card, the number of specific interaction patterns is, for practical purposes, limitless.

One way to understand the effect of a system design in a sample work situation is to examine a detailed work scenario, a sequence of typical system presentations and user actions. The planning and marketing members of the vendor team can play an important role by providing representative scenarios illustrating typical sequences expected in use. These sample patterns can, for instance, highlight the tasks users will want to do while learning (e.g., send short messages) or can highlight sequences that may be important because of high frequency to expert users requiring efficient throughput (e.g., checking spelling). The emphasis in such a scenario is on the flow of work, the way in which the output from one step serves as the input for the next.

Returning to Figure E–1, we can see how user understanding of displayed information and user choice of action are influenced both by the work being done and by the user's knowledge of the system. People will do what they expect it is possible to do with the system. This expectation can be shaped by reading explanatory material, by conversation with co-workers, or by a demonstration. The vendor can consider how to build a workable user expectation by selecting what features are demonstrated and what claims are made.

Usability Includes Ergonomics

Usability of an interactive system is associated with both physical aspects of using the terminal equipment and cognitive (thinking, decision-making, creative) processes within the user. Typical human factors literature addresses questions about visual contrast on the screen, phosphor color, dot resolution, keyboard layout, direction and amount of key motion, and understanding how audio feedback (e.g., key clicks) can increase throughput within keying tasks (Hirsch, 1981; McCormick, 1970). Satisfying these and other physical human factors is necessary but not sufficient for developing an acceptable product. Much of the challenge we must meet lies in providing support for human cognitive processes—understanding, thinking, deducing—as discussed by Card in his chapter.

Usability can only be meaningfully measured during task performance. The information processing required of the user must be studied as well as the mechanical actions necessary to operate the terminal. We can think of usability as relating to mental support for a user. We seek to identify those patterns of system features which will, in actual practice, promote effective user thinking and learning during work in the customer environment.

I focus on what designers and developers must consider to achieve a multifunction system which can be successful in a wide variety of user environments. We seek a balance of trade-offs among task complexity, user characteristics (skill, motivation), and system function. Employers who purchase the system want to draw on the skills of their employees in such a way as to achieve both productivity and user watisfaction.

Classes of Tasks Are Important

In order to establish system goals for function and for usability in a wide variety of markets, marketing analysts frequently establish classes of workers—clerks, typists, administrators, principals—when considering the prospective system users. This can help determine the marketplace potential and sample representative users when testing system quality. However, in the discussion of usability, I concentrate on the TASK or activity that a person will carry out and the skill required (regardless of class membership). For example, people from all four classes mentioned above will use editing functions when interacting with a system designed for production of text documents and for the interchange of messages with other users. Usability has a very personal focus. A given individual will vary in performance over time, and the wide variation in performance skill between individuals is well known. However, it is only after observing individual performances that we can extrapolate to a population of users.

In development we must gather information about the environment, abstract from particular details, and establish the general product focus. This process is reversed by the implementation specialists in particular customer organizations. They look at a range of product offerings and see which general functions can be best adapted to the specific needs of that particular environment. In addition, since many systems offer nearly the same function, implementation specialists are beginning to consider the usability of the products.

Languages of Interaction: Flow Across the Interface

By "languages" I mean the patterns of signs and symbols which the system uses to present information to a person—the Presentation Language (Fig. E–1). I also include the patterns of signs and symbols used to interact with the computer—the Action Language. Elements of the languages may be shown dynamically on a display screen or statically as a layout of keys on a keyboard. The user gives commands by selecting representations displayed on the screen or by moving hardware elements, such as keys, that are assigned a meaning in the Action Language. Thus, the languages include the rules for output on the VDT and the rules the user follows to construct input expressions.

The challenge to the system designer is to provide a Presentation Language which the user finds appropriate for work tasks and which the user can interpret with a minimum of thought extraneous to the task. The quality of the Action Language through which the worker conveys instructions to the system can be measured indirectly by examining the number of required user steps, the information which the user must remember, and the action errors which occur when the worker uses the system.

The hardware and software that form the interface provide the means for the worker to achieve the goals of effective use. Similarly, I make a careful distinction between the *mechanisms* appearing in a particular implementation—such as a menu of allowed commands to support user selection of a particular command, and the *concepts* appearing at the interface—the commands as a way for the user to give directions to the system.

Presentation Language and Action Language are closely linked. For example, Action Language commands may be shown as menu items on the screen. This design approach is consistent with a fact in human performance: it is often easier for the user to recognize and select information presented in a familiar format than it is to recall and type the same information accurately from human memory. This menu approach can be supplemented by allowing the user who recalls the name of a needed command to key it directly without waiting for the system to display a menu containing its name.

A conversationally interactive system might be thought of as a "partner" who will counsel the user and lead the user to a result. We have, however, many technological limitations in our understanding of user work processes, in the physical characteristics of the terminals we have available, and in the computer support software. Therefore, the successful system is usually thought of as a tool, which the worker uses to achieve a desired result rather than as a conversational partner (see Shackel's chapter).

ONE APPROACH TO MANAGING USABILITY

Usability issues tend to be diffused, come into focus over time during the system development process, and are often considered by many developers to be "subjective" or "fuzzy." Thus we may need a variety of mechanisms to derive and manage overall measurable goals. One of the key elements in the development of a user-oriented system is a means to measure user performance. Phrases such as "user friendly" must be given a technical basis if they are to have a predictable effect on design. The remainder of this chapter describes a methodology for formulating and presenting quantifiable usability goals.

Overall usability is often affected by a series of small points or "nits" in the way that the system is used. No one nit is itself enough to cause failure and system rejection, but a whole series of nits can have a devastating effect on user acceptance of the system.

Developers must make a series of technical, economic, and schedule trade-offs while managing usability. The documents guiding the development process will be most effective if they establish measures meaningful to those who will make and manage these trade-off decisions. If we want to achieve measurable results in a measure-sensitive industry, and if we want to avoid an accumulation of usability nits, then everyone concerned had better have a clear idea of how "success" will be gauged.

Usability Analysis

The usability of a particular system depends upon the characteristics of the tasks, the users, the computer support, and the system purpose (as discussed earlier). For this reason, there is no simple definition—or meaningful single measure—of usability. To illustrate how the concepts discussed earlier by Shackel and recapped in the first part of this chapter can be interpreted, I adapt several ease-of-use attributes discussed by R. B. Miller (1971). They illustrate general categories for which system-specific usability measures can be developed, and they put the concepts into a form such that developers can understand requirements and can see opportunities for design trade-offs.

Learnability

1. **Training time for the population of intended users.** If an interface is obvious and fits smoothly into the user's preset or preconceived way of doing things, then the actions taken by the user will be correct, and the training time will be short.
2. **Learning time until a user can enter actions "automatically."** When tasks involve creative thinking, a person's limited cognitive capacity makes it desirable to be able to do the more mechanical actions without thinking about them. The person typing is most efficient when thinking of content, not the location of keys on a keyboard. Having learned how to access the system functions offered through the terminal, the worker will typically require additional time to become facile in order to concentrate attention fully on the work task.

Throughput

3. **Kind and rate of errors.** This can be a revealing indicator of where the "correct" action of the user (based on the model of the system in the user's mind) does not agree with the action expected by the system (the actual model as represented in the design of system hardware and software). The designer can use the pattern of errors as a diagnostic cue and can choose either to change the user's model of the system through training or to change the user interface by redesigning the system.

4. **Time to recover from (user or system) errors.** Whatever the task, people—especially infrequent users—will make mistakes. Concern that work will have to be repeated can inhibit increased computer use. Sure and rapid recovery from an error matters to people who entrust their creative work to a system.

5. **Warm-up time after being away from the equipment.** The wide variety of functions available through a VDT makes it unlikely that a user will always remember immediately how to get useful results. A multi-function system usually contains too much detail for all to be remembered accurately. The amount of "how do I do that?" review is important for workers who use a VDT irregularly or who use a variety of computer-based tools.

Flexibility

6. **System adaptation to a changed work environment.** The new tool, if its potential is realized, will make it possible to support new ways of work. For example, messaging, rather than the telephone, may be used initially to set appointments. Similarly, text processing function may be used initially as a "super typewriter." As work patterns shift to make full use of these functions, people may usefully insert parts of messages and notes used for informal communication (rather than just for appointment setting) in formal documents. Conversely, parts of formal documents under revision can be usefully exchanged as messages and notes when people collaborate.

7. **User adaptation to a style of system interaction.** When first learning to use a new system, many benefit from command selection from menus. As they become familiar with the system, they often want to switch to direct commands when they are ready to take responsibility for precision and correctness. The system can continue to support them by prompting for missing parameters or for uninterpretable parameter values.

Attitude

8. **Feelings about continued use.** The user who feels that the system causes physical or mental strain is likely to resist using it. In fact,

such a person may try to prove that use of the system is not in the organization's best interest.

It should be clear that making trade-offs against these sample indicators (and others listed by Miller) depends on the overall system purpose. These usability indicators take on empirical values during performance, and can be evaluated only during use of the system. These measures are not at all like analytic engineering indicators which can be used to predict electrical or mechanical performance of physical components. The system developer who wishes to design a system that is easy for the worker to use does not have an analytic technology of the kind the developer relies on for making decisions about storage space or data flow rates.

A usability analysis is sometimes made difficult by the fact that people have a remarkable ability to work around all kinds of barriers. If the system gives them an important function unavailable in any other way, they may cope with a poorly designed computer interface. Nonetheless, the consequences of the design will appear as low efficiency, fatigue, and dislike of the system.

Presenting Goals

Tom Gilb, in his book *Software Metrics* (1977), stresses the importance of measurement in maintaining control as development progresses toward goals. Subsequent draft manuscripts by Gilb titled "Computerware Technoscopes" and "Design by Objectives" develop measurement concepts into a methodology for managing development resources. Most of his examples are drawn from consulting experiences with *applications* of computers. Because I am more interested in *development* of the systems that people will use for applications, I have adapted some of Gilb's ideas to apply to system development.

System goals will be abstracted by the requirements people from their analysis of the system's many applications in varied environments. Those goals must be meaningful to both the requirements community and the development community. I place particular emphasis on incorporating usability goals within this framework. The format allows formal inspection of both planned performance goals and of the development steps taken to meet these performance goals.

Distinctions Among Functions, Goals, and Attributes

Typically the process of setting goals begins by identifying system attributes at the highest level, those that will have major impact on success of the system. When we see the need for more detail in order to manage successfully, then we can expand the high-level critical attributes.

A FUNCTION is any capability that the system is to provide. A function performs a transformation on a given set of inputs to obtain an output result.

One example of a system function is a capability to retrieve stored documents. A list of functions defines what the system as a whole is intended to do.

A GOAL is a specific, measurable, testable result that is to be achieved. A goal may refer to the impact of a system when used (e.g., user productivity); it may relate to the work needed to market, sell, and install a system (e.g., field force productivity); or it may specify the level of resources needed to develop the system (e.g., personnel or material). A usability goal related to a retrieval capability might be the specification of the maximum learning time necessary for a set of users to pass a retrieval test.

An ATTRIBUTE serves as a way to elaborate on a function, a goal, or the implementation of a function in order to specify quality. (Examples of attributes for goals will be described below in the explanation of Figure E–5). Attributes provide parameters which enable an observer to make distinctions and to detect differences (in speed, accuracy, or cost) among the various ways of implementing a single function. The parameter categories for a goal make distinctions needed to determine whether a system goal has been reached. The time needed to learn (for the retrieval function) could be one attribute of overall usability, and the parameter would specify the measure to determine if the goal is met. When considered together, a set of attributes, each with its parameters, can make a particular function, goal, or mechanism meaningful.

In order to develop a system which meets goals, each function is implemented through one or more DESIGN DECISIONS—that is, technology is applied to make concepts real at the user interface. Each design decision has attributes that can be assessed as it is incorporated into the system along with other design decisions.

In practice the designer will tend to iterate through analysis of the required functions and the proposed design decisions. This need for iteration in setting goals, making and evaluating design decisions, and testing progress toward goals is emphasized throughout this description. The intention of the development team is to achieve system results that have some specified (implicit or explicit) level of performance. The designer will need to consider the attributes of both individual functions within the system and the aggregated functions that we commonly refer to as "a system."

To summarize, system goals are defined in terms of critical attributes and their parameter values. For example, in order to maintain user involvement in the interactive retrieval process, it might be specified that computer time to begin display of a retrieved document should be less than 8 seconds 90% of the time. In addition, the design decisions used to implement system functions themselves have attributes. For example, access method X has an average time of 5 seconds to begin display of a retrieved document from a data base of size Z.

If we fail to state goals correctly, then we are unlikely to achieve what the prospective users of the system really want. This is especially true for usability goals, currently considered by many designers to be "soft" and "unmeasurable." Although we may not be able to state goals perfectly at the outset, we can refine them through iteration as we establish working communication among system managers, planners, designers, and developers.

The end users will ultimately be the judge of whether the goals were valid and whether the development team has indeed met them. However, since users' evaluations are not available until they can use the system, an important part of achieving usability goals is identifying early warning surrogate measures to alert us to potential problems.

Relating Requirements Specifications to Development Activity

Figure E–2 highlights in a data flow diagram (DeMarco, 1978) the conceptual relationship between the work performed by the members of the System Requirements team and the work performed by the Development team. It also indicates the processes that must take place during development to manage the usability of a system as it evolves.

The list of typical work tasks for intended users is derived from an analysis of work needs in the user community. These serve as input to the SPECIFY SYSTEM REQUIREMENTS process. People in the requirements community typically take responsibility for this work. The output from this process includes a set of System Attribute Specification (SAS) Tables (Figs. E–5 and E–6) containing hierarchically organized goals. In addition, since usability is defined with respect to tasks, users, and system capability, a general scenario of anticipated use is necessary input for the TRACK SYSTEM EVOLUTION process. The usual list of functions, abstracted from study of the customer environment, also serves as input to the DEVELOP THE SYSTEM process.

In order to manage usability during development, we need to establish a basis for communication between personnel who understand marketplace requirements and personnel who understand computer technology. Development people typically have a focus on function, but any proposed design solution requiring interaction with the user will have implications for usability. Effective understanding of these usability implications requires a medium for communication between people to make current assumptions clear and to support the evolution of ideas during all phases of the development process.

In the DEVELOP THE SYSTEM process the design group determines how specific functions will be implemented. All of the process outputs are intended to communicate the implications of a design to those who TRACK SYSTEM EVOLUTION during development.

Communication during the process of stating requirements and the process of proposing designs assures that a technical design meets actual needs. Scope and frequency of this exchange occurs as managers TRACK SYSTEM EVOLUTION. Typically the managers who TRACK SYSTEM EVOLUTION should have the same orientation as the people who SPECIFY SYSTEM

Managing Usability

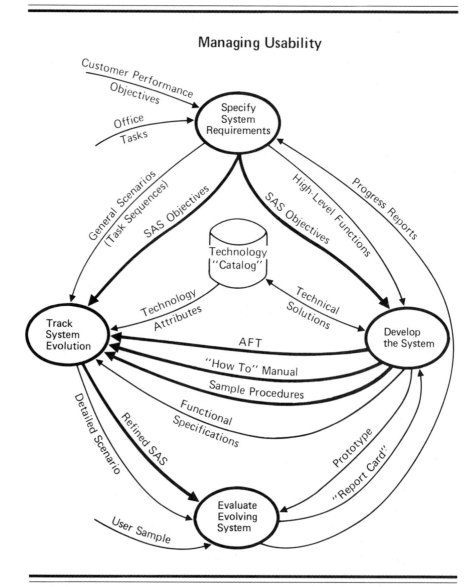

Figure E–2. A data flow diagram illustrating the relationship between the requirements specification and monitoring processes (Specify, Track, Evaluate) and the system development process.

REQUIREMENTS. The staff will need to be supplemented by specialists who can interpret the implications of design decisions (through reference to the Technology Catalog) and can develop the detailed information needed to EVALUATE EVOLVING SYSTEM. A "test" cycle can be performed whenever management suspects that an aspect of the design or the implementation may not meet goals.

Ideally, personnel who TRACK SYSTEM EVOLUTION could rely on a single output from those who DEVELOP THE SYSTEM to provide a complete specification of both system function and of the dynamics of use. However, no such single reference point exists.

The functional specification, the usual document produced by development, is the most complete and detailed source of design information. Unfortunately, it is usually organized to describe and specify function from a development perspective rather than from a user perspective. The reader trying to understand the process of use implied by the design must piece together facts from widely separated pages in order to determine the effect on user tasks. This is challenging for any reader, and it is especially difficult for marketing people untrained in engineering to grasp the implications of these separate design decisions.

Gilb suggests that we provide Attribute/Function/Technique (AFT) Tables to give management an effective overview of design decisions for both hardware and software technology. Such tables show the attributes of the design decisions intended to meet the specified level of performance. However, I address only the design goals here and do not discuss the AFT Tables in this chapter. I describe the other information sources (the "How To" Manual, Sample Procedures) that may be helpful in understanding usability issues in the explanation of Figure E–6.

As they EVALUATE EVOLVING SYSTEM, a team of specialists can answer questions generated by those who TRACK SYSTEM EVOLUTION by working with a user sample to gain test data. A prototype from development (i.e., a paper representation of the user interface or an operating model) can be tested with a sample of intended, representative users to see if detailed goals (represented in another SAS Table) are met. The output serves as a progress report to those charged with understanding system evolution, and it provides an early-warning report card back to the development team. In addition, we can establish a formal information link back to the REQUIREMENTS team. The output from the empirical tests may lead to better understanding of actual user requirements.

Technology Catalog

Central to the diagram in Figure E–2 is a Technology "Catalog." The design team, given an organized list of functions and a set of specified performance goals, must make the design decisions needed to implement the system. What is the source for these design decisions? How can a designer understand the effect of one design decision when it is included with the multitude of other design decisions which make up a system?

At the moment, the answer is that designers must rely largely on personal experience and intuition. Organizations which have designers with extensive design and implementation experience can make use of their staff's creative ability. Less experienced professionals may underestimate the need for considering a wide range of design decisions and may be unaware of the need for design quality control.

The need to consider design options is particularly acute in software. In almost any major area of design (i.e., data elements, file design, maintainability) we are confronted with hundreds of basic technical alternatives. The major difference between these technical alternatives is *not* in their function but in their power to satisfy the quality attributes for a particular product. Since a typical technique has a number of potentially interesting properties, the systematic choice of the most satisfactory alternative may require construction of data tables. This becomes a laborious job, but the body of knowledge can be updated to assist others as experience is gained.

The scientific, medical, and legal professions have coped with similar problems by organizing technical knowledge into technical handbooks. Students training to be professionals have then learned how to use these handbooks. The technology (techniques which serve to implement design decisions) used in the software development community needs to be organized, stored, made available, and updated in quantitative technical handbooks. Such handbooks should include *what* a technique is intended to do, the attributes indicating *how well* the component has done that job in the past, and the circumstances of its use. Typical attributes for a technique or mechanism could be the cost to buy or build, lead-time needed to acquire, time to install, resources needed to operate, etc. Figure E–3 shows in a list format the kind of information that should appear for each entry in such a handbook. A catalog of techniques and mechanisms serves the same role as the parts catalogs currently available to circuit designers.

When they focus on usability of a component, the design team members need information on attributes such as: time needed to learn to use, throughput speed observed, sensitivity to response time, frequency and kind of user errors observed, and user effort required to recover from computer or user error. Observations on the skill level required to use the component and the attitude of users would help the designer decide whether to use the component. Many of these usability attributes are situation-dependent; the designer needs to understand how the component was used in the particular reported situation and needs to estimate whether these conditions will hold in the proposed product. Figure E–4 shows a sample list of the kind of software techniques and mechanisms that might appear in such a catalog.

The chapter by Card describes attributes of the user as a "system component." That is, he effectively discusses how "rough and ready" tests can provide insight into the effects of design decisions. Data gained from this approach can be incorporated into a catalog of annotated techniques.

If we use the "design by objectives" methodology within the development process, we may create a demand for catalogs of software techniques needed to meet specified requirements in a cost-effective manner. Until then, devel-

---

TECHNOLOGY "CATALOG" SOURCE
for DESIGN DECISIONS

1. What a TECHNIQUE or MECHANISM does
   - e.g., a procedure interpreter and
     - associated macro language

2. ATTRIBUTES of this technique or mechanism
   - dollar cost to buy or build
   - time to acquire
   - time to install
   - resources needed to run
   - usability (situation-dependent)
     - time to learn to use
     - throughput speed
       - computer response time
       - user error-frequency observed
       - user error-recovery time
     - attitude toward use

Figure E–3.   A sample entry in a Technology Catalog.

opment teams must rely on members who have such a "technology catalog" stored in their heads as part of their experience.

The System Attribute Specification Table

Figure E–5 shows a sample System Attribute Specification (SAS) table for a hypothetical system. Alhough specific parameters are shown, the format and content of each table can be changed to reveal qualities important for a particular system.

Attributes are given brief descriptions and then further defined by a series of parameter categories across the top of the table. Each attribute takes on real meaning only when we specify how we will measure it in the "unit of measure" column. For example, one approach to measuring personal productivity would be to establish sample tasks known from experience to be important in the job. The set of tasks, carried out by a sample of intended users on a prototype implementation, could indicate the design's ability to support this kind of job. This early simulation of the user interface prevents the belated and unhappy discovery that the intended users cannot perform to specification with the system as designed. In the example in Figure E–5, the unit-of-measure (hours) is chosen to be long enough to give an idea of steady-state user productivity, yet short enough for feasible testing.

SAMPLE CATALOG ITEMS

1. Abstract data types,
   format for each and operations allowed on it
2. Procedure interpreter,
   language for writing procedures
3. Co-routines to support transfer of control
4. Code interpreter
5. Decision-table processor
6. Display management packages
7. Templates to serve as models for a data object
   (e.g., sample conference format with typical content)

Figure E–4.   Sample items in a Technology Catalog.

The next series of Parameter Categories in the sample SAS Table can be used to specify values that establish level of performance. The figure for the Planned Value indicates a satisfactory performance for the final user of the system, and it should be consistent with the Planned Values for all other system attributes. The Worst Case Value marks the borderline between a tolerable and an intolerable system. If the observed value for any one attribute goes beyond the assigned worst case level for that attribute, then the system as a whole may be formally unacceptable. While the system may not be "worthless," it has not met goals. An explicit Current Value provides a basis for comparison. For example, management may be prepared to accept a lower-than-currently-available level for user productivity for a part of a new system if the overall level of system performance, as measured by other high-priority attributes, is greater for the new system.

The Remarks column may contain a reference to source information or to additional details listed in another SAS Table containing an expansion for this attribute.

This method raises three questions. First, how do we set the values shown in each parameter category? At this stage in the development of these concepts, most requirements people are not accustomed to supplying goals specific enough to make careful trade-offs. In addition, development people are not accustomed to receiving such goals. For these reasons, values must be arrived at through iteration and negotiation. At the least, this method places important values "on the record," and thus avoids unpleasant surprises—such as requirements people envisioning an on-the-job training time of three hours and development people assuming that users will attend a 30-hour class.

Second, how do developers make trade-offs intended to meet goals? Again, there is no magic process, but both the target values and the trade-offs made are explicit in this approach. In a private communication, Stuart Card has

DEVELOPMENT GOALS FOR USABILITY OF A SYSTEM

PARAMETER CATEGORIES

Attributes	Means Used to Measure	Unit of Measure	Planned Value	Worst Case Value	Current Value	Remarks
1. Increase user productivity	sample cross-section of users, sample set of tasks	hours to complete	4	8	6 with current means	assume have learned system
2. Add tele-conference function	function test by Assurance Group	check-list, compare with specs.	100% working	95%	not avail.	make sure fits with existing function
3. Hold budget	cost accounting line items	$	x	$2x$	$\frac{1}{3}x$ so far	over-run raises price, reduces no. of users
4. Meet schedule commitment	calendar	month end	June '84	Sept. '84	est. 1/2 complete	a key cust. plans to use Aug. 1

Format adapted from T. Gilb, "Design by Objectives"

Figure E–5. A sample System Attribute Specification (SAS) Table which gives high-level definition to development goals for productivity, function, cost, and schedule. Each goal is made concrete by the values chosen for the parameter category.

pointed out that making trade-off points explicit can have a beneficial effect on use of system resources. For example, it may be very expensive to achieve three-second response time for a particular kind of information retrieval request. If an analysis of goals with respect to work patterns reveals that such a request comes at a natural closure point for users, then the response time can be reasonably adjusted upward for that requirement without damaging the overall usability of the system. If target values and trade-off points are explicit, then there is hope for tracing results observed in the field back to specific design decisions so that we can learn from experience.

Third, how often must progress be monitored? The scope and frequency of monitoring the TRACK SYSTEM EVOLUTION process is a business decision. For example, a minor new release of standard technology for an existing product intended for trained specialists is usually less risky than introducing a product intended for a new user group.

Gilb reports that one top manager's initial reaction to a sample SAS Table was, "That's for the technical people." Gilb countered with, "No, the set of tables is your primary instrument of control." It is not good sense to launch a costly project without getting all members of the team to reach a clear agreement about what they are trying to accomplish.

Some attributes may be considered "unmeasurable." As Gilb suggests, if the existence of a quality can be determined, then it is measurable—if only at the level of "present" or "absent." It is better to have some measure for an important system quality (even if the method to measure it is weak) than to have no measure whatsoever. No measure means no hope of control over that particular quality. If there is no convenient objective measure, then we can make use of sampling and statistical methods from the social sciences in order to quantify opinion.

Note that only the first attribute in the Figure E–5 table is directly related to usability. The "design by objectives" methodology can apply to the management of all attributes affecting quality.

Expanding an Attribute into More Detail

As it stands, the table in Figure E–5 does not give us enough detail for managing to meet the high-level goals. Guided by an understanding of the usability attributes, I expand attribute 1 into subattributes shown in Figure E–6 as a sample SAS Table for usability. A similar expansion can be done for any Figure E–5 attribute, and the process can be carried to any level necessary.

In Figure E–6, Attribute a. relates to learnability. Team members know that the "easy to learn" attribute will be measured by five people using a prototype mockup to perform a sample teleconferencing task. For a particular scenario, the planned estimated time is four hours. A refined measure would give an estimate of expected deviation. The Worst Case Level provides an upper bound value; all agree that something is seriously wrong if, on the average, it takes the user more than six hours to learn the task and perform to the standard. The basis for this measure is not given here, but of course it would have to be available. The table shows that there is no Current Value data available to show the time for learning comparable performance skills with an alternative conferencing tool.

Attributes b., c., and d. focus on throughput. Attribute e. addresses one measure of flexibility as the new teleconferencing function is integrated into people's work patterns. Attribute f. shows how attitude will be measured. Note that this table only gives an overview at a glance. The details for Attributes and for Parameter Categories must be contained in supporting documents.

DEVELOPMENT GOALS FOR USABILITY OF A SYSTEM

PARAMETER CATEGORIES

Attributes	Means Used to Measure	Unit of Measure	Planned Value	Worst Case Value	Current Value	Remarks
a. Basic Conf. tool must be easy to learn	test sample of 5 people using proto-type	hours, score	4	6	no data	must be able to learn
b. Conf. tool leads to results comparable to face-face	sample task suitable for tele-conf.	hours to complete structured interview	2	4	4	a key selling point
c. Relation of errors in Conf. use to errors in other parts	kind and rate of errors	count of errors due to confusion about design	1/hr	5/hr	?	must fit existing style of system use
d. Recovery from errors (system or user)	observe log of user actions	count of errors requiring > 30 sec.	hold to 2/hr	more than 7/hr	1/hr in current system	field reps say is of key import
e. Smooth transitions from menus to commands in use of new function	task set requiring use of new and old function	count actions, time, to make transitions	less than 1/10 overall time	1/3	1/10 time is currently spent overall moving between current system parts	
f. Attitude toward continued use	interview after question-naire	score	80%	50%	current system score 80%	word-of-mouth is key for referral selling

Format adapted from T. Gilb, "Design by Objectives"

Figure E–6. A sample SAS Table showing parameters for usability attributes. Each goal is established by the values chosen for the parameter category. These particular goals are related to learn-ability, throughput, flexibility, and attitude attributes adapted from the section on Usability Analysis.

The question of determining these values, discussed earlier in the explanation of Figure E–5, arises again. The discipline of choosing attributes and setting values can itself clarify what is important for all members of the team.

Returning to Figure E–2, note that we show two outputs from the DEVELOP THE SYSTEM process in addition to the Functional Specifications and the AFT Table. We can see now how these are linked to usability in a table such as the one in Figure E–6.

An outline of the "how to" manual can contribute by focusing on the user process needed to learn the system and to complete important tasks. This outline should contain those concepts which the development group knows must be explained, the required user actions, and the results which the user can achieve—chapter by chapter. The outline highlights both what needs to be taught and what needs to be understood by the user in order to do that level of useful work.

Still another output that can be helpful, if it is produced at early stages of development, is a set of example procedures or "models" recommended by the development group for using the system effectively. Developers know the trade-off decisions that were made, and they can outline the implications of these trade-offs for successful system use. For example, the designers of a particular product may decide not to provide the same file retrieval tools for informal user-to-user messages as are provided for retrieval of formal teleconferencing data (because of cost and schedule constraints). From the point of view of usability, users will rightly expect that the same tools, operating in the same way, will be provided for both. Recognizing this, the designers may suggest a way for users to name messages so that some content indicators appear in the titles which can then be reviewed in a list as an aid to memory. This is clearly a compromise. Those who TRACK SYSTEM EVOLUTION can review the suggested user procedures needed to manage user-to-user messages and can see if they are likely to be acceptable to intended users.

SUMMARY

We are seeing an increased focus on system usability as a factor in overall work productivity and job satisfaction. This chapter has suggested how usability can be defined through measurable, testable attributes given in enough detail to support development trade-offs. These attributes and their measures can be presented in hierarchically arranged tables to support communication between all the people working within the development process. The tables can evolve, be refined, and be tailored to represent the qualities required of a specific system.

At first the people working within the development process may think the effort required to establish "Design by Objectives" tables unnecessary.

Clearly the approach is not a substitute for function nor a substitute for creative design ideas needed to implement function. But, as Brooks observes (1975, pp. 46–47), clear goals allow designers and developers to be creative in applying technical skills to meeting those goals. When the "design by objectives" method is fully developed, and when the full implications of user demands described by Keen and Shackel are realized, the representations and the processes for using the method within the development cycle will prove of great practical value to both requirements and development people.

REFERENCES

Brooks, F. P. Jr. 1975. *The Mythical Man-Month.* Boston: Addison-Wesley.

DeMarco, T. 1978. *Structured Analysis and System Specification.* Englewood Cliffs, N.J.: Prentice-Hall

Gilb, Tom. 1977. *Software Metrics.* Cambridge, Mass.: Winthrop.

————. (1981) Design by objectives. Unpublished paper.

————. (1979) Computerware Technoscopes. Unpublished paper.

Hirsch, R. S. 1981. Procedures of the human factors center at San Jose. *IBM Systems Journal* vol. 20, no. 2: pp. 123-71.

McCormick, E. J. 1970. *Human Factors Engineering*, 3rd ed. New York: McGraw-Hill.

Miller, Robert B. April 12, 1971. Human ease of use criteria and their trade-offs. IBM Corporation report TR 00.2185. IBM Corporation, Poughkeepsie, N.Y.

Shneiderman, B. 1980. *Software psychology: human factors in computer and information systems.* Cambridge, Mass.: Winthrop.

SECTION 2

Using Visual
Display Terminals:
Health Concerns

INTRODUCTION

Controversy exists over whether Visual Display Terminals (VDTs) are a hazard to human health and whether research findings published to date are an adequate basis for understanding and coping with VDT-related health concerns. Are VDTs the cause of the complaints heard from large numbers of workers, or are they a convenient target for reacting against are fundamental changes introduced in the work process by their presence? This question cannot be completely answered as yet, but the articles in this section will enable the reader to understand the issues involved and to draw reasonable conclusions.

Health complaints related to using a VDT can be placed into the following four categories: visual dysfunction, musculo-skeletal problems, emotional disturbances, and psychosocial disorders. Visual dysfunction ranges from temporary acute effects such as eye irritation, visual fatigue, blurred vision, and headaches to concerns about chronic visual disorders such as cataracts or glaucoma. Visual distress is the most common complaint of VDT operators. Temporary problems do occur and are generally caused by poor design of the VDT or work environment or by long intensive work intervals without adequate rest periods. There is no current evidence showing that use of VDTs causes chronic visual disease, or that the vision of VDT operators deteriorates faster than the vision of workers in other jobs. However, this may simply reflect a lack of knowledge about long-term effects from VDT use. While there appears to be no cause for alarm, concern is justified, and further research into the chronic visual influences of VDT viewing is needed.

Musculo-skeletal problems take the form of pain or discomfort in various body parts, including the neck, shoulders, back, arms, hands, and fingers. VDT operators have a higher incidence of complaints than do traditional typists. This may be due to the posture required to view the VDT screen. The design of the VDT unit (e.g., detached keyboard, tiltable screen) and associated furniture (e.g., adjustable chair, variable height terminal stand)

muscles

187

affect the operator's flexibility in assuming a proper posture. This topic is receiving increased attention because of its importance in product marketing. "Ergonomically designed" is a common term now in VDT product literature.

Emotional disturbances occur in two forms. Mood disturbances include anger, frustration, irritability, anxiety, and depression. Psychosomatic disorders include gastrointestinal disturbances, muscle and psychic tension, heart palpitations, and frequent sweating. Very little research has been done in examining emotional disturbances among VDT operators. However, emotional disorders in general appear to be a growing problem. They are recognized today in 19 states as potentially work-related and therefore subject to worker's compensation awards.

Psychosocial disorders reveal themselves in worker complaints about work load, pace of work, poor supervision, and other problems in the work environment. Job dissatisfaction and fear of job loss can create high stress levels. Such job-related stress has been linked to serious chronic ailments, including coronary heart disease, coronary artery disease, stomach and intestinal disorders, emotional distress, endocrine imbalances, and reduced resistance to disease. However, these problems appear to arise from organizational, social, and job design changes related to automation of tasks, rather than from the VDT itself.

The authors of the three chapters in this section are affiliated with very different organizations. The reader will, therefore, encounter varied opinions and interpretations on the same or similar research evidence regarding the health consequences of using VDTs. Michael Smith works for a governmental agency concerned about worker health. Lawrence Stark and Phyllis Johnston are university researchers. O. Bruce Dickerson and Walter Baker are affiliated with a large company that is both a vendor and user of VDTs. These authors present different views on the extent and seriousness of worker complaints, on the causes attributed to such complaints, and on actual health problems resulting from regular use of VDTs. Yet all feel some form of environmental redesign is necessary to ensure worker well-being, and each suggests ways to improve the VDT working environment.

In the first article in this section, Michael Smith reviews studies conducted in the United States and Europe on the potential health problems for users of visual display terminals. He defines the possible health risks, describes factors contributing to observed health complaints, and offers recommendations on ways to make the VDT workplace safer.

In reviewing health concerns, Smith considers environmental design, workstation design, job content, and organizational context. Environmental design includes lighting levels, glare on the VDT screen, readability of displayed characters, and temperature and humidity factors. Workstation design considers the type and nature of adjustment the VDT operator should have available when using the device, including furniture that is adjustable to enable the worker to properly position the body in relation to the VDT keyboard and screen. Smith notes that the nature of the job itself–what the worker is expected to do and how work performance is measured–plays an important role in observed worker complaints. He provides an example of job redesign within an insurance company that led to improved worker morale and productivity. The organizational context in which the worker does his or her job also plays a major role in overall health concerns. How the organization relates to the employee on matters of job security, training, and other issues concerning employee well-being affect job-related stress levels.

After reviewing the potential health risks and their possible causes, Smith provides recommendations on ways to eliminate or minimize them. He concludes his article by pointing out where gaps exist in our knowledge about VDTs and worker health, and by identifying field studies and laboratory research work necessary to fill these gaps.

In the next article, Lawrence Stark and Phyllis Johnston provide a comprehensive look at how the visual system works and what causes visual dysfunction. They acknowlege that visual fatigue is difficult to define or evaluate, and list some suggested operational measures. They proceed to describe the various mechanisms in the visual system that might account for the visual fatigue symptoms reported by VDT operators. Then they review the eye movements necessary to line up on the retina the information to be examined, and the focussing mechanisms (accommodation, vergence, and pupillary action) necessary to make a clear image on the retina. Finally, they describe how these processes relate to visual dysfunction. The processes are described in terms of cybernetic models reflecting both the authors' backgrounds in neurology and Stark's knowledge in electrical engineering.

The Stark/Johnston article makes clear the complexity of the visual system. A number of interrelated components make compensating adjustments when stress and strain are placed on the system. The visual system is shown to be very "hardy"—able to accommodate a significant load before actual dysfunction occurs. However, the VDT places unusual demands on the visual system by using the various mechanisms (eye movement, pupil response) in unaccustomed ways. This may have an exacerbating effect on normal visual strain, thereby causing fatigue. The article ends by recommending ways to enhance the visual environment of VDT operators. These recommendations encompass viewing distance, screen and character color, luminance contrast ratios, VDT refresh rates, and VDT brightness and contrast controls.

In the final article of this section, O. Bruce Dickerson and Walter Baker summarize for the implementor of VDT-based systems the important health issues surrounding VDTs, then describe one company's approach (IBM) in dealing with them. The reader will find many of the topics discussed in the Smith and Stark/Johnston articles revisited, but from a different perspective. Dickerson and Baker view the VDT as a tool available to a worker in accomplishing tasks specified by an employer. They show why many of the health concerns with assembly line workers carry over into the VDT-based work environemt. They note further that there must be shared responsibility in providing a safe working environment. The participants in this sharing are:

- the supplier (manufacturer), who provides products that incorporate what is known about good ergonomic design;
- the employer, who establishes a physical and social environment that is conducive to worker well-being, and who designs job content that is meaningful and rewarding; and
- the employee, who uses his or her work tools properly and who informs the employer about observed health problems.

In reviewing factors linking VDTs to health concerns, such as radiation, lighting, posture, and visual tasks, Dickerson and Baker provide their own opinions on and references to relevant research studies. They are at times critical of the subjective nature of these studies, and they maintain that additional scientifically validated evidence is necessary before defining standards or drawing final conclusions.

The Dickerson/Baker article closes with a brief report on measures IBM has taken in confronting VDT-related health issues. These include developing training courses for health and safety professionals and providing line managers with instructional aids for increasing employee awareness and knowledge about VDT-related health issues. Such aids include a short videotape describing possible VDT problems and solutions, and a 13-page booklet addressing ergonomic and environmental factors in the VDT workplace.

The authors in this section disagree about the findings on visual health problems. Smith asserts there is a consensus, based on both field and laboratory studies, that VDT operators working at normal everyday work tasks experience a variety of acute visual disturbances. He postulates that these acute disturbances may become chronic with daily exposures and that such long-term health effects could impact visual processes permanently. Stark and Johnston point out that the visual system is very hardy and flexible. They believe continuous exposure to VDT work may exercise the visual system but doubt that it will produce permanent negative effects. Dickerson and Baker question the adequacy of the research literature and suggest that evidence is presently insufficient to determine the visual health consequences of VDT viewing.

However, as M. J. Dainoff points out in his article "Occupational Stress Factors in Visual Display Terminal (VDT) Operation: A review of Empirical Research" (Behaviour and Information Technology, 1982): "Nevertheless, whatever asthenopia/visual fatigue/eye strain is, it appears to occur in VDT operators around the world. Although individual studies may have flaws, particularly in regard to adequacy of comparison groups, the high rate of response in VDT operators, as opposed to non-VDT controls, occurs again and again." VDT operators do have an extremely high rate of visual disturbance complaints. Whether or not acute temporary visual problems lead to chronic visual disease has yet to be determined; meanwhile, it would be prudent for employers to improve the VDT workplace so that chronic health problems will not arise.

It is not clear when or if the controversy over VDTs as a hazard to health will be settled. It is clear that the use of VDTs is growing rapidly, and that growth is expected to continue for a long time. The purpose of this section is to identify potential health risks, explain possible causes, and provide guidance on how to reduce or eliminate these risks.

HEALTH ISSUES IN VDT WORK

Michael J. Smith

INTRODUCTION

Why are health and safety practitioners, managers, and union officials concerned about video display terminals (VDTs)? They are concerned because the workers who use VDTs are worried about radiation, visual dysfunction, sore muscles, and emotional disturbances. Whether workers' worries about significant health consequences are legitimate is a complex issue. One of the key elements in this concern, as demonstrated in Figures F–1 through F–3, may be the working conditions of many VDT operators, which are akin to working in factories, with operations like those on an assembly-line, high workload demands, and little decision making or job control. This chapter will investigate some of the potential health consequences of VDT use, their severity, possible causes, and primary solutions.

Interest in video display terminal health issues developed in Sweden in the early 1970s and spread to the rest of Europe during the mid-1970s. Early work by Hultgren and Knave (1973, 1974) indicated that a high percentage of video display terminal operators complained of visual disturbances. Those findings were reinforced by the work of Gunnarsson and Ostberg (1977), who found that 76% of the VDT operators studied had visual complaints. In Austria,

The author would like to acknowledge the technical help and assistance of Dr. Marvin Dainoff. Dr. Dainoff's review of draft material was helpful in developing the final version of this chapter. The author also wishes to acknowledge the editing and typing support provided by Ms. Donna Thorman.

Figure F–1. VDT work area at an insurance company.

Haider and his associates (1975) found that work at a VDT for prolonged time, without a rest break, produced small shifts in visual function. In Germany, Cakir and his associates (1978) found 68% to 85% of operators they studied had visual complaints, depending on the type of VDT job. This European research emphasized the relationship between the work environment and VDT design, and how this produced visual fatigue and associated visual complaints of VDT operators.

In the United States, early interest in VDTs centered on potential radiation hazards that may be produced by the operation of the VDT. This interest was triggered when in two reporters at the New York Times who used VDTs developed cataracts. The National Institute for Occupational Safety and Health (NIOSH) measured the radiation levels to which these reporters were exposed in 1977 and concluded that radiation exposure from the VDT was not responsible for their cataracts. Subsequent investigations of radiation levels emitted by VDTs confirmed that radiation levels were below current standards.

In one particular NIOSH investigation, an experimental psychologist interviewed workers and management about the work environment. He concluded that workplace design, workload, and supervisory styles were of greater concern to VDT operators than radiation. Based on this evaluation, in 1979,

Figure F–2.   VDT work area at a newspaper.

NIOSH initiated a program to examine workplace design and job stress in VDT work.

In summary, interest in VDTs in Western Europe has centered on ergonomic design issues of the work environment and workstation, and how they influence workers' visual and muscular complaints. In the United States, initial concerns focused on potential radiation health hazards, but in the last three years they have shifted to the ergonomic concerns of the Europeans. American research has focused on job stress and work task design issues.

REVIEW OF VDT HEALTH RESEARCH

Definitional Studies

The first VDT studies lacked control groups, which limited the implications of their findings. In particular, it was difficult to determine the seriousness of the problems observed in relation to similar jobs. These studies should be considered definitional and significant indicators of visual and muscular problems among workers using VDTs.

Much of the early VDT health consequences research was conducted in Sweden. Hultgren and Knave (1973) found that about half the number of

Figure F–3. VDT work area at a taxation department.

VDT operators examined at an insurance facility reported visual problems. The investigators related these problems to environmental conditions of inadequate lighting and glare on the VDT screen. Ostberg (1974, 1976, 1977) was one of the first scientists to suggest that VDT operators' complaints may be due to improper ergonomic design of the VDT screen and workstation. In a study of airline reservation clerks by Gunnarsson and Ostberg (1977), ergonomic aspects of workstation and environmental design were evaluated, and the VDT operators were interviewed to identify specific health complaints. The findings indicated that 76% of the VDT operators reported some type of visual complaint, with 47% reporting effects that persisted after work, reinforcing the findings of Hultgren and Knave (1973). As in the earlier study, environmental factors were identified as potential sources of workers' complaints. In addition, workstation ergonomics was implicated as a significant issue, evidenced by the fact that over 65% of the VDT operators reported some form of muscular discomfort.

In other parts of Europe, interest in VDTs was rapidly growing. Trade union concerns about VDT operators' visual complaints brought about research by Haider's group (1975) at the Institute of Environmental Hygiene at the University of Vienna in Austria. This study included a laboratory simulation of VDT activities where 14 subjects worked for 4 continuous hours on one day, and for two 1-hour periods separated by 15 minutes of rest on a second day. This work included the first ophthalmological evaluation of VDT operators under controlled conditions. A majority of the study's participants experienced slight shifts in visual acuity (1/8 to 1/4 diopter) from the beginning to the end of work. The effect was more pronounced after the visually intensive 4-hour session than after the other session. These findings suggested changes in visual functioning when using VDTs and also demonstrated the usefulness of laboratory simulation studies to evaluate VDT health issues.

In Germany, a monumental effort was undertaken by the Technical University of Berlin to examine a wide range of issues (workplace design, workstation ergonomics, job structure) that could influence VDT operators' health. This research culminated in the Armbruster Report (Cakir et al., 1978), which served as the basis of the popular VDT Manual (Cakir, Hart, and Stewart, 1979). This effort differed from earlier ones in Sweden and Austria because it included a wide range of issues and a control group of non-VDT operators. This study, which will be discussed in more detail in the following section, bears special mention here as a significant impetus to research on VDT operators' health around the world.

In the United States, NIOSH pioneered in evaluating the radiation emissions from VDTs in actual field settings (Moss et al., 1978). Specialized instrumentation was used for these studies to characterize VDT emissions accurately. Since 1975, over 500 VDTs have been examined. VDTs have never been found to emit ionizing or nonionizing radiation above the present occupational radiation standards (Moss et al., 1978; Murray et al., 1981).

Comparative Studies

The previous studies identified problems that VDT operators were experiencing, but they did not determine the seriousness of these problems or explain why they were occurring. However, the studies did provide some insight into the nature and extent of the problems. When 50% to 75% of employees in one type of job complain about visual problems, there is cause for concern. These early studies helped to identify what issues should be addressed in subsequent research.

Based on these early efforts, other research into VDT health concerns proliferated in Sweden, Germany, Austria, Switzerland, France, Italy, New Zealand, and the United States. The Technical University of Berlin study (Cakir et al., 1978) was really a series of mini-studies. Each examined a specific VDT issue, such as worker preference to glare controls, VDT workers' health complaints at various job activities, and job design features particularly problematic to various VDT jobs. For some aspects of this work, over 1,000 VDT operators were given opinion surveys on their perception of VDT work. For other aspects, as few as 50 VDT operators were examined. Unfortunately, the reports (Cakir et al., 1978; Cakir, Hart, and Stewart, 1979) describing this work do not provide all of the technical methodology; i.e., how opinions were solicited, response rates, how certain physical measures were taken (glare levels, measures of workstation dimensions). They rely heavily on the authors' opinions, conjecture, and extrapolated findings. While this is not necessarily bad (since that is what we ask experts to do), it is difficult to reconcile their findings and opinions with divergent findings from other research. However, this criticism can be applied to much of the European VDT research, particularly those studies dependent upon the solicitation of worker opinions and health complaints.

Essentially, the Cakir et al. reports (1978, 1979) indicated that complaints of a visual, muscular, and job-design nature varied with the type of VDT task. For instance, copy typists had more neckaches (70%) than other clerical VDT operators (45%), information typists (40%), editors (39%), or programmers (22%). Copy typists also had more headaches (45%, 30%, 23%, 8%, and 6%, respectively). In terms of job design issues, VDT clerical operators paid on a piece-work basis reported feeling more controlled by the computer than programmers or other hourly paid clerical staff. They also reported more mental effort and greater fatigue than the other job categories. However, they reported less monotony than other clerical staff for whom becoming VDT operators represented a downgrading in their jobs.

This research also indicated that different environmental features produced different levels of complaints. For instance, matte keys produced less complaints of glare and eye problems than more reflective surfaces. This research showed that varying working conditions (whether they be workplace design, workstation design or job design) can influence the level of VDT operators' health complaints. Although issue can always be taken with specific findings, such as the most appropriate level of illumination, this research demonstrates that job-specific considerations are important in defining problems and providing appropriate alternatives for VDT operations.

Work in Switzerland, by Grandjean and his associates, also showed that VDT operators' health complaints varied with task factors and workstation design (Grandjean, 1979; Hunting, Laubli, and Grandjean, 1980; Laubli, Hunting, and Grandjean, 1980; Grandjean, 1982; Brauninger, Grandjean, and Fellmann, 1982). Hunting et al. (1980) found that 60% of data-entry operators suffered from sore shoulders in comparison to 30% of conversational terminal operators, 25% of non-VDT typists, or 10% of traditional office workers. This group also found that data-entry operators alone had more problems with the right shoulder than the left shoulder. Laubli (1980) found that the conversational VDT operators (72%) had more visual complaints, followed by data entry operators (65%), non-VDT typists (55%), and traditional office workers (50%). These results demonstrate the strong ties between task requirements and the physical demands which influence health complaints. The data-entry job, with greater keying demands, created more muscular problems; the conversational job, with more visual demands, created more visual problems.

Additional work by Grandjean (1982) has shown a relationship between the severity of VDT operators' visual complaints and the quality of characters and screen characteristics of two different makes of VDTs. Seven percent of operators reported constant eye pains using the VDT with better characteristics, as opposed to 19% using the VDT with poorer characteristics; 4% of the operators reported blurred vision with the good VDT and 15% with the poor VDT. While these percentages are not high, they do demonstrate that specific VDT characteristics can influence visual complaints.

In the United States, NIOSH has taken a leading role in examining VDT health issues. As stated earlier, initial work was concerned with potential radiation health hazards, which were shown to be negligible (Moss et al., 1978; Murray et al., 1981). Later work addressed ergonomic job demand issues that could produce job stress (Dainoff, 1979, 1980; Smith et al., 1980, 1981a; Stammerjohn et al., 1981; Sauter et al., 1981, 1982; Smith et al., 1982). The primary approach to the first NIOSH study of ergonomic job demand factors was to identify high-risk VDT work sites in order to determine the greatest potential hazards for VDT operators. The San Francisco study (Smith et al., 1980, 1981a; Stammerjohn, Smith, and Cohen, 1981) examined VDT operators and control workers, at the request of their unions, who felt that their members were being exposed to undue health hazards. The findings from this study must be tempered since the response rate to the health and job demands questionnaire was quite low (50% for VDT operators and 38% for control subjects). Thus, the response may not be representative of the employees at the companies investigated. In all, 125 professionals using VDTs, 129 clerical VDT operators (data entry, interactive), and 157 nonoperator clerical workers participated in the study.

The results from the questionnaire survey indicated that the clerical VDT operators reported a higher frequency of visual complaints (80% burning eyes, 91% eye strain) than professional VDT operators (60% and 78%, respectively), who had a higher frequency of complaints than the clerical control subjects (44% and 60%, respectively). The clerical VDT operators reported a higher frequency for 14 muscular complaints than both professional VDT operators and clerical controls. The latter two groups differed on only one muscular complaint, with the control group reporting a higher frequency. These findings agree with those from Europe, demonstrating job-specific differences in the levels of health complaints and differences between VDT operators and control subjects.

Of more interest, however, are the findings regarding job demands perceived as stressful by VDT operators and control subjects. A trend similar to that found for the health complaints was observed. The clerical VDT operators considered their jobs more stressful in a number of dimensions than the control subjects and the professional VDT operators. These dimensions included heavy workloads, boring tasks, lack of job control, close monitoring of performance, and fear of job loss. For some dimensions, the clerical controls reported more stress than the professional VDT operators. These included low job autonomy and greater boredom. Such findings may indicate that the job requirements are more stressful than the use of a VDT. However, VDTs often impose new methods for performing tasks, and thus may produce direct effects.

In other NIOSH research, Dainoff (1980) interviewed 113 VDT operators, using an open-ended, nonleading format, to establish those aspects of their jobs that were most liked and most disliked. In addition, a subsample of 13 operators was given an optometric evaluation as well as a mood state questionnaire before and after work each day for five days. Complaints of visual fatigue were made by 45% of all the subjects. In the subsample of 13 VDT operators intensively evaluated, the reported incidence of eyestrain increased from 30% to 62%. However, there were no shifts in visual acuity within a work day, or over the five work days, using objective Orthorater measures. Dainoff also found that VDT operators' comments about their work were most frequently positive, praising the efficiency of the computer system and stating that they enjoyed their job. This demonstrates that many VDT operators perceive good as well as bad features in their jobs and the use of VDTs.

In a controlled study examining 250 clerical VDT operators and 84 matched clerical control nonoperators in state agencies in Wisconsin, Sauter et al. (1981, 1982) evaluated job stress and ergonomic factors that could predict VDT operators' health complaints. While analyses have not been completed on the questionnaire survey's data, preliminary analysis indicates that job-specific factors are extremely important in predicting health complaints. When all VDT operators were compared to the clerical controls, there were very few significant differences in health complaints. However, when only the VDT operators in the most regimented and physically demanding tasks (data entry, word processing, file maintenance) were compared to the controls, differences were observed for neck and shoulder pains (80% vs. 45%), backache (83% vs. 54%), burning eyes (75% vs. 49%), eyestrain (76% vs. 51%), and headache (82% vs. 47%).

Of special interest in this investigation is the finding that regression analyses predict that VDT work does not contribute to physical health complaints, psychological distress, or job dissatisfaction to a greater extent than non-VDT clerical work. This finding differs from other NIOSH studies and European studies, indicating further research into job task effects is necessary. However, two cautions must be put forth. First, these data analyses are preliminary. Further regression analyses may modify or refine the results. Secondly, these analyses were made grouping all VDT operators together. As demonstrated by the health complaints analyses reported earlier, such grouping may "washout" significant effects for specific groups or classes of VDT operators.

In the most recent NIOSH study (Smith et al., 1982), comprehensive ophthalmological examinations and a questionnaire survey were conducted on approximately 280 VDT operators at a newspaper. The questionnaire examined VDT usage, environmental features, ergonomic design issues, job attitude, and job stress. The results indicated that the workstation, environmental problems, and the bothersome visual aspects of the VDT were the best predictors of visual complaints as perceived by the VDT operators. Preliminary analysis of the ophthalmological examination data indicated no relationship between the adequacy of refraction and visual, muscular, or job stress problems. Additionally, there was no relationship between the hours of VDT use per day or years of tenure as a VDT operator and the prevalence of eye abnormalities.

In more current European VDT research, Ghiringhelli (1980) in Italy and Elias et al. (1980) in France, have examined job characteristics that influence VDT operators' physical and mental health. Ghiringhelli (1980) interviewed 62 VDT operators, who reported a high incidence of visual complaints (76%) and mental complaints (anxiety, 43%; depression, 40%; and nausea, 15%). However, muscular complaints for both neck (7%) and back pain (10%) were quite low. The VDT operators identified the main sources of these problems as poorly working equipment (63%), screen reflections (44%), screen luminance (44), screen color (31%), and working postures (18%). Relatively low levels of stress related to job demands were reported: monotony, 7%; machine control, 7%; heavy concentration, 5%; overwork, 5%; isolation, 1%.

Elias et al. (1980) studied 89 offline data acquisition operators and 81 dialogue operators using a questionnaire and eye movement evaluations. They found significant differences between these two types of VDT work. The offline operators reported more visual complaints and psychological distress: anxiety, 67% vs. 38%; depression, 53% vs. 22%; irritability, 68% vs. 42%; chest pains, 37% vs. 20%; palpitations, 43% vs. 23%. The offline VDT operators also reported a greater level of job dissatisfaction: 70% vs. 28%. Evaluation of eye movements for 5 subjects in each job indicated that the offline VDT operators had much shorter uninterrupted looks at the screen (a few seconds versus many seconds), but a greater frequency of sweeping looks at the screen.

The last study to be discussed in this section was conducted by Coe et al. (1980) in New Zealand. This was a field study of 257 VDT operators and 124 control subjects from 19 different companies. The VDT operators carried out four basic types of work: (1) data entry (input), (2) creative, (3) editing and (4) interactive (question and answer). Each participant in the study completed a health questionnaire and was given a visual examination. In addition, environmental evaluations were made of work areas. The findings indicated that visual fatigue complaints, seating discomfort, and muscular discomfort of the arms, shoulders, and neck were greater for VDT operators than for control subjects. Coe's group concluded that the symptoms were related to the visual, environmental, anthropometric, task, and psychosocial aspects of VDT use. As in previous studies, the levels of visual and muscular complaints varied with the type of work. However, few differences were reported between VDT operators (when grouped together) and control subjects concerning job satisfaction and job demands.

SUMMARY OF RESEARCH FINDINGS
REGARDING HEALTH EFFECTS

Visual health concerns dominated the studies examined, and have been the primary concern of the workers using VDTs. The evidence from these studies indicates that VDT operators, as a group, suffer from a high incidence of visual disturbances, including visual fatigue, visual irritation, and headache. In addition, it is clear that the type of VDT work (i.e., data entry versus word processing, and the specific visual demands imposed by that activity) influences the incidence of visual complaints. VDT workers at visually demanding jobs have a much higher rate of visual complaints. Finally, most types of VDT work produce higher levels of visual complaints than traditional office work that is also visually demanding.

Some studies have shown that the acute visual disturbances fail to dissipate within a period of time after leaving work and may, in fact, still be present at the start of the next work day. In particular, soreness and tiredness seem to carry over, while those symptoms that relate to visual performance, such as blurred vision, seem to recover after a short period of time (15 to 30 minutes). In essence, the eyes are able to perform properly but asthenopic symptoms persist.

There is some evidence that the processes of visual accommodation and convergence are influenced by VDT work. Haider et al. (1975, 1980) found slight shifts in acuity (1/8 to 1/4 diopter) after working at a VDT in a visually demanding task for 4 hours. Gunnarsson and Ostberg (1977) and Gunnarsson and Soderberg (1980) have demonstrated a recession in the near point (both accommodative and covergence shifts) during the course of a work day for young VDT workers, but not for older VDT workers. Ostberg, Powell, and Blomkvist (1980) observed shifts in dark focus between air traffic control radar operators and clerical workers. However, based on these studies and the results of other research indicating no such changes (Dainoff, 1980; Kintz and Bowker, 1980), the evidence for functional changes in vision is not convincing.

There is also some evidence concerning the relationship between VDT work and the use of corrective eye wear. Ostberg (1976) indicated that bifocal wearers should have more problems than other VDT workers. Cakir et al. (1978) and Smith et al. (1982) found that this was not true for the VDT operators in their studies. However, VDT operators who wore reading glasses did report more visual health complaints. Sauter et al. (1982) confirm that VDT operators who wear glasses have a greater frequency of visual complaints. Thus, it seems that wearing glasses may have a relationship to the frequency of visual health complaints.

A second major health concern shown by the results of the various VDT studies is a high incidence of musculo-skeletal health complaints in VDT operators. As with the visual complaints, musculo-skeletal complaints vary with the type of VDT work. Most types of VDT work generally produce more muscular complaints than other types of traditional office work, including working on a typewriter. The increased muscular complaints of VDT typists, as opposed to traditional typists, is probably due to the increased postural demands imposed by the viewing requirements of the VDT. The musculoskeletal complaints are of a diverse nature, affecting the neck, shoulders, back, arms, hands, and fingers, possibly demonstrating a systemic influence.

The third area of health complaints reported by VDT operators concerns emotional disturbances. These fall into two categories: (1) those that reflect mood states, and (2) those that reflect psychosomatic symptoms. Only a few studies of VDT operators have evaluated emotional factors. Smith et al. (1980) and Elias (1980) indicated that both mood disturbances and psychosomatic symptoms demonstrate the same pattern as the visual and muscular complaints. That is, they vary with the type of VDT work, and VDT operators as a group report more such health complaints than other office workers.

The mood disturbances observed are typical of neurotic behavior demonstrating anger, frustration, irritability, anxiety, and depression. The psychosomatic disorders reflect a typical distress syndrome, with gastrointestinal disturbances, muscle and psychic tension, heart palpitations and frequent sweating.

The fourth major complaint of VDT operators that has a health implication relates to psychosocial disturbances. In particular, VDT operators in many of the studies complained about specific job demands, such as workload, work pace, and supervision, which can produce health complaints, physical and mental disorders, general job dissatisfaction, and reduced efficiency and performance (Smith et al., 1980; Smith et al., 1982). As with the other types of health complaints, the psychosocial problems also varied with the type of job.

WHAT ARE THE POTENTIAL HEALTH RISKS?

The varieties of acute health complaints of VDT operators, ranging from visual and muscular problems to emotional and psychosomatic problems, have been presented in the previous section. The causes of these acute responses seem to lie in inadequate environmental, workstation, job, and organizational design. However, the seeming lack of seriousness of the reported health complaints might suggest that elaborate control measures are not needed.

This is not the case. While there is no evidence for chronic visual disease in VDT operators, it cannot be concluded that VDT viewing will not cause long-term chronic visual dysfunction. This is because there have been no studies addressing the issue of chronic visual disturbances related to VDT work. Such studies would have to look, retrospectively, at available visual pathology in large populations of VDT users and nonusers with varying jobs and VDT exposures. Likewise, prospective studies could be set up to monitor groups of VDT operators and control groups for a period of years to observe the development of visual pathology. Although NIOSH is currently conducting a limited prospective study, limitations in the sample size (150 VDT users) and the length of time necessary to observe chronic visual changes (5–10 years) suggests that a retrospective study is needed now.

The lack of studies of chronic effects indicates that the potential chronic effects may have to be postulated until this research is completed. There are no statistics on how often VDT operators need to change refractive prescriptions, so we do not know if operators' vision deteriorates faster than that of workers in other jobs. There is also a lack of information on the incidence of cataracts or glaucoma in VDT operators. Therefore, it is not possible to determine if this work is related to such problems. However, the complaints made by a very great number of workers about tired, sore, and irritated eyes must be taken seriously. Due to the current lack of research on chronic visual effects of VDT work, it will be at least five years before we know what the chronic impacts are.

Studies on how basic physiological aspects of vision are affected by VDT work are currently underway at IBM, NIOSH, the University of California at Berkeley, and New York University. However, such studies are not evaluating chronic visual deterioration. At a recent National Academy of Sciences meeting on the visual impact of VDT work, it was suggested that the VDT screen introduces characteristics into the work activity that make it more visually demanding than other types of similar work. It was further suggested that eye movement patterns, accommodative processes, and the pupillary response mechanism were being put under strain by VDT use. Anecdotal evidence from the U.S. military academies and Young's work on monkeys (Young, 1977a, 1977b, 1978) suggests that chronic eyestrain may produce significant changes in acuity (up to 9 diopters in monkeys), reflecting unnatural shifts in the accommodative process (myopia rather than presbyopia with increasing age). While evidence for chronic visual deterioration with prolonged VDT viewing is not currently available, there is some reason to suspect that such effects could occur, especially under the most visually taxing of work tasks, in poorly designed work environments, and with poorly designed VDTs. This should be an impetus for further research into the chronic visual influences of VDT viewing.

In terms of musculo-skeletal issues, the same pattern occurs as for visual complaints. High numbers of VDT operators report a variety of postural and manipulative muscular complaints. No research evidence of chronic disease has been shown for VDT operators, but, again, no such studies have been undertaken. However, unlike the vision problems, which lack a strong theoretical base and data that can identify potential chronic problems, there are good models for the estimation of what VDT operators' chronic musculo-skeletal problems could be. Repeated trauma, produced by keying-in data, have been linked to a very high incidence of carpal tunnel syndrome and disabling wrist disorders (Arndt, 1981). The frequency and type of VDT operators' wrist and finger complaints are highly predictive of this syndrome.

Low back injury occurs more frequently and is responsible for more lost time than any other form of occupational injury. The etiologies of the group of disorders involved in low back injury are not completely understood. However, repeated loads on the neck, shoulders, and back are related to this trauma. Of particular significance to VDT work is the static loading of the major postural muscles in fixed positions for extended periods of time. This type of loading can produce musculo-skeletal complaints indicative of a low back pain syndrome.

Emotional disturbances of an acute, neurotic nature (distress syndrome) are at epidemic proportions in the U.S. according to the latest statistics from the National Institute of Mental Health. These disorders are characterized by mood disturbances and psychosomatic symptoms, such as those exhibited by some classes of VDT operators. Such disorders accounted for more than 15% of the total workers' compensation costs in California in 1980 and have steadily grown each year. Today 19 states recognize such emotional disorders as being potentially work related and award compensation.

However, the greatest concern is with the high levels of job stress shown in some VDT users, which reflect high job dissatisfaction, feelings of work pressure, and fear of job loss. Such job stress factors have been linked to serious chronic disease, such as coronary heart disease, coronary artery disease, stomach and intestinal disorders, emotional distress, and endocrine imbalances as well as a reduced resistance to disease (Smith, 1981b). This is the most serious concern regarding VDT operators. However, it is not likely that the VDT is at fault in producing job stress. More likely, the organizational and job design changes related to computer automation are at fault—just as they were at fault with the automation of many blue collar jobs during the 1950s.

FACTORS CONTRIBUTING TO OBSERVED HEALTH COMPLAINTS

Since VDT operators have a high incidence of some types of health complaints, what factors have been identified in studies as contributors to these problems?

Environmental Design

Three of the most often cited causes of vision problems are improper illumination, glare on the VDT screen, and improper contrasts in luminance. Figures F–4 and F–5 illustrate glare and contrast problems associated with VDT use. These environmental problems usually occur together, although any one could conceivably produce visual disturbances. Hultgren and Knave (1973) found lighting levels at 76% of the workstations examined exceeded 700 lux (30% over 1,000 lux), while at 53% of the workstations VDT operators reported disturbing reflections on the screen, and 59% of the VDT operators reported trouble reading images on their VDT screen. Generally, the luminance ratios between the screen background and characters exceeded 3:1, thereby provid-

Figure F–4.   Glare on VDT screen from overhead lights.

ing the minimum necessary contrast for character recognition. However, there were large contrasts between the screen and surrounding room surfaces at some workstations exceeding 1 to 500, and thereby potentially taxing pupillary response and, hence, visual accommodative processes.

Findings similar to these have been shown by Cakir et al. (1978) and Laubli, Hunting, and Grandjean (1980). However, variations have been observed in some studies. For instance, Gunnarsson and Ostberg (1977) found illumination levels varied between 150–500 lux. In the NIOSH San Francisco study (Stammerjohn, Smith, and Cohen, 1981) over 85% of the workstations examined had illumination levels between 300–700 lux (which are considered to be appropriate illumination, depending on the VDT task). As with the other studies, glare was observed on a high percentage of VDT screens (87%). When asked about aspects of their workstation that they found bothersome, 85% of the VDT operators cited screen glare, 70% character brightness, 69% readability of screen, 68% screen flicker, and 62% screen brightness. Coe et al. (1980) also found that 90% of the workstations examined had lower illumination levels than those observed in European studies (500 lux or lower). In fact, it was observed that there were more visual complaints when the lighting level

Figure F–5.   Glare on VDT screen that diminishes contrast.

was below 500 lux, than when it was above 500 lux. However, again, glare was a significant problem (42% of the VDTs). It seems that VDT operators still complain about visual problems when illumination levels are below 500 lux and above 200 lux. Thus, it would appear that glare and/or contrast problems are more critical elements in VDT operator visual complaints than illumination level.

Even with reasonable illumination levels, vision complaints occur if glare and contrast problems are not controlled. Laubli, Hunting, and Grandjean (1980) found a correlation between the measured intensity of glare reflections and reported annoyance by the VDT operators but no relationship between the luminance of the reflections and reported visual impairment. On the other hand, Stammerjohn, Smith, and Cohen (1981) found a clear relationship between glare and visual health complaints.

Temperature and humidity are two areas that commonly evoke complaints from office workers. Cakir, Hart, and Stewart (1979) found that about 50% of the VDT operators complained of the heat in nonair-conditioned offices. In air-conditioned offices, 30% complained of the heat. In addition, almost two thirds of the VDT operators complained that the air was too dry, even though the relative humidity in their workplaces was between 30 and 40%. In the NIOSH San Francisco study (Stammerjohn, Smith, and Cohen, 1981), 63% of all employees rated summer temperatures as too high, while 41% rated winter temperatures as too low, even though measurements of the temperatures and relative humidities at the work sites were within established limits for comfort (between 21–25° C and 35–80% respectively). Coe et al. (1980) found that 80% of the VDT operators and 75% of the controls reported that the temperature of their work areas was uncomfortable.

Workstation Design

Many aspects of the VDT, the desk, and the chair have been examined to determine relationships to health complaints. In terms of the screen, the issue of adequate contrast between the characters and screen background has already been discussed. In many of the field studies these contrast ratios were much less than optimal (7:1 to 10:1), and in some cases were less than adequate (3:1) (Stammerjohn, Smith, and Cohen, 1981). Grandjean (1982) has demonstrated that the quality of the screen characters can influence the level of health complaints. Although most field studies have found that the large majority of VDTs examined have the capabilities to meet minimum requirements for contrast ratios and character size, many do not achieve these minimum requirements in the field due to screen glare. There has been some laboratory research to indicate that a negative contrast screen (dark characters on a light background) produces better performance and more visual comfort (Radl, 1980; Bauer and Cavonius, 1980). However, these studies were conducted under very constrained conditions and the implications for health complaints are limited. These studies and Grandjean's (1982) suggest that the characteristics and quality of the screen characters could have an impact on operators' visual complaints.

A number of studies have identified the workstation as contributing to both visual and musculo-skeletal health complaints. In particular, the height of the working surface has an impact on the height of the arms, wrists, and hands, as well as wrist and neck angles (Sauter et al., 1981). Figure F–6 illustrates a workstation where the keyboard is too high for the operator, thus imposing undue biomechanical loads. In addition, the height of the chair and the amount of support that it provides for the lumbar region of the back have been postulated as factors contributing to workers' musculo-skeletal complaints.

Chairs may fail to provide adequate back support, thus affecting worker posture and biomechanical load on the back. Studies by Stammerjohn, Smith, and Cohen (1981); Cakir, Hart, and Stewart (1978), Coe et al. (1980); and Sauter et al. (1982) all demonstrate that a majority of VDT operators are

Figure F–6. Inadequate workstation due to excessive keyboard
   height.

exposed to undue muscular loads (postural and manipulative) because of
poorly designed, or improperly used, workstation furniture.

Job Design

If all ergonomic design aspects of the environment and workstation were maxi-
mized, would VDT operators still have visual and musculo-skeletal complaints?
The answer is yes. It's quite clear that job demands, both physical and
psychological, influence the type, severity, and frequency of VDT operators'
health complaints. It's also logical to assume that the psychological demands
can produce physical as well as emotional complaints. Some support for this
view is suggested by the fact that, in three major studies (Gunnarsson and
Ostberg, 1977; Smith et al., 1981a; and Sauter, Gottlieb, and Jones, 1982), the
amount of time working at the VDT was not very predictive of the frequency
of visual or musculo-skeletal health complaints, while the type of VDT work
activity was, with the more mundane, repetitive VDT jobs showing higher
levels of both visual and muscular problems.

The evidence as to whether VDT operators have greater job demands than other occupations is mixed. In most cases, the evidence is confounded by other ergonomic factors, as well as the lack of adequate study designs. Gunnarsson and Ostberg (1977) found that when VDT operators had little control over job tasks, 72% complained of monotony; while in another group that had greater control, only 10% complained of monotony. Cakir et al. (1978) used a standardized test battery to evaluate VDT operators' psychomotor and psychosocial responses and found that their stress levels were not higher than other occupations. However, they were cautious about interpreting these data. Comparisons between different studies are often confounded when evaluating the results of studies with varying methodologies. In a second study, Cakir, Hart, and Stewart (1979) found that piece-rate paid VDT operators reported less sociability, poorer frame of mind, greater stress, fatigue, and less inner security than hourly paid VDT operators. NIOSH (Smith et al., 1981a) evaluations indicated that clerical VDT operators reported less job involvement, job autonomy, self-esteem, staff support, and peer cohesion, but more work pressure, workload, workload dissatisfaction, supervisory control, role ambiguity, and job future ambiguity than professional VDT operators. For all these dimensions except staff support, job involvement, and role ambiguity, the clerical VDT operators also indicated more stressful responses than clerical control subjects. Coe et al. (1980) found differences in the level of work pressure between VDT operator groups. Editors showed the most work pressure, and interactive operators showed the least. However, control subjects showed greater work pressure than all VDT operators, except the editors. For bordeom and frustration, there were no differences between the groups.

Sauter, Gottlieb, and Jones (1982) found that a heterogeneous group of VDT operators did not differ greatly from clerical controls on similar dimension of stress as those reported by NIOSH (Smith et al., 1981a). However, the job stress factors were highly predictive of health complaints, job satisfaction, and emotional status for both VDT operators and clerical controls. Sauter states, "This means that the conditions denoted in this model affect VDT users and nonusers in the same way. This does not mean that VDT use is not a stressor; rather that where VDT use is associated with degraded working conditions, the effect on job satisfaction would be the same for nonusers working under similarly degraded conditions." There were differences between VDT operators with regard to control, future certainty, and environmental problems.

Finally, Johansson and Aronsson (1980) found that there were slightly higher levels of adrenaline excretion in a group of VDT operators than in a clerical control group. In addition, the pattern of adrenaline excretion during the course of the work day varied between the groups, with VDT operators starting high and dropping to a middle level during the course of the day, while the clerical controls started at a high level, dropped to a low level at mid-day, then rose to starting levels at the end of the day. However, the VDT operators' middle levels of adrenaline excretion persisted at home after work, while the clerical workers' adrenaline dropped substantially to a low level after work.

It appears that job design factors, primarily highly paced work, lack of control, and pressures such as deadlines, are more prevalent in some types of VDT work than in others. These factors are related to many of the health complaints reported by VDT operators and could be linked to serious health disorders.

Organizational Design

The organizational factors that have been associated with VDT work as sources of distress are: (1) lack of worker participation in VDT implementation, (2) inadequate employee training, (3) job security issues (such as downgrading, advancement, and job loss), (4) the monitoring of employee performance, (5) the influence of close employee monitoring on supervisory style, and (6) incentive pay schemes. These have been identified in studies by Cakir et al. (1978), Smith et al. (1981a); Johansson and Aronsson (1980); and Sauter, Gottlieb, and Jones (1982).

SOME SOLUTIONS

Environmental Design

There are significant variations in what experts feel are appropriate lighting levels for VDT work (Ostberg, 1974; Cakir et al., 1978; Cakir, Hart, and Stewart, 1979; Coe et al., 1980; NIOSH, 1981). This may be because the studies researched different work activities and thus perceived divergent lighting needs. This may also be due to different philosophies on lighting. It is quite clear that different VDT tasks require different lighting characteristics. For instance, work that requires the operator to look only at the screen and not at any hard copy calls for less illumination than work that requires the operator to read hard copy. Some experts feel that general illumination levels should be kept low, and if additional illumination is necessary for a particular work activity, then task lighting (illuminating just the material to be read at a higher level) should be installed and used. As a general rule, work activities that require the operator to look only at the screen (no hard copy reading) require about 300 lux for general room illumination. When the requirement of reading hard copy is included in the work activity, then the general room illumination level should be increased to between 500 and 700 lux, depending on the quality of the hard copy. Quality should be rated by the amount of contrast between the characters and background (e.g., carbon copies of credit card receipts many times have poor contrast) and the legibility of the characters (e.g., poor handwriting).

In some operations, VDT operators perform different jobs; some are screen intensive, while others are hard copy intensive. In such cases, it is preferable to have a lower level of general room illumination (300–500 lux) to accommodate the needs of the screen-intensive workers. Then, task lighting can be used for those tasks requiring more illumination.

Glare is the single most detrimental environmental factor for VDT operators because it reduces contrast and increases the amount of visual effort. Glare is best controlled by eliminating its sources, or modifying the source. Glare sources include luminaries, windows, and reflective surfaces in the environment. Placing the video display screen to eliminate reflections from glare sources is the most effective means of glare control. Therefore, positioning VDT screens parallel to windows, as well as parallel and between luminaries, will eliminate or reduce the amount of screen glare considerably.

When positioning is not feasible, then modifications must be made to the glare source. In the case of windows, curtains, blinds, or shades can be installed and drawn to block out the incoming light. However, use of very dark curtains or shades and the complete elimination of all window light or view of the outdoors can have an adverse psychological impact on employees, which may override any positive effects from the glare reduction. The purpose of shades is not to make the work area into a dungeon but to reduce a major light source sufficiently to control glare.

For luminaries, it is possible to install fixtures that focus the light downward, such as parabolic wedge reflectors. These act to reduce the amount of light dispersion and hence the amount of reflected glare.

If glare persists, some modification must be made to the VDT. The most effective method is to use a filter over the screen, which absorbs incoming light rays and reduces the amount of reflections from the screen surface. Such filters can be put on the screen during the original manufacturing process, or they can be added at a later date. It should be pointed out that some filters reduce contrast, degrading the character images on the screen. Most filters also cut down luminance of the characters on the screen, requiring the operator to increase the brightness level.

Another method of glare control is to install a hood over the screen to block the screen from all angular reflections. Thus, all glare sources except those directly behind the screen are no longer accessible to the screen. Problems with such hoods include a difficulty looking between the screen and source documents due to a tunnel vision effect, and problems of excessive contrast variations. Because the operator is forced to focus solely on the screen, when the operator looks away from the screen, the difference in contrast between the screen and the lighter room surfaces is accentuated.

With regard to contrast problems, most VDTs provide sufficient contrast between the characters and background (3:1 minimum) for adequate character recognition. As VDTs age, however, the ability to maintain adequate contrast is reduced. This could pose some problems. For this reason, it is recommended that VDTs be serviced on a routine basis to ensure proper working order. When operators observe that a VDT is losing some contrast capability, repairs should be made so that it always meets the minimum contrast requirements.

Other contrast problems relate to environmental sources of reflected glare or luminance, which are much higher than the VDT screen. Most experts feel that these contrasts should not exceed 10:1 (ANSI, 1973). As a working approach, any environmental glare source or luminance source that is bright enough to be uncomfortable to view is probably too bright and should be controlled. This can be done by covering the source or redirecting the luminance.

Temperature and humidity should be kept within the normal comfort zone. Temperatures should be between 20–30° Centigrade; but can vary from 18–27° Centigrade, if operators are allowed to dress appropriately to adapt to the temperature. It is easier to modify clothing for cooler temperatures than for warmer. Relative humidity should be between 40% to 50%. This humidity level will help control electrostatic shock and will also help keep operators' skin from drying out.

Workstation Design

The operator should be able to adjust the display terminal. Most importantly, the VDT must have a keyboard that can be detached from the screen so that each can be independently adjusted in height. In addition, the brightness and contrast should be easily controlled. Some experts feel that the VDT should tilt backward to reduce neck angle. However, tilting the VDT back exposes the screen to greater amounts of glare, thus helping the neck while hurting the eyes. If the screen is detached from the keyboard, it can be adjusted to the proper height so that the neck will be in the optimum position and tilting the screen will be unnecessary.

The characters on the VDT must be easily recognized. The spacing between characters should be sufficient to recognize words and the spacing between the lines sufficient to distinguish one from line another in a paragraph. All of this presupposes that we know the appropriate character size (height and width), font (type face), and spacing requirements. Unfortunately, too little is known about what is best so that minimum requirements only can be suggested. Gould (1968) has demonstrated that a 5×7 dot matrix is marginally acceptable for adequate performance. However, this holds true only for performance and may not be true for visual discomfort or fatigue. Grandjean (1982) has demonstrated that different character shapes and sizes, varying distances between characters and lines, and differing luminances produce different levels of eye complaints. However, this work is merely suggestive of the relationship between screen and character qualities and visual problems. It will be some time before we can determine what are the most appropriate character sizes, shapes, spread, etc. in terms of visual comfort.

The desk on which the VDT sits should provide for independent adjustment of the keyboard and the screen. The keyboard and the screen should be adjustable to accommodate the 5th and 95th percentile male and female. Currently, adjustable VDT workstations are available (for instance

IBM Synergetic furniture, Wrightline dual adjustable workstation, Facit adjustable workstation, NKR adjustable workstation) that provide for the independent adjustment of keyboard and screen. Figure F–7 illustrates an adjustable workstation with an adjustable chair. Some of this furniture is better than others, in terms of the range of adjustability, durability, accessibility of controls, and safety features (load capacities, rounded edges). The individual purchaser will have to determine which meets his needs for the particular VDT application or task being performed.

The VDT work desk should not only be adjustable, but should also have a sufficient work area for the VDT task to be carried out in a smooth manner, without excessive twisting, turning, or stretching of the trunk, shoulders, neck, or arms. Many of the ergonomic workstations listed above have accessory work areas that can be added to the basic work desk to provide extra space for papers, reference books, etc. Copy holders should also be provided for job tasks where hard copy is used. This reduces the number of head and neck movements and turns, thus reducing muscular strain to the neck, shoulders, and back. The copy holder should be adjustable in height and direction so that it can be repositioned when an operator shifts posture, or when a different operator works at the VDT.

All VDT workstations should be equipped with a wrist-rest. This will reduce the angle between the keyboard and the keying level of the wrist, thus lessening the pressure on the muscles, tendons, and nerves of the wrist, hand, and arm.

Finally, each workstation must have an adequate chair. Since a VDT produces unique postures, which have been shown to cause muscular complaints, it is essential that a chair be provided that allows for height adjustment, and gives support to the lumbar area of the back. It is preferable that all adjustments can be made while the VDT operator is seated in the chair, in a standard straightforward posture, without having to bend, stoop, or reach excessively. It is also preferable that the chair seat be moderately padded for comfort. For safety purposes, to prevent tipping accidents, a chair with five legs is recommended.

Job Design

It is clear from the literature that the greatest job design difficulties in VDT work occur in jobs that had little job content before automation, and even less after automation, such as clerical work. The work must have meaningful content for the individual to derive a sense of accomplishment and a positive feeling of self esteem. Many clerical VDT jobs are fragmented and simplified versions of traditional clerical activities. Computerization has diminished the little content that was in these clerical jobs to such an extent that very little meaning or satisfaction is left. Therefore, boredom and fatigue predominate. To enhance this type of activity, meaning has to be built into the job content. This can be accomplished by enlarging the use of workers' skills, as opposed to

Figure F–7.   Adjustable workstation with adjustable chair.

simplifying the work. Work should not be overly repetitive, to the extent that
the VDT operator uses only simple perceptual motor skills and no cognitive

skills. In addition, job tasks should be designed to utilize existing skills, as much as possible, to enhance worker confidence and performance.

Control of the work process is a significant factor in job stress. Lack of job control is one of the primary causes of psychological and physiological dysfunction (Smith, 1981b; Karasek, 1979; Cooper and Marshall, 1976) and looms as one of the major characteristics of computerized work processes. The introduction of computer automation often reduces the operator's control of the work process and increases stress. Increasing operators' decision making and permitting alternative work procedures reduces the stress imposed by computerized work processes. It also enhances the job's content, giving more individual meaning and satisfaction with individual accomplishments.

Workers may be concerned about their lack of control over performance feedback. If the worker considers the computer to be a "fink" that is reporting performance information to the supervisor, who then uses this information to intimidate the employee, the employee will perceive a lack of control over the work process. Rather than providing performance feedback to the supervisor, it may be better to give this information directly to each employee on his/her own VDT screen on a frequent basis (at least hourly). There is a large body of literature that indicates that such direct performance feedback to the employee has a positive influence on performance (Smith and Smith, 1966). On the other hand, having the supervisor provide the performance feedback may create tension and stress, and thus have a negative influence on performance.

Completeness, which also makes work meaningful, is often missing in computerized office work. As work is fragmented through simplification, the relationship of the task activity to the organization and the end product is diminished. Thus, workers fail to identify with the work process and the product. They fail to appreciate that a lack of quality in their small component of the product can have a major impact on the completed product and their fellow co-workers' performance. Fragmentation of work must be avoided so that employees can attain a personal identity with the organization, a product identity, and an organizational pride. If work tasks must be simplified and fragmented, then it is imperative that employees understand their contribution to the end product and the organization. They must feel that their contribution is significant and meaningful for a positive feeling of self esteem. Otherwise, health and productivity will suffer due to increased job stress. Obviously, the best approach is not to fragment the work tasks, as this will produce boredom and diminished job satisfaction. Rather, the operators' tasks should be broad enough to provide some closure, and, therefore, understanding of the significance of the work.

Computerized systems often isolate individual operators to a much greater extent than traditional nonautomated processes. This isolation at a fixed workstation greatly reduces social interaction, which has traditionally been one of the major benefits of clerical office work. It is well established that social support of co-workers is an important buffer in controlling the health consequences of job stress (LaRocco, House, and Frech, 1980). As this social support is removed by isolation, the positive benefits in stress control are eliminated. However, with the use of VDTs, it is often not possible to have social interaction while working. Therefore, social interaction during nontask periods must be enhanced and encouraged. This can be accomplished by providing special work break facilities in close proximity to the work areas, and by allowing groups of workers to go on break together.

An example of a job design application to a VDT work activity may provide a clearer understanding of the issues just presented. A company in the health insurance business has recently redesigned VDT jobs. Prior to redesign there were VDT operators who entered insurance claims as they came in, those who updated claims, claims examiners who called up the files for customer information, and claims examiners who determined payments and issued checks. In the redesigned VDT jobs, each operator was assigned a group of claims as they came in and handled the claim throughout the entire process. They entered the claim information, updated the files, answered customer queries, paid claims, and issued checks.

What did this redesign accomplish? It changed fragmented, simplified work tasks into more complex and meaningful work activities that involved greater use of skills and decision making. This also provided closure, by allowing the employee to deal with the entire product, thus enhancing the employee's knowledge of and identification with the product and the organization. Most certainly this not only reduces job stress, but also enhances customer relations and productivity.

The final job design issue deals with the determination of reasonable workload for VDT operations. The research literature has shown that workload for VDT operators is often set by the limits or capacity of the computer system rather than by the capacity of the operator. This occurs because computer operations are set-up by systems analysts and computer programmers, who have an understanding of the computer system capabilities, but no idea of what people are capable of doing. In addition, computer sales representatives market systems as able to produce tremendous gains in productivity. These claims are also made based on the capabilities of the computer and not the human operator. Sometimes the productivity claims are greatly exaggerated. Given that computer systems are an expensive investment for any company, it is understandable that production goals are often set based on the cost of the computer system, and the need to improve productivity. However understandable this action, it is not based on sound engineering or psychological principles for determining the proper workload and often produces excessive workloads. The end result is that one of the greatest complaints of VDT operators is their excessive workload.

To determine the appropriate workload, industrial psychologists and industrial engineers must be part of the team that designs the computer system. Workload for individual jobs has to be set taking into consideration human cognitive, physical, and perceptual motor capabilities, not just the capabilities of the machinery.

Organizational Design

There are many different organizational styles used to operate a company. The following methods for controlling VDT operator job stress and health concerns are designed to be used in a variety of organizations with differing methods of management.

A major factor, which produces worker resistance to automation, is that automation often appears at the workplace "out-of-the-blue" without worker knowledge of the impending change in the work process. It is very important for the successful implementation of computer automation, and subsequent enhancement of worker health and performance, that organizations have a transition policy that includes worker participation in all stages of the automation process. That is, workers should participate from the initial discussions about automation, through selection of equipment, to the daily operation of the computer system.

First, worker representatives should be involved in the planning phase of automation. This will aid in employee acceptance of the changes in work processes and ensure that employee concerns are aired. Secondly, the employee representatives should be involved in the design of the computer system to ensure that human concerns and capabilities are included, as well as the computer capabilities. Finally, employees who are affected by the automation should be involved in the implementation of the automation. This will provide them with a fuller understanding of the computer system, its capabilities, and their role in the work process.

Training of the operators in their new job requirements is one of the most neglected aspects of computer automation. Of course, all companies introduce the equipment to the operators and explain what the various features are. Additionally, the manufacturer typically provides a manual that explains how the system works and how specific functions can be carried out. Often, the extent of operator training is to be told to read the manual and to start working. In some cases, there may even be classes held for one whole day or part days, for one or two weeks, to go over the material in the manual and to practice with the equipment. However, this limited training is neither sufficient to develop skills nor to build operators' confidence in their ability to perform the job adequately.

Because VDT technology represents a completely new way of carrying-out the work activity, it increases the need to have comprehensive training procedures, which will develop skills and enhance worker confidence and self esteem. Training should start with an explanation of why the new technology is needed, and its benefits to the company and to the worker. The equipment and computer system should be thoroughly explained, indicating the strengths *and* weaknesses of the system. Then, there should be intensive training from the manual that explains how the system works and its specific functions. Each classroom teaching or individual reading session should be followed up by practice, with a skilled operator available to coach the trainees.

After the trainee has successfully passed the training course, he/she should not be required to work at full speed until becoming accustomed to the work situation. This could take from one day to a month, depending on the complexity of the work activities. In addition, all operators should have periodic retraining (at least every six months) to keep skills and confidence at peak levels. While this training regimen is more complex than usually undertaken, it will enhance operator skills and will reduce the psychological fears of obsolescence and job loss, since trained operators will perceive themselves as important investments.

As indicated in the discussion of psychosocial stress problems, fear for job security is one of the greatest concerns of VDT operators. This is natural, since it is commonly believed that automation displaces workers even though history has demonstrated that automation typically redistributes workers to other jobs. As indicated above, a company that invests time and energy in developing the skills of workers demonstrates a desire to keep a valuable resource, thus reducing workers' fears of job loss. However, there are other job security problems related to computerization. One is the possibility of being downgraded because the computer system takes over some of the worker's functions, making the job less complex. There is always a temptation to reduce labor costs by simplifying work. However, such efforts almost always are doomed to failure, as they produce extensive morale and motivation problems in workers, which directly influence productivity. The main purpose of computerization is to do work more efficiently and productively not just to simplify it. Thus, companies should establish a policy that workers not be downgraded when VDTs are installed, since the workers will be more productive than they were before computerization at their company took place.

In addition, companies must develop career paths for VDT operators so that advancement can be attained for those who are good performers. Being locked into a highly repetitive job, which has very little content or meaning, with no chance for advancement is a major source of job stress, and a demotivating force for many VDT operators. Companies will have to be innovative in advancing operators through a career path to enhance performance and reduce job stress.

It is quite clear from the research literature that monitoring employees by computers creates a dehumanizing work environment in which the worker feels controlled by the machine. When performance monitoring is used by supervisors to control performance, workers' perception of work pressure and workload is very high, thus producing stress responses. In many cases, keystroke-by-keystroke information is kept on operators, and then used by first-line supervisors to pressure employees into increasing their performance. This creates two problems. The first problem is improper use of performance feedback, which has already been discussed in the job design section. The second problem is that it creates an adversarial relationship between the supervisor and the employee. This is especially troublesome, since the supervisory/employee relationship may have been quite positive before the introduction of computerization and performance feedback.

To attain the most effective employee performance and to enhance stress reduction, supervisors should use positive motivational and employee support approaches. This suggests that first-line supervisors should not be involved directly in the performance feedback system. Secondly, supervisors should be skilled operators who can assist those operators having technical difficulties. Thirdly, supervisors should receive training in employee support approaches, thus helping to buffer the effects of other stressful job demands. It must be understood by companies that this approach changes the basic role of the first-line supervisor by removing production pressures from the supervisor and establishing this individual as a positive link between employees and other levels of management.

The last organizational interventions are of an administrative nature and are aimed at dealing with the direct physical effects of VDT use, as well as some of the psychosocial issues. The first area concerns the scheduling of work activities. To increase workers' control over the work process, it is best to allow for flexible working hours, i.e., schedules where an individual can start and end work when desired, as long as the required number of hours are worked (or the required amount of work), and they do not interfere with other operational requirements (e.g., the need to have telephones covered during certain working hours). This flexibility is not possible in many VDT operations, but there may be other forms of flexibility in daily task scheduling or in selection of coffee break time, etc. that can provide the employee some feeling of control.

It must be remembered that shift work (at night, or that rotates between night and other time periods), will exacerbate fatigue and stress problems. Thus, VDT operators working such schedules must be given even greater consideration in terms of administrative, organizational, job, workstation, and environmental design controls.

Work/rest breaks are one form of administrative control that can be used to deal with workers' physical and psychological fatigue. That VDT operators demonstrate visual, muscular, and psychological fatigue is well established. Since fatigue reduces workers' performance and could increase health problems, it is logical to provide minimum work/rest requirements to guard against excessive fatigue. It is quite clear from the work of Coe et al. (1980) that frequent, short, self-determined rest breaks are the most effective in dealing with VDT operator fatigue. These breaks occur when an operator feels the need to rest his/her eyes, muscles, or mind. However, many work activities are too rigid or complex to allow individual operators to determine when they are going to take a break; therefore, some minimum requirements need to be established.

For work activities requiring more than 60% viewing time or that require constant, rapid muscular action or fixed postures for extended periods of time, or that are highly repetitive and boring, it is advisable that a 15-minute rest break be taken after 60 minutes of work. For those VDT work activities with lesser requirements, a 15-minute rest break should be taken after 120 minutes of work.

The final administrative control deals with visual examinations for VDT operators. The following are current NIOSH recommendations taken from the publication *Potential Health Hazards of Video Display Terminals* (NIOSH, 1981): The American Optometric Association (AOA) (1980) has conducted a review of rules promulgated by the States regarding standards for minimum optometric testing. They indicate that the following procedures are among those usually mandated as minimum optometric testing:

1. Complete case history (ocular, physical, occupational, and other pertinent information).
2. Naked visual acuity/or visual acuity of each eye uncorrected and with best correction.
3. Detailed report of external findings (lids, cornea, sclera, etc.).
4. Ophthalmoscopic examination (media, fundus, blood vessels, disc).
5. Corneal curvature measurement (dioptric)/keratometer (ophthalmometer) readings.
6. Static retinoscopy/objective refraction of each eye.
7. Amplitude of convergence and accommodation.
8. Phoria and duction findings; horizontal and vertical, distance and near.
9. Subjective findings/subject refraction of each eye for distance and near vision with phoropter or adequate trail case and trail frame.
10. Fusion and stereopsis.
11. Color vision.
12. Visual fields and/or tonometry.

In terms of preplacement visual testing, Hirschfelder (1980) of the National Society for the Prevention of Blindness states:

> Although the majority of industrial jobs require more extensive test of eyesight, especially where machining, measuring, and assembling to very close tolerances are concerned, the following primary visual skills, at the very least, should be checked:
> Central visual acuity (sharpness of vision) at distance (ability to see test targets well at 20 feet).
> Central visual acuity (sharpness of vision) at near point (ability to see test targets well at 13 to 16 inches).
> Muscle balance and eye coordination (ability to keep eyes in balance, to prevent one eye from deviating vertically or horizontally; ability of eyes to relay images from various distances which the brain can fuse without difficulty).
> Employees or job candidates who wear corrective lenses, including those of the contact types, should be tested both with and without them.

Hirschfelder (1980) goes on to say, "In all cases, however, the key purpose of testing is to measure individual visual skills in relation to individual seeing demands of specific jobs."

Based on evidence of acute vision problems in VDT operators (Haider et al., 1975; Haider, Kundi, and Weissebock, 1980; Gunnarsson and Ostberg, 1977; Gunnarsson and Soderberg, 1980; Laubli, Hunting, and Grandjean, 1980; Dainoff, 1980; and Smith et al., 1980), we feel that there is a need for mandatory vision testing for VDT operators. In addition, the high visual demands of VDT work tasks define a requirement for properly corrected vision for adequate performance and reduced visual strain. The suggested vision testing programs of the National Society for the Prevention of Blindness (Hirschfelder, 1980) and those reviewed by the AOA are a logical basis for vision testing requirements for VDT operators. The proposed visual testing program is primarily for ensuring that operators have the appropriate corrected vision for performing their VDT work tasks. In some cases, the job tasks will require a different correction factor than is needed for daily living activities, such as reading the newspaper or driving a car. Determinations of the proper corrected vision have to be made with the viewing requirements of the job tasks in mind.

It is recommended, given the mounting anecdotal evidence of ophthalmologic complaints associated with VDT use and paucity of research pertaining to the incidence, etiology, or pathophysiology of these events, that at the very least VDT workers should have a comprehensive preplacement vision examination. Either the American Optometric Association or Hirschfelder's recommendations could serve as a basis for the exam. We also recommend that those individuals who become symptomatic, even after the initial exam, should receive appropriate medical care, and that a general exam should be repeated periodically. The periodicity of these repeat exams should depend on the natural history of VDT ophthalmic pathology (information that is not yet available). Current NIOSH and other investigative research should clarify this issue.

FURTHER RESEARCH NEEDS

It is quite clear from reviewing the studies on VDT health problems that the body of knowledge in this area is incomplete. This suggests that additional research is necessary to understand more fully the problems and to develop more complete solutions than those presented in this chapter.

Field Studies

A number of field investigations should be carried out. First, there is a need for a large scale epidemiological study to examine the *chronic* health effects of VDT work. To date, no such study has been conducted. This gap in

VDT research is the primary reason that only minimal efforts are being put forth to deal with VDT health issues. If chronic effects are not present, then employers do not want to invest a lot of money in environmental and workstation design. They need proof. Such studies should look at visual pathology, musculo-skeletal disease, stress-related concerns, and reproductive outcomes. With regard to reproductive problems, questions have been raised recently about possible linkages between VDT use and spontaneous abortions/birth defects. Reported cases of these occurrences need to be investigated from an epidemiological standpoint to disclose causal factors.

There is a need for further field evaluations of acute health and performance effects of VDT work. Current studies suffer from inadequate VDT operator samples, poor control groups, poor response rates, improper statistical analysis, and generally poor methodology. Highly controlled field studies of large VDT operator populations and controls using adequate methods and analytic approaches are needed. To conduct such studies requires the cooperation of industry, labor, educational institutions, and government.

There is a need for demonstration projects which will illustrate the effectiveness of currently known interventions for defineable health problems.

These demonstration projects will provide hard data on the cost/benefit of control procedures and will be the basis for motivating employers to undertake control programs. They also will provide information on successful interventions in an active way. We cannot afford to wait five years before we start controlling our VDT problems. Demonstration projects give us a chance to have an impact quickly.

Laboratory Studies

There is also a great need for some basic research on specific concerns that cannot be adequately explained or controlled in field studies. A major need is to develop methodologies and instrumentation for evaluating VDT-related health problems. In particular, methods for examining visual processes, in a dynamic fashion, while an operator is working at a VDT are needed. Also, there is a need for studies that can provide information on specific effects on workers' vision, musculature, and emotions as they are affected by particular aspects of computerized work, when all other aspects are controlled. This will determine the most significant components which will need the most control efforts. Such laboratory studies should evaluate specific ergonomic features, such as adjustable workstations, to determine their ability to reduce physical stress. Other laboratory studies should examine cognitive elements of VDT work to define their influences on psychological stress, as well as potential solutions. Like demonstration projects, laboratory studies can be done in a much shorter time frame, and thus provide solutions more quickly than large field studies.

NOTE

Disclaimer: Mention of company names or products or their illlustration in pictures does not constitute endorsement by the author or by the National Institute for Occupational Safety and Health.

REFERENCES

American Optical Association (AOA). 1980. Written personal communication. December, 1980.

ANSI. 1973. American national standard practice for office lighting. *The Journal of IES.*

Arndt, R. 1981. The development of chronic trauma disorders among LSM operators. Paper presented at the American Industrial Hygiene Conference, Portland, Oregon. Copies available from author at Dept. of Preventive Medicine, University of Wisconsin, Madison, Wis.

Bauer, D., and Cavonius, C. R. 1980. Improving the legibility of visual display units through contrast reversal. In *Ergonomic Aspects of Video Display Terminals,* ed. E. Grandjean and E. Vigliani, pp. 137–142. London: Taylor and Francis.

Brauninger, U.; Grandjean, E.; Fellman, T.; and Gierer, R. 1982. Lighting characteristics of VDTs. In *Proceedings of Zurich Seminar on Digital Communication.* Zurich, Switzerland: Federal Institute of Technology.

Cakir, A.; Reuter, H.; Von Schmude, L.; and Armbruster, A. 1978. *Unterschung Zur Anpassung Von Biloschirmarbeitsplatew an dic Physche und Psychische Functionweise des Mensche Forschungbericht Humanisierung des Arbeitslegens.* Bonn: Bundesminiter fur Arbeit und Sozialordund.

Cakir, A.; Hart, D. J.; and Stewart, T. F. M. *The VDT manual.* Darmstadt, Federal Republic of Germany: Ince-Fiej Research Association (IFRA).

Coe, J. B.; Cuttle, K.; McClellon, W. C.; Warden, N. J.; and Turner, P. J. 1980. *Visual display units.* Wellington, N. Z.: New Zealand Department of Health Report No. W/1/80.

Cooper, C. L., and Marshall, J. 1976. Occupational sources of stress: a review of the literature relating to coronary heart disease and mental ill health. *Journal of Occupational Psychology.* 49:11–28.

Dainoff, M. 1979. *Occupational stress factors in secretarial/clerical workers.* Cincinnati: National Institute for Occupational Safety and Health.

———. 1980. Visual fatigue in VDT operators. In *Ergonomic aspects of visual display terminals,* ed. E. Grandjean and E. Vigliani, pp. 95–100. London: Taylor and Francis.

Elias, R.; Cail, F.; Tisserand, M.; and Christman, M. 1980. Investigations in operators working with CRT display; relationships between task content and psychophysiological alterations. In *Ergonomic Aspects of Visual Display Terminals,* ed. E. Grandjean and E. Vigliani, pp. 227–32. London: Taylor and Francis.

Gould, J. D. 1968. Visual factors in the design of computer controlled CRT displays. *Human Factors* 10:359–76.

Grandjean, E. 1979. *Ergonomical and medical aspects of cathode ray tube displays.* Zurich, Switzerland: Federal Institute of Technology.

————. 1982. Ergonomics related to the VDT workstation. In *Proceedings of Zurich Seminar on Digital Communication*. Zurich, Switzerland: Federal Institute of Technology.

Gunnarsson, E., and Ostberg, O. 1977. The physical and psychological working environment in a terminal-based computer storage and retrieval system. Stockholm, Sweden: National Board of Occupational Safety and Health, Report 35.

Gunnarsson, E., and Soderberg, I. 1980. Eye-strain resulting from VDT work at the Swedish telecommunications administration. Stockholm, Sweden: National Board of Occupational Safety and Health.

Haider, M.; Hollar, J.; Kundi, M.; Schmid, H.; Thaler, A.; and Winter, N. 1975. *Stress and strain on the eyes produced by work with display screens: report on a work-physiological study performed for the union of employees in the private sector*. Vienna, Austria: Austrian Trade Union Association.

Haider, M.; Kundi, M.; and Weissebock, M. 1980. Worker strain related to VDUs with differently colored characters. In *Ergonomic Aspects of Visual Display Terminals*, ed. E. Grandjean and E. Vigliani, pp. 53–64. London: Taylor and Francis.

Hirschfelder, D. 1980. Better industrial vision testing and safety. *Occupational Health and Safety* 49:30–4.

Hultgren, G., and Knave, B. 1974. Discomfort, glare, and disturbances from light reflections in a office landscape with CRT display terminals. *Applied Ergonomics* 5:2–8.

Hunting, W.; Laubli, T.; and Grandjean, E. 1980. Constrained postures and VDU operators. In *Ergonomic Aspects of Visual Display Terminals*, ed. E. Grandjean and E. Vigliani, pp. 175–184. London: Taylor and Francis.

Johansson G., and Aronsson, G. 1980. *Stress reactions in computerized administrative work*. Stockholm: University of Stockholm.

Karasek, R. 1979. Job demands, job decision latitude, and mental strain: implications for job redesign. *Administrative Science Quarterly* 24:285–308.

Kintz, R. T., and Bowker, D. O. 1980. Accommodation response during a prolonged visual search task. Paper presented at Ergonomic Aspects of Visual Display Units Workshop. Milan, Italy, March 1980.

LaRocco, J. M.; House, J. S.; and Frech, J. R. P. 1980. Social support, occupational stress and health. *Journal of Health and Social Behavior*. 21:202–18.

Laubli, T.; Hunting, W.; and Grandjean, E. 1980. Visual impairments related to environmental conditions in VDU operators. In *Ergonomic Aspects of Visual Display Terminals*, ed. E. Grandjean and E. Vigliani, pp. 85–94. London: Taylor and Francis.

Moss, C. E.; Murray, W. E.; Parr, W. H.; Messite, J.; and Karches, G. J. 1978. An electromagnetic radiation survey of selected video display terminals. Cincinnati: National Institute for Occupational Safety and Health, Publication No. 78–129.

Murray, W. E.; Moss, C. E.; Parr, W. H.; and Cox, C. 1981. A radiation and industrial hygiene survey of video display terminal operations. *Human Factors* 23:413–20.

National Institute for Occupational Safety and Health (NIOSH). 1981. *Potential health hazards of video display terminals.* DHHS (NIOSH) Publication No. 81–129. Cincinnati: National Institute for Occupational Safety and Health.

Ostberg, O. 1974. Fatigue in clerical work in CRT display terminals. *Goteborg Psychological Reports* 4:19:1–14.

——. 1976. Office computerization in Sweden: worker participation, workplace design considerations, and the reduction of visual strain. Paper presented to the NATO Advanced Study Institute on Man-Computer Interaction, September 1976.

——. 1977. Towards standards and TLVs for visual work. Paper presented at the 2nd World Congress of Ergophthalmology. Stockholm, June 1977.

Ostberg, O.; Powell, J.; and Blomkvist, A. 1980. *Laser optometry in assessment of visual fatigue.* Lulea, Sweden: Department of Human Work Sciences, University of Lulea, Report 1980: 1 T.

Radl, G. W. 1980. Experimental investigations for optimal presentation-mode and colours of symbols on the CRT-screen. In *Ergonomic Aspects of Visual Display Terminals*, ed. E. Grandjean and E. Vigliani, pp. 127–36. London: Taylor and Francis.

Sauter, S. L.; Harding, G. E.; Gottlieb, M. S.; and Quackenboss, J. J. 1981. VDT-computer automation of work practices as a stressor in information-processing jobs: some methodological considerations. In *Machine Pacing and Occupational Stress*, ed. G. Salvendy and M. J. Smith, pp. 355–60. London: Taylor and Francis.

Sauter, S. L.; Gottlieb, M. S.; and Jones, K. C. 1982. A general systems analysis of stress-strain in VDT operations. Paper presented at the Conference on Human Factors in Computer Systems, Gaithersburg, Maryland, 1982. Copies available from S. Sauter at Dept. of Preventive Medicine, University of Wisconsin, Madison, Wis.

Smith, K. U.; and Smith, M. F. 1966. *Cybernetic principles of learning and educational design.* New York: Holt, Rinehart and Winston.

Smith, M. J.; Stammerjohn, L. W.; Cohen, B. G. F.; and Lalich, N. 1980. Job stress in video display operations. In *Ergonomic Aspects of Visual Display Terminals*, ed. E. Grandjean and E. Vigliani, pp. 201–10. London: Taylor and Francis.

Smith, M. J.; Cohen, B. G. F.; Stammerjohn, L.; and Happ, A. 1981a. An investigation of health complaints and job stress in video display operations. *Human Factors* 23:387–400.

Smith, M. J. 1981b. Occupational stress: an overview of psychological factors. In *Machine Pacing and Occupational Stress*, ed. G. Salvendy and M. J. Smith, pp. 13–19. London: Taylor and Francis.

Smith, A. B.; Tanaka, S.; Halperin, W.; and Richards, R. D. 1982. *Cross-sectional survey of* VDT *users at the Baltimore Sun.* Cincinnati: National Institute for Occupational Safety and Health.

Stammerjohn, L.; Smith, M. J.; and Cohen, B. G. F. 1981. Evaluation of workstation design factors in VDT operations. *Human Factors* 23:401–12.

Young, F. A., and Leary, G. A. 1977a. Visual characteristics of apes and persons. In *Apre Research*, pp. 207–225. New York: Academic Press.

Young, F. A. 1977b. The nature and control of myopia. *Journal of the American Optometry Association* 48:451–7.

———. 1978. Accommodation and the control of myopia. *The Optician* 176:7–9.

VISUAL FATIGUE
AND THE VDT WORKPLACE

Lawrence W. Stark
with the editorial assistance
of Phyllis Grey Johnston

VISUAL FATIGUE

As emphasized in reviews of VDT-associated health complaints (see the article by Smith in this volume), visual fatigue is the most common source of complaints by terminal operators. In both the United States and Europe, problems related to visual health (eye strain, headaches, etc.) have received the most attention in research studies. The purpose of this article is to review the mechanisms of the human eye, and the methods by which visual fatigue may be evaluated.

Can We Define Fatigue?

The concept of "visual fatigue" is one that has escaped canonical scientific definition. We are, therefore, reduced to different definitions that summarize the careful work that has been done in this difficult field. Some would like

Acknowledgments: The authors are pleased to acknowledge partial support from the NCC 2–86 Cooperative Agreement, NASA-Ames Research Center and from the National Institute for Occupational Safety and Health, Order No. 82-2002, and wish to thank Dr. Marvin Dainoff, Dr. Michael Smith, Shirley Arao, and Emily Holden for their help.

to discard the term "visual fatigue" and use "visual discomfort" and "ocular-motor fatigue" as more specific descriptors for somewhat different subjective complaints. Fatigue may relate to the subjective effort necessary to reach a given level of performance more often struggling with central nervous system boredom or *habituation* than with a muscular disability.

The decrement in motor response performance to a stimulus may be due to adaptation of sensory organs, habituation of the central nervous system, or muscular fatigue. It is clear that motivation may often overcome subject fatigue and decreased performance. For example, Cameron (1972) suggested that efficiency, the ratio of response to effort, is a more appropriate measure of fatigue than response decrement. Fatigue has also been divided into acute fatigue, resulting from a stress situation; chronic fatigue, resulting in disability; and task fatigue, with boredom, monotony, and habituation.

Four operational measures of fatigue have been suggested (Smith, 1979):

1. *Subjective fatigue* has been studied with respect to the VDT, and two clusters of symptoms have been separated by means of factor analysis (Laubli, Hunting, and Grandjean, 1980): (a) ocular irritation includes burning and pain in the eyes, redness of eyes, headache; (b) visual-motor deficit comprising blurring of near or far vision and double images, and flickering vision. The New Zealand study (Coe et al., 1980) compared VDT workers with a control group and found that effects of irritation (itchy, dry, gritty, stinging, watery eyes) were not increased, but asthenopic fatiguelike effects (hot, heavy, tired, twitchy, aching eyes) were increased. This agreement suggests both studies are valid, but, of course, field studies relating VDT use to symptoms of ocular-motor fatigue and irritation have complex methodologies and are difficult and expensive to conduct. An excellent review has been contributed by Dainoff (1980).

2. *General physiological measures not related to the sensory or motor performance organs.* These include increased heart rate, sweating, and other signs of general physiological fatigue.

3. *Visual performance* itself has often been carefully measured during performance of the visual task. Noncumulative deterioration of psychophysical measures such as visual acuity and errors or slowed reaction time have been documented.

4. A correlation with subjective reports of fatigue has been found with a number of measurable *ocular-motor functions*—blinking, pupillary oscillations, restriction of accommodative and vergence ranges, and other eye movement changes. This fourth category relates closely to our assignment, and we will take up these functions in our review (sections II and III below) of literature involving any or all of the following tasks: VDT (relatively few recent papers), reading hard copy, microfilm reading and tracking movement.

Can Objective Measures Define Fatigue?

Many investigators have turned to this "objective cluster" of ocular-motor responses as objectively recorded measurements of the process associated with the subjective complaint of fatigue.[1] We shall see that to the thinking person this may *not* be so. A recorded change, for example, in accommodative near point may be a consequence of an unmeasured and even unnoted change in pupil size; pupil constriction which increases depth of focus, makes unnecessary as much accommodative amplitude as required with a small depth of focus. A recorded change, for example, in accommodation may be a normal, healthy "adaptive" response to an ongoing task without any implied or actual decrement in performance—much as a skilled truck driver may not apply as much force in holding the steering wheel as an inexperienced driver. Or a recorded change in accommodation could be the response of a person with some idiosyncratic or minor ophthalmological defect in refraction or binocular vision that may interact with their task requirements. Indeed, the brochure *Humanizing the VDT Workplace,* published jointly by the Newspaper Guild and the International Typographical Union (1981), recognizes the possible role played by minor ophthalmological defects of VDT operators (Mahto, 1972).

It has been difficult using clinical and epidemiological methods to find consistent relationships between subjective complaints and different optometric refractive errors (simple astigmatism with or against the rule, oblique astigmatism, compound astigmatism with myopia or with hypermetropia, anisometropia, and also minor amounts of myopia or hypermetropia) (Mahto, 1972; Simmerman, 1950; Vaithilingam and Khare, 1967; Borish, 1970).

EYE MOVEMENTS

Considering three levels of extraocular-motor performance clarifies, to some extent, the eye movement changes that are responsive to sustained ocular-motor performance.

(1) Saccadic Trajectory

The first level, the fine neurological control structure of the saccadic trajectory, has been shown to decompose rapidly (within minutes) in repetitive tracking in at least two quite different ways. Central nervous system habituation allows the appearance of *double saccades*, each component of which falls naturally on the "Main Sequence," relating saccadic velocities and amplitudes (Bahill and Stark, 1975). This fitting to the main sequence provides evidence that even lower level pulse shaping neurons in the brain stem as well as, of course, neuromuscular and muscular factors are all functioning quite normally. Also, *pulse-step mismatches* in the controller signal envelopes of

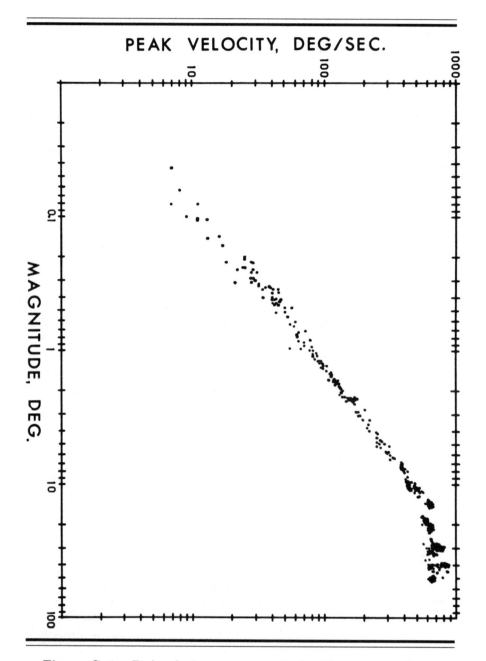

Figure G–1. Peak velocity versus magnitude of human saccadic eye movements.

neuronal bursting and tonic firing of nerve impulses occur and result in "glissades," which often violate Hering's Law of equal innervation to cor-

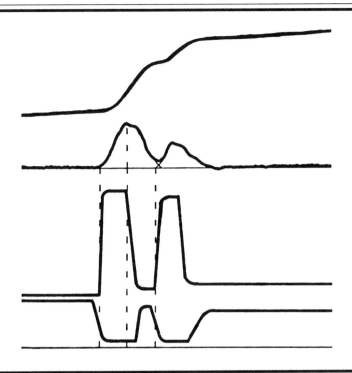

Figure G–2. Overlapping saccades and their proposed motoneuronal controller signals. Shown, from top to bottom, are the eye position, eye velocity, nervous activity for the agonist pool, and nervous activity for the antagonist pool, all as functions of time.

responding muscles (Bahill and Stark, 1975; Bahill et al., 1976). The more peripheral neuromuscular fatigue type of decomposition of the saccadic trajectory produces generally slowed movements below the main sequence velocity-amplitude relationship and also irregular fragments showing erratic profiles of velocity and acceleration. These fragments have been found in patients with peripheral neural and neuromuscular diseases (Feldon et al., 1981) and lie above the main sequence as a result of "truncation" (similar to the truncation that occurs in the overlapping voluntary nystagmus saccades) (Zuber, 1981).

Reading VDT displays is largely performed by repetitive saccades at a rate of approximately 4 saccades per second. Thus, there are similarities and differences between reading eye movements and repetitive tracking eye movements. Students of reading eye movements use tracking movements as a related but simpler form of sequential reading eye movements. Indeed, Pavlides (1981) has suggested that a deficiency in tracking accompanies abnormalities in reading eye movements. (Reading eye movements are discussed below.)

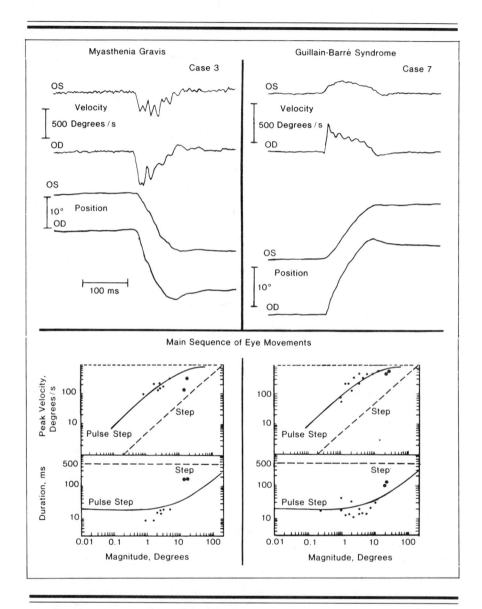

Figure G–3. Similar saccadic trajectories are shown for myasthenia gravis (top left) and Guillain-Barre syndrome (GBS) (top right). Series of small, rapid changes in eye position separated by periods of little or no eye movement is termed "stutter."   Bottom: main sequence plots for myasthenia (left) and GBS (right) traces demonstrate that overall trajectories have long durations and slow peak velocities (large solid circles). Subcomponents, however, are often of shorter than expected duration and may show low, normal, or high peak velocities (small solid circles).

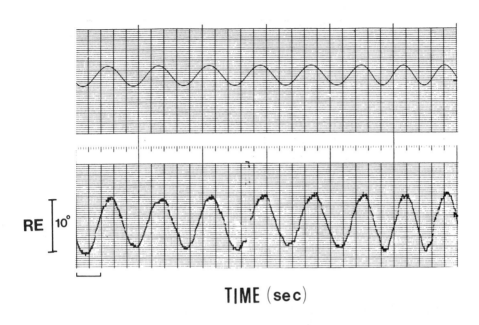

TIME (sec)

Figure G–4. The smooth pursuit eye movement of a normal subject (above) following the target (below).

(2) Dual Mode Tracking Eye Movements

A second level of eye movement performance has to do with both smooth pursuit and saccadic eye movements in tracking. Here a single entire saccadic response may drop out and the sequence of responses then continues in phase (Lion and Brockhurst, 1951). In addition, the tracking quality may deteriorate with gradually increased reaction times and abnormal sequences of saccades (Stark, Vossius, and Young, 1962). Saccadic smooth pursuit also may occur as a compensatory adaptation when the gain of smooth pursuit decreases. [Restoration may occur after a brief rest period (tens of seconds) or a startle dishabituation stimulus.] Recall that visual feedback is a crucial element in the control of eye movements at this level.

The *tracking* task is a paradigm human factors experiment to define human operator activities such as in controlling vehicles. It has been studied with conceptual and mathematical tools of the control engineer (Young and Stark, 1963). Thus, it fits nicely into extensive and quantitative studies of task performance and its deterioration with sustained activity. It is important to remember here Cameron's notion of efficiency: effort may compensate for decreased response and maintain performance in highly motivated subjects.

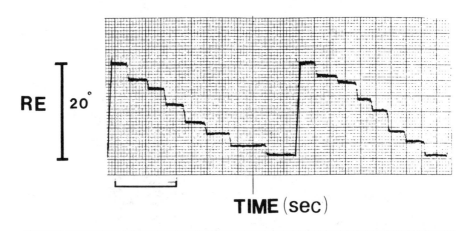

Figure G–5. The reading eye movement of a normal subject reading text on a VDT.

(3) Higher Level Eye Movement Pattern

Reading. A third level of eye movement performance comprises reading and looking, composed of sequential patterns of saccadic eye movements. The *reading* task is a complex one with cognitive, linguistic, visual, and eye movement factors all interacting (Rayner, 1973). Many studies have demonstrated poorer reading performance with nonoptimal typography or illumination (Demilia, 1968; Tinker, 1939; Tinker and Paterson, 1939). However, several experienced and careful researchers have found no significant decrement in reading performance even after six hours of reading such concentrated material as Adam Smith's *Wealth of Nations* (Carmichael, 1951; Carmichael and Dearborn, 1947). Although subjective "fatigue" was reported after this task, 60 out of 80 subjects felt they could continue to read if provided with a rest. Many studies have shown that poor readers with or without specific *dyslexia* often have prolonged fixations and irregular reading eye movement patterns. These and backward staircases have been found in peripheral motor dyslexia secondary to the diplopia of a peripheral ocular-motor paresis. One may speculate that minor forms of dyslexia in VDT operators surface and produce complaints. The eye movement component of the reading task involves mainly a sequential pattern of saccades, about one for each word, although small common words (a, of, the) are often skipped. About 10%–20% of the saccades are regressions or backward saccades, generally to a linguistically critical word in the syntax of the sentence. Indeed the French word "verification" for a regression assumes this linguistic role. At the end of a line, a larger saccade sweeps the eye to the left margin of the next line; here numerous corrective saccades occur, especially vertical ones to place the eyes

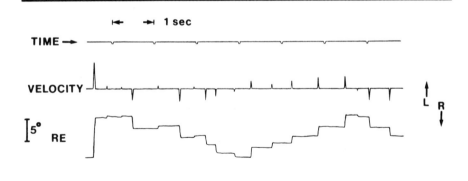

Figure G–6.   The reading eye movement of a young specific dyslexic
     showing an occurrence of a complete reverse staircase. Note the
     prolonged fixation pauses within the reverse pattern.

correctly on the line. Vergence and accommodative response have not been
thoroughly studied during reading. Reading rates of 300 words per minute
are near maximum. The maximum rate of saccadic generation is 5 per second;
this is equivalent to a reading rate of 300 words per minute (Adler-Grinberg
and Stark, 1978). (We roughly equate the extra number of regression saccades
to the number of skipped small words.) This high frequency of saccades must
be considered as a possible source of interaction with flicker produced by video
refresh rates.[2] Also large saccades (i.e., looking from a dark VDT to a sheet
of lighted hard copy) may act as a light stimulus to the pupil and also may
quickly change focal distance and stimulate an accommodative response.

   Looking. Actual looking scanpath eye movements are larger, irregular,
often oblique, and somewhat less frequent (3–4 saccades/second). The scanpath is a nonrandom sequence of saccadic eye movements that scan a picture
in an idiosyncratic pattern for each subject (Noton and Stark, 1971a, 1971b,
and 1971c). Scanpaths appear to be generated by internal cognitive models in
a checking phase of pattern recognition. Recent evidence for this comes from
the work of Noton and Stark (1971a, 1971b, and 1971c) and Stark and Ellis
(1981) who used ambiguous and fragmented figures and asked subjects to signal their alternating perceptions. With the same subject and the same physical pictures, the eye movement scanpath developed different patterns, each
associated with a particular perception. Scanpaths are modified with continued examination of the same pattern (Yarbus, 1967), but implications are
not known and minor changes may not be noticed. Drivers engaged in long,
continued driving tasks show central concentration of fixations rather than
the normal, wider-spread active looking and searching patterns (McDowell
and Rockwell, 1978). The question of preview control, how far ahead the
driver looks, and its relationship to the fatigue situation may be important
(Tomizuka and Rosenthal, 1979; Zwahlen, 1977).

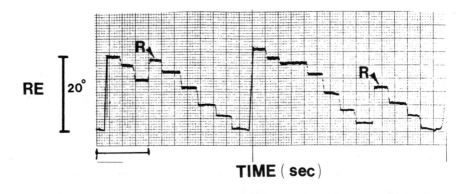

Figure G–7.   The reading eye movement with regression while reading
text at a VDT.

(4) Gaze and the Vestibular-Ocular Reflex

The vestibular-ocular reflex is a primitive phylogenetic mechanism that sta-
bilizes the direction of gaze in space. In the brainstem there are connections
between the ocular-motor system and the vestibular apparatus that monitor
balance and posture with respect to gravity. If a head movement occurs, a
signal that generates a compensatory eye movement (in the absence of voli-
tion) is sent from the vestibular apparatus to the ocular-motor system. Thus,
when attending a visual target, an operator may turn body or head without
losing visual contact (Baloh and Honrubia, 1979; Henn, Cohen, and Young,
1980; Wilson and Melville-Jones, 1979).

Coordinated gaze movement normally has an initial eye-in-orbit saccade
onto the target followed by a synkinetic and much slower head movement.
At the level of the electromyographic (EMG) signal latencies are synchronous;
but because the viscoinertial dynamics of head and neck muscles are different
from the viscoelastic dynamics of head and extraocular muscles, the saccade is
over before head position has changed. The vestibular ocular reflex generated
by head acceleration drives the compensatory eye movement, eye-in-orbit, in
the opposite direction so that gaze, eye-in-space, remains on target. Thus,
gaze movement has the advantage of the rapidity of the eye saccade and at
the end of the movement the eye is in primary position in the orbit and the
target is in the straightforward position, since directional sense is determined
by head position.

Diseases of the ocular-motor system, the vestibular apparatus, or the
central nervous system may cause incomplete visual compensation for body
movement. In such circumstances a disequilibrium may result because visual
space does not correspond with the subject's egocentric image of space. This
sensation results in nausea, vomiting, and vertigo. The same symptoms may

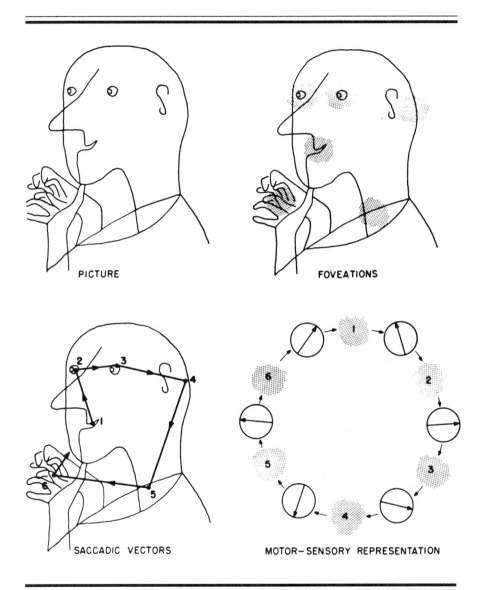

Figure G–8. Feature ring. Feature ring proposed by Noton and Stark as a format for internal representation of a picture. Picture is identified by its principal subfeatures and by successive saccades composing scanpath. Feature ring consists of sensory memory traces of subfeatures and motor memory traces of saccades composing scanpath. Scanpath is generated from this cognitive model by successively reading out subfeatures and motor vectors in this checking phase of pattern recognition.

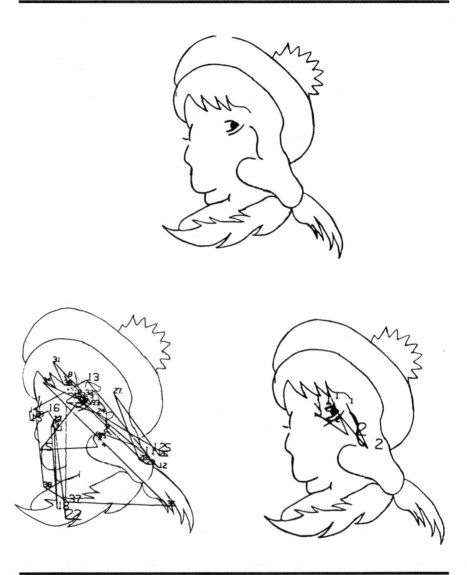

Figure G–9. Triply ambiguous figure. Upper picture shows old man with mustache, old woman with gnarled chin and nose, and young woman seen in profile with eyelash extending from silhouette (Fisher, 1971). Lower left figure shows eye movements and fixations during experimental run. Lower right figure shows eye movements during three successive occurrences with subject in that cognitive state wherein he saw the old man.

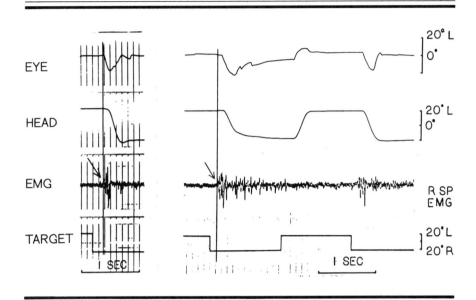

Figure G–10. Gaze responses. Left panel—unpredictable 40 degree horizontal target shift to right; eye movement preceded head movement (45 ms), whereas neck electromyogram (EMG) of right splenius (RSP) started about 10 ms before initial eye position changes. Right panel—predictable target shift; first target shift only slightly predicted, whereas next two repetitions showed increased prediction head more than eye; first shift latencies (eye 205 ms, head 225, EMG 155); third shift latencies (eye 165 ms, head 190, EMG 115). Note slowed eye saccade because of ongoing compensatory eye movement (CEM), a consequence of relatively decreased head latency. Note also different rations of initial eye amplitude compared with head amplitude; quick phase-like interruptions in CEM were not due to visual feedback but were related to the fast phases of vestibular nystagmus that can also occur in the dark.

occur in the absence of disease if the operator uses psychotropic drugs such as tranquilizers, sedatives, or alcohol (Westheimer and Rashbass, 1961).

(5) Blinking

A quite different movement, blinking, may be considered here (Hung, Hsu, and Stark, 1977). Very often *excessive* blinking has been associated with difficulty with a linguistic higher level processing task as, for example, when reading difficult text. Perhaps blinking should be considered a "cybernetic windshield wiper" for the retina! By this we mean that transient quenching of the light input to the rods and cones of the eye by an eye blink must have some resetting effect on the excitability of, not only these receptors, but of all the retinal and CNS visual neurons. The visual information processing 'computer' includes not only rods and cones, but also bipolar, horizontal, amacrine, and ganglion cells of the retina and neurons in the lateral geniculate body, the visual cortex, the parietal cortex, and the frontal eye fields. Blinking has been associated with fatigue at least since 1895 (Katz in Leningrad as reported by Kravklov (1974) and documented by Luckiesh (1947); Krivohlavy, Kodat, and Cizek (1969); and Bartley (1942) but denied by Bitterman (1945, 1946, 1947), Wood and Bitterman (1950), Holland and Tarlow (1972), and Brozek, Simonson, and Keyes (1950)). An abnormally high or abnormally low rate of blinking may be related (although no clinical evidence as yet exists) to the ocular irritation syndrome of redness and injection of sclera and cornea, sensation of heat and burning of the anterior portion of the eye, and headache. Tear production is necessary to prevent drying of the eye; an abnormal blink rate may adversely influence this factor.

TRIAD

(1) Accommodation

a. Normal function. Blur is the stimulus to accommodation (Phillips and Stark, 1977) and has some very important properties which help us to understand the accommodation system as a whole. Blur is appreciated by the foveal cones under photopic light conditions. It is an even error signal, and accommodation is a hill-climbing controller which accepts large steady-state errors. (Even error has magnitude but not sign or direction. A hill-climbing controller attempts to minimize error, but does not try to correct to zero error.)

The "dual indirect active" theory of the accommodative mechanism put forward by Helmholtz (1867) has received support over the past century. There is an extra-lenticular mechanism whereby the active ciliary muscle applies tension and stretches the peripheral portion of the elastic ciliary ligament or zonule of Zinn. This then allows the lenticular portion of the system, the surrounding elasticity of lens and capsule, to produce the accommodated state. It is a *dual* mechanism because of the participation of both extra-lenticular and lenticular elements. It is an *indirect* mechanism since the ciliary muscle does not act directly on the lens as a sphincter, but only indirectly by unloading the axial portion of the ciliary ligament. It is an *active* mechanism since activity in the ciliary muscle produces an increase in accommodation.

The accommodative control mechanism has, besides the hill-climbing controller, many other nonlinear characteristics (Stark, 1968). It also has a leaky integrator (Krishnan and Stark, 1975) or leaky memory with about a 10-second time constant. There is a control *bias level* with a normal value or

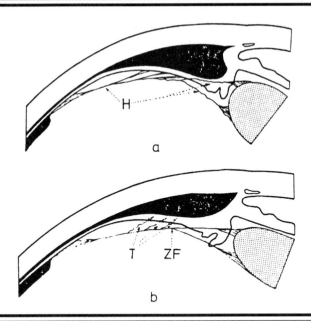

Figure G–11. Illustrating Rohen and Rentsch's concept of the structure of the zonular fibers. The accommodated state: H are the holding fibers which split at the zonular fork, ZF. Branching from the holding fibers are the tension fibers, T, inserting into the ciliary epithelium.

set point of 1 diopter. The accommodation mechanism drifts to this bias point if, and only if, the system is made to be an *open loop* system by electronic methods (Phillips and Stark, 1977), or if illumination is reduced to below photopic levels (night myopia), or if a focusable image is absent (space myopia). Space myopia was described by Whiteside (1957) and has been shown to be important in decrement of visual detection ability in pilots. The normal accommodative mechanism drift bias point may be called a "lead" if the subject was previously focusing at a near point. So called "dark focus" is incorrectly named. It is not peculiar to darkness, but relates equally to space (empty field) and to open loop conditions; it is not a focused state of accommodation but is that state of accommodation to which the accommodative mechanism is set by synkinetic control from the vergence system (CAC).

This triadic synkinesis (O'Neill and Stark, 1968) is an essential part of the control of accommodation. Accommodation produces an accommodative pupillary constriction, which in turn increases the depth of focus. This provides for a lessened requirement for accommodation on a near target; without measuring the pupil size and calculating the depth of focus, it is *not* possible to state that a certain measured accommodative state is or is

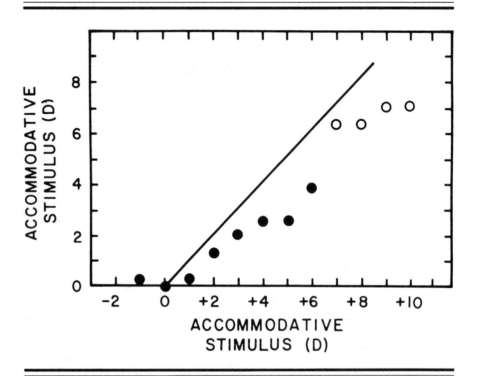

Figure G–12. Two accommodative stimulus-response curves measured with Fincham optometer. Response (circle) shows focusing ability of a normal 25-year-old patient. Note that from 0 to 7 D of accommodative stimulus, the patient follows the target quite well and manifests typical "lazy lag of accommodation." Beyond 7 D of accommodative stimulus, the patient approaches the "presbyopic zone" (latent zone), and the plateau gives a measure of accommodative amplitude. In contrast is the response (square) of another 25-year-old patient who complained of focusing difficulties at near distances and clearly exhibits an impaired focusing ability. At the time of testing, the patient was wearing poorly fitting soft contact lenses and had slightly reduced and variable visual acuity.

not optimal. Vergence also drives accommodation (Krishnan, Shirachi, and Stark, 1977); this turns out to be a main mechanism for a change of focus. Disparity, the binocular parallax that is a signal to the vergence system, can be computed even when the disparate images are blurred, indeed, disparity itself throws the stimulus off the fovea and thus creates an open-loop blur stimulus to accommodation. Thus, in ordinary daily vision, as in switching from VDT to nearer work or distance vision (and, of course, neglecting predictive capabilities and "proximal" factors), it is not the defocussed image that derives

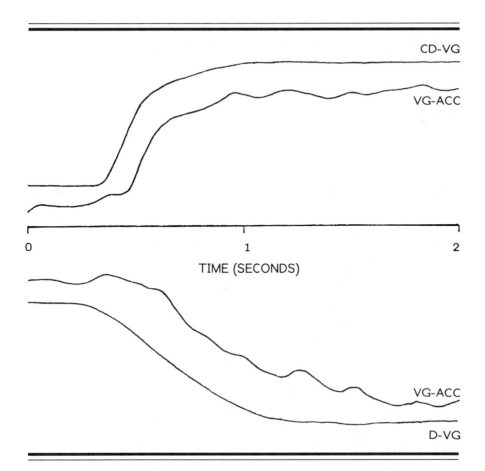

Figure G–13. With a step disparity stimulus of 4.5 deg, starting at time zero, vergence accommodation (VG-ACC) and disparity vergence (D-VG) responded similarly—an initial fast phase followed by a slower phase. The subject's responses were averaged for the indicated number (N) of total trials. Curves were normalized for comparison. Amplitude of VG-ACC is approximately 1.8 D. The subject, DKS, is a 30-yr-old male orthopore with 2.5 D of myopia and 0.50 D of astigmatism in each eye and corrected acuity of 20/20.

accommodation but the disparate images driving vergence and, via vergence-accommodation (CAC), the accommodation state.

 b. Static factors in accommodation. The range of accommodation is up to 16 diopters in children but only about 10 diopters in young adults. The gradual restriction of range of accommodation with maturity (or age) is called *presbyopia*; since it begins in childhood, it is clearly not a degenerative condition. The ciliary muscle has normal strength and activity (Saladin and Stark, 1975), but since the growth of the lens continues producing a larger lens with a decreased curvature and increased radius, there is a recession of the near point. By the age of 40, normal adults need reading glasses as a static refractive prothesis. "By the time one understands the mechanism of accommodation, the pupil is one's mechanism of accommodation!" By this we mean that the increased depth of focus produced by pupillary constriction is then the only method by which the near point can approach the presbyopic subject.

Certain other static disabilities are seen clinically. Accommodative spasm, which produces a fixed accommodation level at the near point, most often is not muscular, since it usually also involves vergence. On the other hand, accommodative asthenopia is characterized by fixed accommodation at the far point with no evident or effective accommodative effort. (Because these static conditions occur most frequently in persons aged 30–40, they may be related to the incidence of complaints of ocular discomfort in VDT operators.)

c. Dynamic factors in accommodation. The latency and time constant of accommodation vary idiosyncratically for the same subject under different operating conditions (Shirachi, Liu, Lee, Jang, Wong, and Stark, 1978). Methods of experimentally and clinically analyzing these dynamics include ergographic recordings and more recently the laser optometer. In these methods the subject positions the target so as to fall within his depth of focus and this positioning may be recorded as a measure of subjective appreciation of blur or laser speckle direction. A new laser ergograph method depends upon subjective appreciation of directional movement of a "speckle pattern" secondary to separation of the conjugate plane of the image from the retina. The image is formed by a rotating drum illuminated by a laser. On the other hand, objective methods include: the lensometer principle, which measures the blur of a target on the retina; the Scheiner method, in which blur is converted to prismatic shift (Malmstrom et al., 1981); retinoscopic methods, which use directional image motion as an indication of accommodation error; and the third Purkinje image method (O'Neill and Stark, 1968), which directly measures lens anterior pole position.

Disfacility of accommodation, less severe than static accommodative spasm or accommodative asthenopia, has been studied recently by means of such dynamic objective instrumentation. Time constants can be slowed or responses delayed beyond the usual latencies (Liu, Lee, Jang, Ciuffreda, Wong, Grisham, and Stark, 1979). Responses reach the required accommodative levels but then drift back; oscillation in level of accommodation can also occur. It should be kept in mind that some oscillation is a normal feature of the accommodative control mechanism.

Both prepresbyopes and children can show accommodative disfacility. It has been shown with subjective (Hofstetter, 1943) and objective (Liu et al., 1979) observations, that disfacility can be successfully treated by exercise.

d. Fatigue and accommodation. The earliest work on fatigue and accommodation consisted of only clinical impressions, and there continues to be a clinical literature (Weber, 1950).

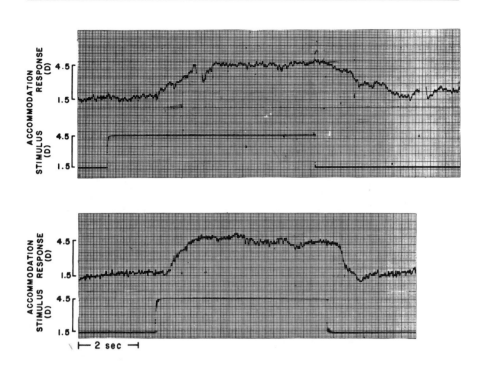

Figure G–14.   Accommodation responses of Subject 2. Upper records show slow response dynamics for positive accommodation and slow, multiphasic response dynamics for relaxation of accommodation before orthoptics training.   Bottom records show the patient's improvement after training with faster velocities in both directions of accommodation. Note two discontinuous spikes in upper record when patient blinked; stimuli for each are unpredictable step changes, between targets set at 1.5 and at 4.5 D.

The ergograph was designed to measure objectively and record a sequence of continual movements so that if fatigue occurs and the amplitude of the movement decreases, this can be noted. Ergographic studies have been performed for the last 50 years (Lancaster and Howe, 1912; Blatt, 1931; Berens and Stark, 1932; Kurts, 1937 and 1938; Hofstetter, 1943), and more recently the laser ergograph had been employed by Ostberg (1980) and Kintz and Bowker (1981).

Accommodative ergograph studies uniformly display changes, usually recessions of the near point, with fatigue; all have quite variable results. For example, Gunnarsson and Soderberg (1980) report recessions of the near point for younger VDT workers and some transient approach of the near point

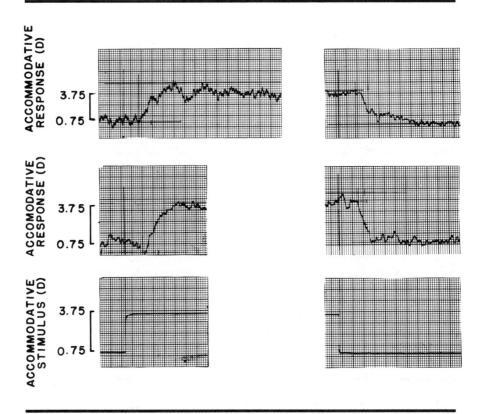

Figure G–15. Accommodation responses of Subject 3. Upper record taken before undergoing orthoptics program and, middle record, afterward. Bottom record denotes stimulus positions set at 0.75 and at 3.75 D. Only statistically significant improvement shown by Subject 3 was decreased time constant for relaxation of accommodation. Drift and low frequency noise seen in upper record for positive accommodation occurred irregularly.

during the early part of the day for older VDT workers. Tanaka and Oshima (1981), however, report approach of near point with younger workers.

Various authors are of the opinion that what is lacking in their research is a distinction between fatigue and boredom and especially control of motivational factors that might combat performance decrements. Hofstetter (1943) feels his results, especially rapid restoration with attention, indicate that the locus of fatigue is in the central nervous system and not in the muscles. That fatigue shows up in a nonseeing eye almost to the same extent as in a seeing eye (Berens and Sells, 1954) rules out fatigue in sensory processes. A serious defect in all of these studies is that they do not measure the 1 pillary aperture. The pupil is known to constrict with sleepiness, boredom, or fatigue and, if constricted, would increase the depth of focus, reducing the requirement for accommodation. A basic issue is the question of whether the objective measurements define abnormally functioning accommodation or simply demonstrate a healthy *adaptive* response. That is, to an overly learned task involving muscular effort, a healthy, intelligent (if unconscious), and sensible response is to reduce muscular effort to the lowest level compatible with task performance. Perhaps a skilled VDT operator shows this ability and reduced ocular-motor movement should not at all be construed as an objective medical sign of fatigue.

Another important aspect of accommodative amplitude is that it makes sense for it to be reduced when the pupil is small and thus produces a large depth of focus to the eye. None of the studies reported above measures the pupillary aperture, a requirement for the quantitative consideration of this factor.

Dynamic studies with fatigued subjects have been performed by a few authors: Kreuger (1980) has a good review of the physiology and the clinical approach to accommodation. Malmstrom et al. (1981) used a tracking test in which subjects followed sinusoidal targets for a 13-minute period; logical defects in this study include the absence of a necessity to maintain a sharp focus on the target and also the lack of control of possible pupillary constriction. Krivohlavy (1969) showed, using subjective methods, that accommodation was slowed because of increased time to cycle between near and far targets and that this was significantly correlated with decremented performance on a reading task. Mourant, Lakshmanan, and Chantadisai (1981) indicated that eye movements from a near to a far target slowed a small amount with duration of a task. Their work is marred by their definition of "in-focus" and "out-focus" times; they used video cameras to estimate eye fixation directions and had no measure at all accommodation. That accommodation was very likely not a factor is indicated by the alternate distances they chose—2.2 Diopters and 0.16 Diopters. Both could easily have been within the depth of focus of their subjects' eyes at the same time. Additional evidence supporting this interpretation is the similarity in responses of their presbyopic subjects without accommodation and their younger subjects with accommodation! Finally, in considering the ergonomic aspects, Haider (1980) pointed out that multi-colored displays might include colors that are less effective than those usually used in enabling accommodation to clear blur.

(2) Vergence

Vergence is one of the most interesting of the ocular-motor control systems. As an object moves closer or farther away the two eyes move to maintain bifixation on the point of interest. Vergence, in which the eyes move disjunctively and symmetrically, utilizes the same muscles as version, in which the eyes move in the same direction toward objects with different horizontal

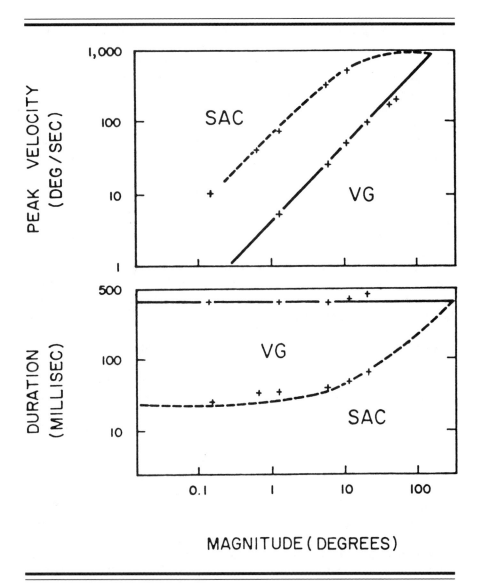

Figure G–16. Main sequence of eye movements.

and vertical locations with, of course, different patterns of "corresponding" muscles. However, the vergence system moves much more slowly than the versional (or turning) system, probably because of the synkinetic coordination of vergence with pupillary and accommodative changes which smooth intraocular muscles. Vergence is by far the easiest ocular-motor system to fatigue. Luckiesh and Moss (1935a and 1935b) showed in two studies that two

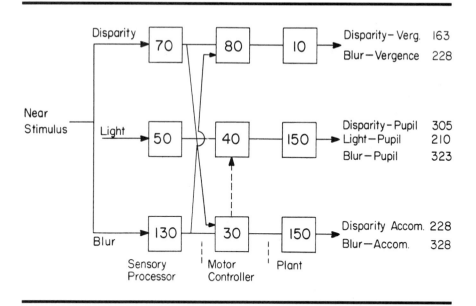

Figure G–17. Block diagram of the near response triad. Average response latencies in milliseconds for subject NE are given at the right. Numbers in the blocks represent the "component" latencies in milliseconds. Component latency assignments are based on topological and physiological considerations (see text). This block diagram is not intended to be interpreted anatomically.

aspects of the vergence system are changed with fatigue. The tasks used were reading, especially of small type, and also inspection tasks lasting up to four hours. The amplitude of convergence, the dioptric distance from infinity to the point at which bifixation no longer becomes possible as a target moves closer and closer, was reduced with fatigue. Muscle imbalance was also increased by fatigue. Muscle balance was tested by Cobb and Moss (1925) by covering one eye and estimating the amount of eso- or exophoria (turning in or turning out) of the covered nonfixating eye. The decreased amplitude of convergence under fatiguing visual inspection work was also shown by Brozek, Simonsen, and Keyes (1950). Mahto (1972) observed in a clinical study that convergence insufficiency was the usual cause of eye strain complaints in a series of patients he studied. The association of close work with these complaints was also noted. In an important, interesting physiological drug study (Rashbass, 1959; Westheimer, 1963; Westheimer and Rashbass, 1961), the vergence system has been shown to be much less robust to drugs than the versional system; thus, the well-known phenomenon of double-vision, a primary sign people use to determine that they have had too much alcohol to drink!

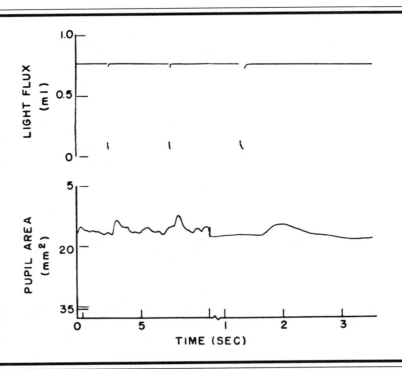

Figure G–18.   Experimentally obtained pulse responses.

(3) Pupil

a. Pupil as part of the eye's optical system. Depth of focus is controlled by the pupil, synkinetically driven by accommodation and convergence. In the earlier section on accommodation, it was pointed out how this asymmetrical interaction between the control of accommodation and pupillary constriction could reduce the need for accommodation amplitude. Indeed, as discussed above, studies of accommodation that do not define the state of constriction of the pupil are suspect.

b. Pupil as a regulator of light level. The pupil is only effective, that is, acts as a high gain control mechanism, for rapid small changes of illumination. Larger changes in illumination which indeed can vary over many log units, are handled by multiple retinal adaptive mechanisms. A recent study by Cakir et al. (1978) has suggested that "transient adaptation glare" may be a significant pupillary factor in visual fatigue. They noted that viewing of positive contrast VDT (light letters on a darker background) is often alternated with negative contrast hard copy (dark letters on a white sheet of paper) and designed an experiment to explore this factor. They found significant transient changes in pupil size produced by the alternation. Rupp (1978) criticized this study and suggested that the "pupillary response may well have been caused by the brief period of darkness on the display appearing

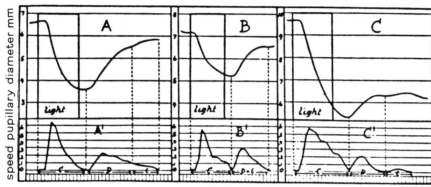

Time in 0.1 seconds

Figure G–19. Influence of timing of the psychosensory stimulus on psychosensory restitution in normal man. (**A**) The subject was emotionally excited. The first reaction to light shows a V-shape with shorter than normal contraction time. The fourth reaction shows parasympathetic disinhibition with increased extent and speed of contraction. The sensory (sound) stimulus (S) reverses this development; the fifth reaction shows V-shape. (**B**) The subject was calm and the pupil fatigued by 10 successive light stimuli. The sensory (sound) stimulus elicited at S (2 sec before the following light stimulus) produces full restitution of the light reaction. (**C**) The subject was calm and the pupil almost exhausted by 24 light stimuli. A strong sympathetic (sound) elicited immediately before the 25th light stimulus completely inhibits the light reflex. (**D**) After active sympathetic dilation has come to an end, the following (26th) reaction to light is restituted.

between the alternating fields" and further reports preliminary experiments confirming his conjecture.

    c. Pupil as a factor in fatigue. Bartley (1938) showed that slow flicker (1–6 flashes per second) was still often too fast a frequency for pupillary movement to follow. However, maintained constriction occurred (Troelstra, 1968), and discomfort and fatigue were produced. More recent control studies of the pupil have shown that the pupil can follow at least up to 3 hz, so that it is not clear whether the static constriction or a small, fast oscillation not indicated by older methods underlies this "Bartley effect." In a very interesting experiment, Halstead (1941) used the mydriatic scopolamine, which blocks pupillary constriction, when he repeated the Bartley paradigm. Under these conditions *no* ocular strain was reported by his subjects! Fugate and Fry (1956), Fry and King (1975), and King (1976) performed a different but related experiment. They used very bright light flashes well above sensory threshold and the definition of BCD—the "border between comfort and discomfort". They also believed that pupillary constriction was the source of discomfort and when they used atropine to block both the sphincter and ciliary muscles, they reduced the discomfort in their subjects! These studies, of all the thousands on visual fatigue, are the only ones that clearly implicate an ocular-motor mechanism, repetitive pupillary constriction, in visual fatigue and discomfort and demonstrate relief by eliminating that mechanism with drugs.

In apparent partial contradiction to these studies, Heaton (1966) found that hyoscine, a mydriatic and blocker of ciliary muscle, did not relieve various complaints of pain with eyestrain. His main finding was that pain after administration of eserine, a miotic drug, was different but not greater nor less than that due to eyestrain.

d. Pupillary hippus as a sign of fatigue. Hippus, or random fluctuations in pupillary aperture, is a well known clinical phenomenon and, indeed, is present in all normal persons. Stark and colleagues (Stanten and Stark, 1966; Stark, 1959; Stark, 1968; Stark, Campbell, and Atwood, 1958; Usui and Stark, 1978) have considered hippus as central nervous system *noise* with low band-pass characteristics. The amplitude of hippus (and pupillary gain in general) is dependent upon the size of the pupil. It is highest at moderate pupil sizes and decreases for both large and small values.

In another study, Lowenstein and Loewenfeld (1952) showed a continually diminished responsiveness with fatigue, sleepiness, and boredom. Immediately after a sudden alerting stimulus, they obtained psychosensory dilation of the pupil and increased constriction response to a light flash. Irregular large amplitude hippus has long been associated with a vague list of ailments, and Lowenstein, Feinberg and Loewenfeld (1963) have related this large amplitude hippus to fatigue in a variety of clinical, normal, and abnormal settings. Again, they point to the possibility of immediate recovery either by instructions to the subject or by psychosensory stimuli; this immediate dishabituation suggests that the fatigue is habituation of central nervous system origin. Another factor is the interplay between parasympathetic (pupil constriction and accommodation) and sympathetic (pupil dilation and relaxation of accommodation) innervation in controlling both the smooth muscles of the iris and the ciliary mechanism.

e. Pupillary constriction as a sign of fatigue. The problem of pupil constriction as a sign of fatigue in a working environment has been approached by Geacintov and Peavler (1974). They showed significant pupillary diameter decrease over the day's work in operators using microfiche or telephone books. There is also a large and growing literature on pupillary constriction as indicative of work load vs. pupillary dilation as indicative of emotional interest or arousal. Remember again that pupillary constriction produces a larger depth of focus; a larger depth of focus permits the accommodative mechanism to work less in accommodating a near target or in alternating accommodation between near and far targets.

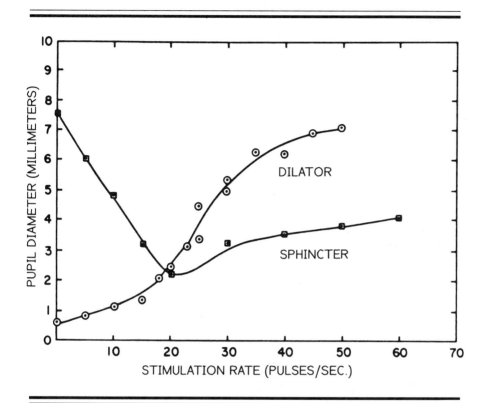

Figure G–20. Static characteristics of the isolated pupil motor system in cat produced by electrical stimulation of sympathetic (dilation) and parasympathetic (sphincter) final common pathways.

RECOMMENDATIONS

In order to diminish strain on accommodation, it is recommended that consideration be given to the distance and position of the VDT with respect to the range of accommodation and vergence. VDT position and position of room lighting each contribute to specular glare, which stimulates two quite different levels of accommodation and vergence. It is further recommended that "well-constructed" black characters on a white background be used to increase resolution and so reduce accommodative effort and that a terminal be used with good spectral match to vision, again for easy accommodation and reading eye movements, both of which depend upon foveal vision.

In order to aid in obtaining optimal size of the pupil, it is recommended that it be easy to adjust the terminal to optimize contrast and brightness and thus allow pupillary size to provide for adequate depth of focus and better resolution for accommodation and reading. (Opposing this concept is possible confusion in allowing the VDT operator too much flexibility.)

In order to help the *pupil* to adjust optimally, adaptive glare should also be reduced. This is feasible with black characters on a white background and by following the "1:3:9" rule, where 1 is the luminance of the black characters, 3 is the luminance of the white screen, and 9 the general room luminance lit by bright ceiling lamps or external window lighting. In order to reduce a direct fatiguing effect of pupillary oscillations or hippus, it will be required in the future to reduce flicker by using over 100 Hz refresh rates. Finally, one must consider the Helmholtz-Bridgeman effect of a saccade possibly accentuating the flicker effect by smearing it over the retina.

SUMMARY

Few clear conclusions result from this review of the literature on fatigue and ocular-motor function. Only the pupil oscillation experiments point to a specific phenomenon associated with fatigue; two independent, established investigative groups suggest that drugs paralyzing the pupil and stopping pupillary oscillations also minimize subjective feelings of fatigue.

The rest of the battery of ocular-motor tests—for accommodation, vergence, saccadic eye movements at several levels of integration, and blinking—all seem to reflect and confirm subjects' verbal reports of eye fatigue. It is important to note that an objective measure, i.e., recession of accommodative near point, may be seen as an objective finding of fatigue or may equally be interpreted as a sign of helpful *adaptation* to the task, whereby skill and practice allow effort to be minimized while still permitting adequate (perhaps even error-free) task performance to be maintained. We need to define fatigue and the motivationally controlled compensatory mechanism. Until then, our biomedical engineering apparatus may only confuse the issue. Dozens of papers, hundreds of experiments, and thousands of objective recordings throw a web of only tangential evidence on this confusing subject.

Perhaps quoting from the Miles Report, the National Research Council's *Conference on Visual Fatigue* will reassure us that we are at least no worse off than in 1939!

Socially we find ourselves on familiar territory in talking about this experience of visual fatigue but scientifically we seem to be lost in the woods... The subject of visual fatigue while remaining scientifically hazy and perhaps rather unattractive is forced on our attention by certain practical considerations... The general picture obtained from a battery of tests by being more comprehensive and sampling the performance of various types of eye mechanisms should provide the basis for later evaluation of the efficacy of individual tests. Experimentation in this field should not neglect the important datum of subjective reports and it must be remembered that motivation is a crucial element in most visual work that is continued for long periods of time. We cannot afford to neglect the fact that mental fatigue of the work detriment type seems from previous research to be mostly fatigue of the inner stimuli rather than of the physiological capacity to react.

NOTES

[1] Dr. Key Dismukes and his National Academy of Science committee have suggested the term "visual fatigue" be restricted to the subjective complaint. Even this should be detailed to enable fine distinctions such as ocular irritation vs. visual motor deficits. The task and operating condition that bring forth the subjective complaint should be stated and defined rather than loosely characterized as a "fatiguing situation." The reduced or failing performance of the individual should be defined as increase in error rate, decrease in speed, rather than be reported as a "fatigue response." The subjective nature of the motivation effect to combat the "subjective fatigue" should again be detailed and described as fully as possible.

[2] Professor Bruce Bridgeman, 1981: personal communication.

REFERENCES

Classification Code for Selected References

    I.   Definition of fatigue

    II.   Eye movement

    . b = blinking

    III.   Triad

    . a = accommodation

    . v = vergence

    . p = pupil

    IV.   Recommendations

    V.   Illumination and visual factors

    . f = flicker

    VI.   Ergonomics

*Additional references not cited in the paper.

Adler-Grinberg, D., and Stark L. 1978. Eye movements, scanpaths, and dyslexia. *American Journal of Optometry and Physiological Optics.* 55:557–70.

*Bagnara, S. 1980. Error detection at visual display units. In *Aspects of Visual Display Terminals*, eds. E. Grandjean and E. Vigliani, pp. 143–6. London: Taylor and Francis.

Bahill, A. T. R.; Ciuffreda, K. J.; Kenyon, R.; and Stark, L. 1976. Dynamic and static violations of Hering's law of equal innervation. *American Journal of Optometry and Physiological Optics* 53:786–96.

Bahill, A. T., and Stark, L. 1975. Overlapping saccades and glissades are produced by fatigue in the saccadic eye movement system. 00*Experimental Neurology* 48:95–106. II. Double saccadic components and mismatched saccadic components as signs of fatigue (habituation). Otherwise supports Dodge data on slowing and inaccuracy.

Baloh, R. W., and Honrubia, V. 1979. *Clinical neurophysiology of the vestibular system*. Philadelphia: F.A. Davis Co.

Bartley, S. H. 1942. A factor in visual fatigue. *Psychosomatic Medicine* 4:369–75. II. Maintenance of eccentric fixation with a difficult stimulus resulting in discomfort, blinking, and body postural shifts. Fatiguing complaints and eccentric fixation also reported in Zeevi et al., 1979. IIIp. Repetitive stimulation of pupil leading to uncomfortable and fatiguing complaints, especially at low rates of stimulation.

———. 1938. Subjective brightness in relation to flash rate and the light-dark ratio. *Journal of Experimental Psychology* 23:313–19.

*Bartley, S. H. 1976. Visual fatigue. In *Psychological aspects and physiological correlates of work and fatigue*, ed. E. Simonson and P. C. Weiser, Springfield, Ill.: Charles C. Thomas.

*————. 1947. The basis of visual fatigue. *American Journal of Optometry* 24:372–84.

*Bauer, D., and Cavonius, C. R. *Improving the legibility of visual display units through contrast reversal.* In press. IV. Evidence in favor of positive lettering.

Berens, C., and Sells, S. 1954. Experimental studies on fatigue of accommodation. I. *Archives Ophthalmology* 31:148–59. IIIa. Recession of near point. Monocular working eye loses more accommodation than synkinetically driven occluded eye, but this also loses accommodation.

*————. 1950. Experimental studies of fatigue of accommodation. II. *American Journal of Ophthalmology* 33:47–57. IIIa. Decrement in near point of accommodation following 30 min. of visual task in 57 motivated subjects. Refractive error, age, and phoria were not significant factors. Motivation may be an important factor.

Berens, C., and Stark, E. K. 1932. Studies in ocular fatigue. IV. Fatigue of accommodation, experimental and clinical observations. *American Journal of Ophthalmology* 15:527–42. IIIa.

*Bitterman, M. E., 1944. Fatigue defined as reduced efficiency. *American Journal of Psychology* 57:569–73. I.

————. 1945. Heart rate and frequency of blinking as indices of visual efficiency. *Journal of Experimental Psychology* 35:279–92. IIb.

————. 1947. Frequency of blinking in visual work: a reply to Dr. Luckiesh. *Journal of Experimental Psychology* 37:269–70. IIb.

Bitterman, M. E., and Soloway, E. 1946. Frequency of blinking as a measure of visual efficiency. Some methodological considerations. *American Journal of Psychology* 59:676–81. IIb.

*Bitterman, M. E.; Ryan, T. A.; and Cottrell, C. L. 1948. Muscular tension as an index of visual efficiency: a progress report. *Journal of the Illuminating Engineering Society* 43:1074–81. I. Controlled rate of work with measurement of general muscular tension.

*Bjorset, H. H., and Brekke, B. 1980. The concept of contrast. A short note and a proposal. In *Ergonomic Aspects of Visual Display Terminals*, ed. E. Grandjean, and E. Vigliani, pp. 23–24. London: Taylor and Francis.

Blatt, N. 1931. Weakness of accommodation. *Archives of Ophthalmology.* 62:362–73. IIIa.

*Blount, W. P. 1927. Studies of the movements of the eyelids of animals: blinking. *Quarterly Journal of Experimental Physiology* 18:111–25.

Borish, I. M. 1970. *Clinical refraction,* Vol. I. Chicago: The Professional Press, pp. 325–44.

Brozek, J.; Simonson, E.; and Keyes, A. 1950. Changes in performance and in ocular functions resulting from strenuous visual inspection. *American Journal of Psychology* 63:51–66. I. Subjects complained of difficulties in focusing. Letter recognition decreased and variability increased. II.

Confirm effects Dodge showed on eye movement although ophthalmological testing showed ADD actually improved. No change in blink rate. IIIv. Convergence near point reduced after 4 hours with poor illumination. Vf. Decreased flicker fusion rate.

Cameron, C. 1973. A theory of fatigue. *Ergonomics* 16:633–48. I. Review of performance measures of fatigue. Relates fatigue to sleep deprivation.

Carmichael, L. 1951–1952. Reading and visual work: a contribution to the technique of experimentation on human fatigue. *New York Academy of Science* 14:94–7. II. Little change in eye movement after 6 hr. reading.

Carmichael, L., and Dearborn, W. F. 1947. *Reading and visual fatigue.* New York: Houghton Mifflin.

Cobb, P. W., and Moss, F. K. 1925. Eye fatigue and its relation to light and work. *Journal of the Franklin Institute* 202:239–47. III. Muscle balance (phoria) changed during 30 minutes of visual task.

Coe, J. B.; Cuttle, K.; McClellan, W. C.; and Warden, N. J. 1980. Visual display units: a review of potential health problems associated with their use. Wellington, New Zealand: Regional Occupational Health Unit, New Zealand Department of Health.

*Collins, J. B., and Pruen, B. 1962. Perception time and visual fatigue. *Ergonomics* 5:533–8. V. A suggested measure of fatigue.

Dainoff, M. J. 1980. Occupational stress factors in video display terminal operation: a review of empirical research. Prepared for the Department of Health and Human Services Centers for Disease Control. I. Field assessment of fatigue related complaints.

*———. 1979. Occupational stress factors in secretarial/clerical workers. Cincinnati: U.S. Department of Health, Education and Welfare. pp. 1–55. I. Excellent review of occupational stress factors and large bibliography. Separate annotated bibliography.

*Dainoff, M. J.; Happ, A.; and Crane, P. 1980. Visual fatigue in VDT operators. *Proceedings of the Human Factors Society* 24:392–3. I. Visual fatigue and complaints not related to optometric state or to hostility to computers or to job pressures.

Demilia, L. 1968. Visual fatigue and reading. *Journal of Education* 151:4–34. II. Recent review by graduate student on factors in visual fatigue in reading, such as word perception, legibility, and typography.

*Department of the Army. 1979. Vision and eye effects of video display devices. I. Operator complaints.

*Dodge, R. 1917. The laws of relative fatigue. *Psychology Review* 24:890–113. I and II. Important paper with excellent measurements of eye movement showing accuracy and decreased coordination of eye movement. Also discusses problems of mental fatigue as not due to exhaustion.

*Dooley, A. 1980. CRT Radiation Not Harmful: NIOSH. *Computerworld* June:2.

*Doran, D. 1980. CRT-keyboard VDUs—implementing the solutions that already exist. In *Ergonomic Aspects of Visual Display Terminals*, ed. E. Grandjean and E. Vigliani, pp. 245–249. London: Taylor and Francis. IV.

*Ergonomics Society. 1978. An Edited Transcript of the One-Day Meeting on Eyestrain and VDUs. Mechanical Engineering Building, University of Technology, Loughborough, United Kingdom. December 15, pp. 1–58

Feldon, S. E.; Stark, L.; Lehman, S. L.; and Hoyt, W. F. 1982. Oculomotor effects of intermittent conduction block in myasthenia gravis and Fisher's syndrome: an oculographic study with computer simulations. *Archives of Neurology* 39:497–503.

*Ferguson, D. A.; Major, G.; and Keldoulis, T. 1974. Vision at work. Visual defect and the visual demand of tasks. *Applied Ergonomics* 5:84–93. I. Defects in vision interact with visual demands of tasks.

Fry, G. A., and King, V. M. 1975. The pupillary response and discomfort glare. *Journal of the Illuminating Engineering Society* 4:307–324.

Fugate, J. M., and Fry, G. A. 1956. Relation of changes in pupil size to visual discomfort. *Journal of the Illuminating Engineering Society* LI:537–49. IIIp. Contraction of iris or paralysis may result in good deal of discomfort which might account in part for discomfort of visual fatigue.

Geacintov, T., and Peavler, W. 1974. Pupillography industrial fatigue assessment. *Journal of Applied Psychology* 59:213–16. IIIp. Reduced pupillary diameter (.5 mm) during 3 hr. work period.

*Geldard, F. A. 1928. The measurement of retinal fatigue to achromatic stimulation. I. *Journal of General Psychology* 1:123–35. V.

*Gilet, A.; Grall, Y.; Keller, J.; and Vienot, P. A. 1978. Le Travail sur Terminal à Écran. (Work with VDTs.) Archives des Maladies Professionnelles, de Medecine du Travail et de Securité Sociale. 39:357–73.

*Gould, J. D. 1968. Visual factors in the design of computer-controlled CRT displays. *Human Factors* 10:359–73. IV. Recommendations with respect to VDT displays. II. Finger movement for fatigue performance assessment.

*Grandjean, E. 1970. Fatigue. *American Industrial Hygiene Association Journal* July-August:401–11. I. Physiological effects of fatigue related to neurophysiological theories.

*———. 1980. Ergonomics of VDUs: review of present knowledge. Department of Hygiene and Ergonomics, Swiss Federal Institute of Technology, CH–0092 Zurich, Switzerland.

*———. 1980. Ergonomics and medical aspects of VDU workplaces. *Displays* July:76–80.

*Grandjean, E.; Hunting, W.; and Laubli, T. H. 1980. Constrained postures of VDU operators. Department of Hygiene and Ergonomics, Swiss Federal Institute of Technology, Zurich, Switzerland.

*Grandjean, E., and Vigliani, E. 1980. *Ergonomic Aspects of Visual Display Terminals*. London: Taylor and Francis.

Gunnarsson, E., and Soderberg, I. 1980. *Eyestrain resulting from* VDT *work at the Swedish Telecommunications Administration. Eye changes and visual strain during various working procedures.* Stockholm, Sweden: National Board of Occupational Safety and Health.

*————. 1979. Work with visual display terminals (VDTs) in newspaper offices. A visual ergonomic survey. (Report 1979:21). Stockholm, Sweden: National Board of Occupational Safety and Health.

Haider, M.; Kundi, M.; and Weissenbock, M. 1980. Worker strain related to VDUs with differently coloured characters. In *Ergonomic Aspects of Visual Display Terminals*, ed. E. Grandjean and E. Vigliani, pp. 53–64, London: Taylor and Francis. V. Minute changes in accommodation suggested.

Halstead, W. C. 1941. A note on the Bartley effect in the estimation of equivalent brightness. *Journal of Experimental Psychology* 28:524–8. IIIp.

*Hamar, N., and Novak, E. 1971. A telemetric method for assessing mental performance. *Ergonomics* 14:120–35.

*Hartridge, H. 1947. Some fatigue effects on the human retina produced by using coloured lights. *Nature* 160:538–9. I. Sensory adaptation.

*Heaton, J. M. 1966. The pain in eyestrain. *American Journal of Ophthalmology* 61:104–12.

Helmholtz, H. 1867. *Handbuch der Physiologische Optik.* Leipzig:Leopold Voss.

Henn, V.; Cohen, B.; and Young, L. R., eds. 1980. Visual-vestibular interaction in motion perception and the generation of nystagmus. *Neurosciences Research Program Bulletin* 18:1-651.

Hofstetter, H. W. 1943. An ergographic analysis of fatigue of accommodation. *American Journal of Optometry* 20:115–35. IIIa.

Holland, M. K., and Tarlow, G. 1972. Blinking and mental load. *Psychology Reports* 31:119–27.

*Hultgren, G. V., and Knave, B. 1974. Discomfort glare and disturbance from light reflections in an office landscape with CRT display terminals. *Applied Ergonomics* 5:2–8. V. Discomfort glare and specular glare increase subjective complaints.

Hung, G.; Hsu, F.; and Stark, L. 1977. Dynamics of the human eyeblink. *American Journal of Optometry* 54:678–90.

*Jackson, E. 1921. Visual fatigue. *American Journal of Ophthalmology* 4:119–22.

*Johansson, G., and Aronsson, G. 1980. *Stress reactions in computerized administrative work.* Stockholm: University of Stockholm, pp. 5–47. VI.

Kenyon, R. V.; Ciuffreda, K. J.; and Stark, L. 1980. An unexpected role for normal accommodative vergence in strabismus and amblyopia. *American Journal of Optometry and Physiological Optics* 57:566–77.

King, V. M. 1972. Discomfort glare from flashing sources. *Journal of the American Optometry Association* 43:53–6.

———. 1976. Effects of mydriatics and a miotic on ocular discomfort and pupil responses. *Journal of the American Optometry Association* 47:937–42.

Kintz, R. T., and Bowker, D. O. 1981. Accommodation response during a prolonged visual search task. Preprint. IIIa. Results showing well known accommodation lag. DOF is determined by many factors such as pupillary diameter.

Koch, C., and Kurtz, J. I.1937. The general and ocular fatigue problem. *American Journal of Optometry* 14:273–80.

*———. 1937. The general and ocular fatigue problem—Part Two. *American Journal of Optometry* 14:308–17.

*———. 1938. An experimental study of ocular fatigue. *American Journal of Optometry* 15:86–117.

*Kolers, P. A.; Duchnicky, R. L.; and Ferguson, D. C. 1981. Eye movement measurement of readability of CRT displays. *Proceedings of the Human Factors Society* 23:517–27.

*Kravklov, S. V. 1974. The hygienic basis of standards of illumination. Types of visual fatigue. NASA-TT-F-16066, 1–15. I. Russian review of visual fatigue. Reduced constancy of vision over 4 hr. with close work. Increased blinking with poor lighting condition. Reference to Katz, 1895.

Kreuger, H. 1980. Ophthalmological aspects of work with display workstations. In *Ergonomic Aspects of Visual Display Terminals*, ed. E. Grandjean and E. Vigliani, pp. 31–40. London: Taylor and Francis.

Krishnan, V. V., and Stark, L. 1975. Integral control in accommodation. *Computer Programming in Biomedicine* 4:237–45.

Krishnan, V. V.; Shirachi, D.; and Stark, L. 1977. Dynamic measures of vergence accommodation. *American Journal of Optometry and Physiological Optics* 54:470–3.

Krivohlavy, J.; Kodat, V.; and Cizek, P. 1969. Visual efficiency and fatigue during the afternoon shift. *Ergonomics* 12:735–40. II and IIIa and v. Minor changes in accommodation and vergence and increased blink rate in small number of female machinists.

———. 1938. An experimental study of ocular fatigue. I. General Fatigue. *American Journal of Optometry* 15:86–117. IIIa. One out of 6 subjects with exophoria had reduced amplitude of accommodation. Ten percent showed reduced reading rate plus subjective complaints.

———. 1937. The general and ocular fatigue problem. Part One and Part Two. *American Journal of Optometry* 14:273, 308. IIIa.

*Lancaster, W. B., and Williams, E. R. 1914. New light on the theory of accommodation with practical applications. *Transactions of the American Academy of Ophthalmology* 19:170–95.

Laubli, T.; Hunting, W.; and Grandjean, E. 1980. Visual impairment in VDU operators related to environmental conditions. In *Ergonomic Aspects of*

Visual Display Terminals, ed. E. Grandjean and E. Vigliani, pp. 85–94. London: Taylor and Francis. I.

*Lion, K. 1952. Oculometric muscle forces and fatigue. *Journal of the Illuminating Engineering Society* 47:388–90. II.

Lion, K. S., and Brockhurst, R. J. 1951. Study of ocular movements under stress. *A.M.A. Archives of Ophthalmology* Sept.:315–18. II. Eye movements with fatigue retain fine structure but skip stimuli completely at times.

Liu, J.; Lee, M.; Jang, J.; Ciuffreda, K.; Wong, J.; Grisham, D.; and Stark, L. 1979. Objective assessment of accommodation orthoptics. I. Dynamic insufficiency. *American Journal of Optometry and Physiolological Optics* 56:285–94. IIIa. Dynamic insufficiency of accommodation treated successfully by exercise.

Lowenstein, O., and Loewenfeld, I. E. 1952. Disintegration of central autonomic regulation during fatigue and its reintegration by psychosensory controlling mechanisms. I. Disintegration. II. Reintegration. Pupillographic studies. *Journal of Nervous and Mental Disorders* 115:1–21, 121–145. IIIp.

Lowenstein, O.; Feinberg, R.; and Loewenfeld, I. E. 1963. Pupillary movements during acute and chronic fatigue. *Investigative Ophthalmology* 2:138–57. IIIp. Large pupillary hippus with tiredness and sleepiness. Pupillary constriction just before sleep.

*Lubart, N. D. 1980. Resolution model for a VDU-based person/machine interface: an overview. In *Ergonomic Aspects of Visual Display Terminals*, ed. E. Grandjean and E. Vigliani, pp. 25–30. London: Taylor and Francis.

Luckiesh, M. 1947. Reading and the rate of blinking. *Journal of Experimental Psychology* 37:266–8. IIb.

Luckiesh, M., and Moss, R. K. 1935a. Muscular tension resulting from glare. *Journal of General Psychology* 8:455–60. V. Early paper on glare.

———. 1935b. Fatigue of the extrinsic ocular muscles while reading under sodium and tungsten light. *Journal of the Optical Society* (American) 25:216–17. IIIv. Amplitude of convergence reduced 7% after reading for 1 hr at 5-fc.

*———. 1935c. Fatigue of convergence induced by reading as a function of illumination intensity. *American Journal of Ophthalmology* 18:319–23. IIIv, IV. Low illumination (1-fc) results in decreased amplitude of convergence.

*Maas, J. B.; Jayson, J. K.; and Kleiber, D. A. 1974. Effects of spectral differences in illumination on fatigue. *Journal of Applied Psychology* 59:524–6.

Mahto, R. S. 1972. Eyestrain from convergence insufficiency. *British Medical Journal* 2:564–565.

Malmstrom, F. V.; Randle, R. J.; Murphy, M. R.; Reed, L. E.; and Weber, R. J. 1981. Visual fatigue: the need for an integrated model. *Psychonomic*

Society Bulletin 17:183–6. II. Modest decrease in pursuit eye movement amplitude during a 6 min. tracking task following 2 hr. eye movement experiment. No phase difference. IIIa. Small decrease in accommodation amplitude over 6 min. period tracking task. Since subject knew what target was, there was no requirement for high quality focusing.

*Matula, R. A. 1981. Effects of visual display units on the eyes: a bibliography (1972, 1980). *Journal of the Human Factors Society* 23:581–6.

McDowell, E. D., and Rockwell, T. H. 1978. An exploratory investigation of the drivers' eye movements and their relationship to the roadway geometry. In *Eye Movements and the Higher Psychological Functions*, ed. J. W. Senders, D. F. Fisher, and R. A. Monty, pp. 329–345. New Jersey: Erlbaum Associates.

*Meyer, J. J.; Rey, P.; Korol, S.; and Gramoni, R. 1978. La fatigue oculaire engendrée par le travail sur écran. (Ocular fatigue produced by work with CRTs.) *Medecine Sociale et Preventive* 23:295–6.

Mourant, R. R.; Lakshmanan, R.; and Chantadisai, R. 1981. Visual fatigue and cathode ray tube display terminals. *Journal of the Human Factors Society* 23:529–40.

*Muscio, B. 1921. Is a fatigue test possible? *Journal of Psychology* 12:31–46. I. Critical cryptic comment on fatigue.

National Research Council. 1939. *Conference on visual fatigue.* Walter R. Miles, presiding, and A. Ames, Jr., A. Bielshowsky, P. W. Cobb, W. F. Dearborn, D. B. Dill, C. H. Graham, S. Hecht, H. M. Johnson, R. A. McFarland, F. K. Moss, P. G. Nutting, B. O'Brian, I. Stewart, G. Wald attending, May 20–21, 1939.

Newspaper Guild and International Typographical Union, The. 1981. *Humanizing the VDT workplace.*

Noton, D., and Stark, L. 1971a. Scanpaths in eye movements during pattern perception. *Science* 171, 308–311.

——— . 1971b. Eye movements and visual perception. *Scientific American* 224:34–43.

——— . 1971c. Scanpaths in saccadic eye movements while viewing and recognizing patterns. *Vision Research* 11:929–42.

*Ohtani, A. 1971. An analysis of eye movements during a visual task. *Ergonomics* 14:167–74. II. Saccadic latencies with visual task show increase in short involuntary saccades.

O'Neill, W. D., and Stark, L. 1968. Triple function ocular monitor. *Journal of the Optical Society* (American) 58:570–3.

——— . 1980. Accommodation and visual fatigue in display work. In *Ergonomic Aspects of Visual Display Terminals*, ed. E. Grandjean and E. Vigliani, pp. 41–52. London: Taylor and Francis. IIIa.

Pavlides, G. T. 1981. Sequencing, eye movements and the early objective diagnosis of dyslexia. In *Dyslexia Research and Its Applications to Education*, ed. G. T. Pavlides, and T. R. Miles, pp. 99–163. Chichester, UK: John Wiley and Sons.

Phillips, S., and Stark, L. 1977. Blur: a sufficient accommodative stimulus. *Documenta Ophthalmologica* 43:65–89.

*Rados, B. 1981. VDTs—Pass medical tests. *FDA Consumer* April:11–13.

*Radl, G. W. 1980. Experimental investigations for optimal presentation-mode and colours of symbols on the CRT-screen. In *Ergonomic Aspects of Visual Display Terminals*, ed. E. Grandjean and E. Vigliani, pp. 127–135. London: Taylor and Francis. IV. Experiments to improve video screen display of information suggests "framing" helps performance. Dark characters and colored symbols bring an advantage but multicolored displays may cause problems.

Rashbass, C. 1959. Barbiturate nystagmus and the mechanisms of visual fixation. *Nature* 183:897–8.

Raynor, K. 1978. Eye movements in reading and information processing. *Psychology Bulletin* 85:618–60.

*Rey, P., and Meyer, J. J. 1980. Visual impairments and their objective correlates. In *Ergonomic Aspects of Visual Display Terminals*, ed. E. Grandjean and E. Vigliani, pp. 77–83. London: Taylor and Francis. I.

*Rupp, B. A. 1978. Human factors of workstations with display terminals. IBM Tech. Report 6320-6102-0, May 1978.

*Saito, M.; Tanaka, T.; and Oshima, M. 1981. Eyestrain in inspection and clerical workers. *Ergonomics* 3:161–73. IIIa. Minimal changes in flicker fusion in clerical and inspection workers.

Saladin, J. J., and Stark, L. 1975. Presbyopia: new evidence from impedance cyclography supporting the Hess-Gullstrand theory. *Vision Research* 15:537–41.

*Seppala, P. 1975. Visual fatigue in reading microfilm. *Agressologie* 16:147–50. IV. Evidence and support for black lettered (positive) microfiche.

Shirachi, D.; Liu, J.; Lee, M.; Jang, J.; Wong, J.; and Stark, L. 1978. Accommodation dynamics: 1. Range nonlinearity. *American Journal of Physiology* 55:631–41.

Simmerman, H. 1950. Visual fatigue. *American Journal of Optometry* 27:554–61. I. Raises question of subclinical visual impairment related to fatigue.

*Simonson, E., and Brozek, J. 1948a. The effect of spectral quality of light on visual performance and fatigue. *Journal of the Optical Society* (American) 38:830–40. V. Greenish coating appeared to be optimal with a battery of tests.

*———. 1948b. Effects of illumination level on visual performance and fatigue. *Journal of the Optical Sociecty* (American) 38:384–97. V. Optimum level 100 fc. established by a battery of tests.

*Smith, M. J.; Cohen, B. G. F.; and Stammerjohn, L. W. 1981. An investigation of health complaints and job stress in video display operations.

Journal of the Human Factors Society 23:387–400. I. Field assessment of visual fatigue.

Smith, W. J. 1979. A review of literature relating to visual fatigue. *Proceedings of the Human Factors Society.* 23rd Annual Meeting, pp. 362–6.

Stanten, S. F., and Stark, L. 1966. A statistical analysis of pupil noise. *IEEE Transactions in Biomedical Engineering* 13:140–52.

Stark, L. 1959. Stability, oscillations, and noise in the human pupil servomechanism. *Proceedings of the Institute of Radio Engineering* 47:1925–39.

———. 1968. *Neurological control systems: studies in bioengineering.* New York: Plenum Press.

Stark, L., and Ellis, S. R. 1981. Scanpaths revisited: cognitive models direct active looking. In *Eye Movements, Cognition and Visual Perception,* ed. D.F. Fisher, R.A. Monty, and J.W. Sanders, pp. 193–226. New Jersey: Erlbaum Press.

Stark, L.; Campbell, F. W.; and Atwood, J. 1958. Pupil unrest: an example of noise in a biological servomechanism. *Nature* 182:857–8.

Stark, L.; Vossius, G.; and Young, L. R. 1962. Predictive control of eye tracking movements. *IRE Transactions on Human Factors in Electronics* HFE-3, pp. 52–7.

Tinker, M. A. 1939. The effect of illumination intensities upon speed of perception and upon fatigue in reading. *Journal of Educational Psychology* 30:561–71. II.

Tinker, M. A., and Paterson, D. G. 1939. Influence of type form on eye movements. *Journal of Experimental Psychology* 25:528–31. II.

Tomizuka, M., and Rosenthal, D. E. 1979. On the optimal digital state vector feedback controller with integral and preview actions. *Transactions of ASME* 101:172–8.

Troelstra, A. 1968. Detection of time-varying light signals as measured by the pupillary response. *Journal of the Optical Society* (American) 58:685–90.

*Turnage, R. E. Jr. 1966. The perception of flicker in cathode ray tube displays. *Information Display* May/June:38–52. Vf. Phosphor persistence could reduce flicker.

Usui, S., and Stark, L. 1978. Sensory and motor mechanisms interact to control amplitude of pupil noise. *Vision Research* 18:505–7.

*U.S. Army Environmental Hygiene Agency. 1979. Vision and eye effects of video display devices. Aberdeen Proving Ground, Maryland, Department of the Army.

Vaithilingam, E., and Khare, B. B. 1967. Ocular headache and the optometrist. *Journal of the American Optometric Association* 38:477–9.

Weber, R. A. 1950. Ocular fatigue. *Archives of Ophthalmology* 43:257–64. IIIa.

Westheimer, G. 1963. Amphetamine, barbiturates and accommodation vergence. *A.M.A. Archives of Ophthalmology* 70:830–6.

Westheimer, G., and Rashbass, C. 1961. Barbiturates and eye vergence. *Nature* 191:833–4.

*Weston, H. C. 1953. Visual fatigue, with spectral reference to lighting. *Transactions of the Illuminating Engineering Society* (London) 18:2:39–66.

Whiteside, T. C. D. 1957. *The problems of vision in flight at high altitude.* London: Pergamon Press.

*Wilkins, A. J. 1978. Epileptogenic attributes of TV and VDUs. In *Proceedings on Eyestrain and VDUs.* Loughborough, UK: Loughborough University.

Wilson, V. J., and Melville-Jones, G. 1979. *Mammalian vestibular physiology.* New York: Plenum Press.

Wood, C. L., and Bitterman, M. E. 1950. Blinking as a measure of effort in visual work. *American Journal of Psychology* 63:584–8.

Yarbus, A. L. 1967. *Eye movements and vision.* New York: Plenum Press.

Young, L. R., and Stark, L. 1963. Variable feedback experiments testing a sampled data model for eye tracking movements. *IEEE Transactions on Human Factors in Electronics* HFE-4, pp. 38–51.

*Zeevi, Y. Y.; Peli, E.; and Stark, L. 1979. Study of eccentric fixation with secondary visual feedback. *Journal of the Optical Society* (American) 69:669–675.

*Zuber, B. L. 1980. *Models of oculomotor behavior and control.* Boca Raton, Florida: CRC Press.

HEALTH CONSIDERATIONS AT THE INFORMATION WORKPLACE

O. Bruce Dickerson

and Walter E. Baker

INTRODUCTION

In the many activities involved in what *Business Week* (June 30, 1980) calls the "reindustrialization" of the United States, and in various labor management negotiations and discussions, three key issues seem to be involved: worker satisfaction, worker health and safety, and worker productivity. These three issues taken together are sometimes called QWL, or quality of work life (Mills, 1975). Behavioral science developed in the United States in the thirties has provided the basis for this approach. People like Mayo, MacGregor, Hertzberg, Bennis, Likert, and others (Rush, 1969) have developed a theoretical background for establishing ways of improving and managing worker satisfaction, health and safety, and productivity. This process is often called work redesign (Rush, 1971; McCormick, 1979).

Information systems provide a means of enhancing human capability and redesigning work, and will affect many jobs (Norman, 1981). The tool used to interface with and control those systems today is predominantly the visual display terminal (VDT). It is projected that by 1986 one in every ten workers will be using a VDT (Branscomb, 1982). Moreover, VDTs are becoming common in the home as the TV screen is extended to include information systems, video recording, games, and home computing.

A number of observational studies have purported to identify health problems related to visual display terminals (Dainoff, 1981; Dainoff, Happ, and

Crane, 1981; Grandjean and Vigliani, 1980; Smith, Cohen, and Stammerjohn, 1981). These studies have dealt with complaints related to eyestrain, musculo-skeletal dysfunction, and even psychological trauma. Most reports are based on subjective responses to questionnaires concerning perceived health effects from use of a VDT. In general, such studies suffer from problems intrinsic to observational research; i.e., confounding and multivariant analyses are often not properly taken into account. When studies are properly designed, the VDT may be found merely to be a surrogate for, or correlate of, some other underlying factor, such as workplace lighting, constrained postures, or poor task design.

This is not to say that people do not find working with a terminal different from other jobs using more traditional methods of data communication. But, we have yet to establish a scientific basis for many of the conjectures that have been made regarding introduction of terminals into the workplace.

INTERACTIVE MODEL

To understand human factors relating to any job, we believe it imperative to understand the relationship between the tool, the workstation and environment, and the task. Let us look at two examples to define and demonstrate these relationships.

In a human factors model of an assembly task, the tools consist of power and hand tools—power driven screw drivers and wrenches, and hand assembly tools. The workstation is the workbench, the parts bins, the assembly gimbal, and the location itself as defined in terms of heat, light, and other comfort requirements. The task is the job to be done—the application.

Let us now look at the visual display workstation. The tools are the screen and the keyboard. The workstation and environment are the table or desk on which these tools are placed, the chair on which the operator sits, and the location itself as defined in terms of appropriate lighting, heating, and other requirements. The tasks may range from sophisticated programming analysis to routine data entry. In the model we propose, several factors need to be considered in each of the three areas (Fig. H–1).

In our assembly task example, among other factors we need to consider are the biomechanical aspects of the hand tool—grip, weight, body and arm position, and movement. In the case of the VDT—since it is vision that plays the key role—the physical characteristics of the display itself will determine whether visual information is presented in such a way as to avoid visual strain. In the keyboard, we need to consider characteristics that will generate appropriate tactile feel and feedback.

If we look at the assembly workstation, there are biomechanical requirements to be satisfied there also, e.g., the position of the parts bins, movements required, and physiological effects therefrom. There are also anthropometrical requirements: Does the chair fit and satisfy the requirements of the user?

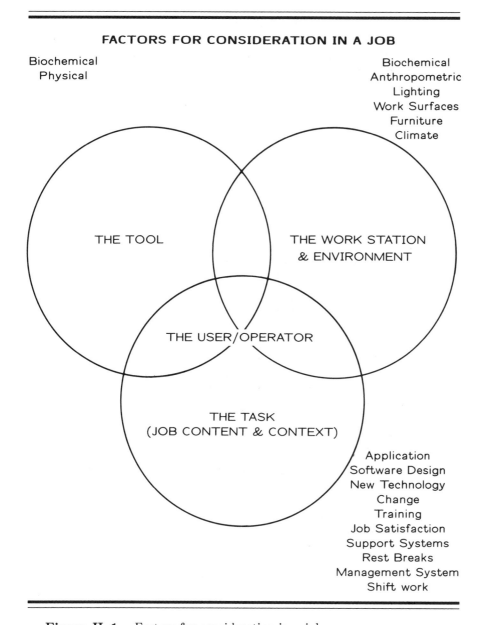

Figure H–1. Factors for consideration in a job.

(Since people have different shapes and requirements, the chair should usually be adjustable to satisfy the individual.) Are the work surfaces positioned appropriately so that the body is in a comfortable, less strained position? Then there are the environmental conditions of the workplace, such as lighting, noise, space, and climate.

In any task, both job content and job context are important. With regard to job content, several factors contribute to satisfaction and motivation, e.g., skill variety required, the identity of the task and its significance, the autonomy given to the operator, feedback, challenge, and opportunity—factors that help make the job itself challenging and meaningful (Hackman and Oldham, 1975). Job context includes management support systems, opportunity for socialization vs. isolation, training and worker participation in change, etc. (Myers, 1970; Walton, 1974; Sayls and Strauss, 1981). The combination of job content and context factors relate to psychological and psychosocial health. A satisfied and motivated worker is more likely to be a healthy, safe, and productive worker (Steers and Porter, 1979, pp. 392-410). For this reason, the application of these principles to the workplace interests health and safety professionals.

All areas of occupational safety and health have certain factors in common. Thus, to achieve appropriate levels of occupational safety and health in industry, three distinct participants share responsibility: the provider of equipment (the manufacturer), the employer, and the employee operating the equipment. To assure proper health and safety on the job, all three must fulfill appropriate roles with interdependent responsibilities.

Manufacturers should consider the ergonomic requirements of the equipment they provide. For example, are the tools biomechanically designed for ease of use, minimizing physiological stress? Are the anthropometric characteristics suitable? In the case of the VDT screen, the equipment should provide proper symbol legibility, image stability, and absence of flicker.

The employer plays a key role in establishing the workstation and its environment. Is the ambient lighting sufficient? Are reflections from work surfaces, walls, ceilings, and floors controlled to provide comfortable viewing? Are musculo-skeletal requirements taken into account? (A well-designed chair is one of the most important parts of any workstation, whether it is at a desk, a terminal, or an assembly bench.)

The employer also has a key role in designing the task. New tools must be comfortably integrated into the organization by properly educating the operator. In any job, a natural link exists between the nature of the job and operator satisfaction. Employee acceptance of the new tool and familiarization with the task are important in this process.

Finally, utilizing the adjustments built into the tool and the workstation enhances the operator's role. In true participatory manner, the employees can provide input as to their needs in order to perform effectively and well.

STRESS

Stress is a normal human condition that provides motivation for many human activities; to some degree it is essential for well-being. There are, however, many stressors in life. The American Academy of Family Physicians reported a study of six different office occupations in which two-thirds of the clerical workers polled described their work as unusually or always stressful. Most of the tasks did not involve VDTs.

Holmes and Rahe (Holmes and Rahe, 1967, pp. 213–18; Rahe, 1972) identified the 43 most stressful changes that might occur in a person's life, and found it possible to predict the subsequent health of those assessed. Included on that list are job security, job change, job responsibility, and management structure.

The Institute of Medicine of the National Academy of Sciences conducted the most recent extensive study of stress and health, concluding that individuals who experience a wide variety of stressful events or situations are at an increased health risk. Such events and situations in the work environment include responsibility, work load, security, change, and interpersonal or role conflicts. Any study, then, to assess the health effects of tools, workstations, and their environments must recognize the effect of these stress factors.

FACTORS INVOLVED

Radiation

All electronic devices are capable of producing electromagnetic radiation. Studies conducted by scientists at a number of universities and research laboratories (Wolbarsht and Sliney, 1980; Petersen, Weiss, and Minneci, 1980; Weiss and Petersen, 1979) and by NIOSH (Pub. No. 81-129,) and BRH (Pub. No. 81-8153) show that for most VDTs—even under worst case conditions—the electromagnetic ionizing and nonionizing radiation emissions are several orders of magnitude below the safety levels accepted worldwide (Fig. H–2.) Additionally, many systems are designed to fail if the high voltage increases significantly, and in all machines such an occurrence would cause the image to be so distorted as to render the device unusable. There are no known deleterious biological effects from electromagnetic radiation associated with VDTs.

Lighting

One of the key factors in the workstation environment is lighting. A number of scientists (King, 1981; Sauter, Gottlieb, and Jones, 1982; Smith, et al., 1982) have all identified lighting as the chief source of visual complaints. Reflective glare from the VDT surface may make the image more difficult to read, and in some cases the user may have to assume an awkward position to avoid the glare. Glare can be significantly reduced by installing VDTs at right angles to windows and other light sources, by providing drapes or blinds, and by informing employees about their use (Rush, 1969). Glare from overhead lighting can best be reduced by installing parabolic louvers that have the effect

Type of Radiation	Level of Radiation Emitted by IBM Terminals
Gamma and x-ray	Six one-thousandths of safety level
Ultra-violet	One one-thousandth of safety level
Visible	One one-thousandth of safety level
Infrared	One one-thousandth of safety level
Micro-wave	One billionth of safety level
Radio frequency	At most, one ten-thousandth of safety level

Figure H–2.   Safety factors in VDT emission.

of directing light vertically downward and minimizing the glare produced by horizontal light (Fig. H–3).

Much discussion has been devoted to absolute light levels—a factor which is application and user dependent. Individuals have different preferences for light levels. One way of meeting these differing requirements is through reduced ambient lighting, coupled with individually adjustable task lighting to allow maximum flexibility.

Posture

Specially designed terminal furniture (Fig. H–4) enables the user to adjust the height of the screen and the keyboard to suit individual posture (Fig. H–5). This solution best suits those employees who use a terminal for long

RECOMMENDED POSITIONING

Windows	Overhead Lighting
Terminal screens viewed parallel to windows.	Terminal screens viewed parallel to, and between, overhead lights.

Figure H–3. Recommended positioning of windows and overhead lights.

periods of time. The chair should also be designed to accommodate individual differences. A chair can favorably affect posture, leg circulation, and the amount of pressure on the spine; hence, ideally it should be adjustable to allow for differences in operators' height and build. Such features as an adjustable backrest, swivel base, cushioned seat pads, backrests, and footrests are also desirable. However, it is equally important that users be trained in the use of such flexible furniture and adjustments built into the terminals.

Efforts are continuing to define specific dimensions with regard to the terminal table. Grandjean states that his recent results concerning work heights were a surprise to him, since they did not correspond to the actual ergonomic recommendations he and others had made in 1979 and 1980 (Hunting, Laubli, and Grandjean, 1981, pp. 917–31). Obviously, setting standards before scientific evidence is complete can be premature. (Grandjean is extending his study to include musculo-skeletal physiological measurements while performing VDT tasks.)

Figure H–4.   Specially designed terminal furniture.

Rest Breaks

In most tasks, natural breaks or pauses occur as a consequence of the inherent organization of the work and help to maintain performance by preventing the onset of fatigue. In some tasks, such naturally occurring breaks are less frequent. Certain data entry jobs, for example, require continuous and sustained attention and concentration, together with high data entry rates. In situations where this type of task cannot be organized in another way, and where natural breaks do not occur, rest pauses may help to maintain work attention and concentration.

The validity of this approach has been supported by the Swedish Telecommunication Administration research, which concluded that visual strain is more frequently observed among those whose work was highly structured, inflexible, and performed under conditions of stress (Gunnarsson and

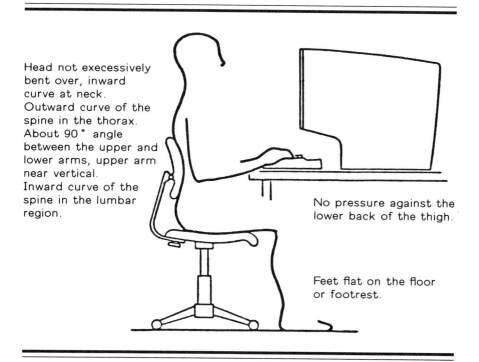

Head not execessively bent over, inward curve at neck.
Outward curve of the spine in the thorax.
About 90 ° angle between the upper and lower arms, upper arm near vertical.
Inward curve of the spine in the lumbar region.

No pressure against the lower back of the thigh.

Feet flat on the floor or footrest.

Figure H–5.   Posture.

Soderberg, 1980). Of two groups, one took informal breaks and reported a lower visual strain than did the other group. We feel it difficult to specify the optimum length of a rest pause. Strictly prescribed rest pauses will often be found to be unnecessary, prolonged, and frustrating for some, and of insufficient length to prevent the onset of fatigue for others. The most satisfactory length of the pause can best be determined by consideration of the individual user and his or her job.

In Europe, researchers have discussed the maximum lengths of time a user should work at a terminal—a question which we feel is dependent on the specific job. Setting time limits is premature; however, sensible use of such concepts as rotating jobs and building job satisfaction into the task should prevent problems from occurring.

Visual Tasks

While VDT users can experience symptoms of visual fatigue, this is not a new phenomenon, nor is it confined to VDT work exclusively. Many industrial and clerical tasks make similar visual demands upon the individual in terms of difficulty and duration. Some improperly corrected impairments in visual acuity can contribute to visual fatigue, and individuals who transfer into a more visually-demanding task may be more aware of such visual problems. In such cases, corrections should be made to meet the specific requirements of the task.

The final report of the NIOSH West Coast study concludes that job-related factors contribute to health complaints (Smith, Cohen, and Stammerjohn, 1981, pp. 387–400), and an extensive study involving factorial analysis by A. Smith, et al. (1982) found that job attitudes associated with VDT work are characteristic of the job rather than the VDT itself.

A comprehensive study by Sauter at the University of Wisconsin includes multivariant analysis to see if group differences in health complaints disappeared when group differences in reported job demands were controlled statistically (Sauter, Gottlieb, and Jones, 1982). Sauter has reported that his study found no evidence of health problems specifically associated with VDT use. Rather, eye complaints were largely the result of improper lighting conditions.

VDT and Other Tasks

In looking at VDT tasks, we know that every VDT application will require different consideration. Bertinuson (1981) has defined at least five different categories of VDT use, each varied as to eye use, postural need, and type of worker involvement. The studies of Laubli, Hunting, and Grandjean (1981, pp. 933–44) indicate that VDT data entry tasks cause more health complaints than other VDT tasks, which have about the same level of complaints as typing tasks. This should come as no surprise, since from the very first days of keypunches, data entry tasks resulted in health complaints associated with repetitive motion tasks. Some countries, in fact, passed legislation limiting the number of keystrokes permitted an employee per day. Similar problems have been reported among telegraphic operators in Australia because the usual keyboard layout entailed constrained posture which could lead to impairments of the locomotor system.

There does not seem to be a good, properly controlled study that compares a job done with a VDT and an identical job done with hard copy. Gould is currently conducting a study in which subjects perform the same proofreading task using a VDT and then hard copy (Gould and Grischkowsky, 1982). Participants complete the questionnaire giving their opinions of any health effects, and these subjective measurements are related to objective measurements of their visual performance. Such measurements as contrast sensitivity—a more comprehensive measure of acuity than the standard Snellen test—are being used.

Vision

As Rogowitz (1982) pointed out, the human visual system is a collection of interacting subsystems. Their complete understanding requires the disciplines of psychophysics and neurophysiology. Many of the VDT studies erroneously assume that a minor change in visual distance must be accompanied by a change in accommodation before comfortable viewing is obtained, and, if this is not achieved, stress results. However, the depth of field of the eye is nearly two diopters (Hamasaki, 1956; Campbell, et al., 1979, p. 145; Young, 1977). Much of the work on adaptation and VDTs has been limited to pupillary response and photopigment bleaching. Both of these, however, are relatively unimportant at the light levels in VDTs. Moreover, photopigment bleaching is not the controlling mechanism for retinal sensitivity, as has been shown by the work on neural adaptation (Barlow and Andrews, 1973; Macleod, 1978; Werblin and Copenhagen, 1974, pp. 88–110; Werblin, 1973, p. 228/1; Ratcliff, 1972, p. 226/6).

One area requiring more study is the relationship between the actual temporal modulation of the image—which may or may not be perceived as flicker—and health. New tests to quantify perceived flicker are being considered, which might become the future standard for comparative studies. Rogowitz is currently investigating the interaction and effects of temporal and spatial variants important in computer generated displays (IBM Doc. No. G320-6102-1, 2nd ed.).

At this time we do not describe and evaluate the necessity of the visual skills needed for a particular job; visual screening programs for all visually-demanding tasks might be considered.

ONE COMPANY'S PERSPECTIVE

IBM has long recognized the importance of the individual in the organizational system, and training and development programs for managers emphasize that principle.

Ergonomics Management Development Module

Ergonomics is an important aspect of a manager's role, and the application of its principles to workplace design can increase productivity and improve work quality, health, safety, and job satisfaction. The module, made available to all managers, consists of a 16–minute video describing some ergonomic principles in terms of applications already in place in specific IBM plant and office locations, a presenter's guide to assist in the presentation of and follow-up to the video, and an 80-page ergonomics handbook that describes in relatively elementary terms the concepts involved in ergonomic design.

Two types of training courses are offered: a three-day session for engineering personnel specifically tailored to application for each location, and a five-day session for health and safety professionals. The program has already produced measurable positive effects in specific cases; however, we seek to achieve long-term effects, in which all designers consider the human/machine interface as a matter of course.

VDT Installation

The basic principles of VDT installation that need to be considered for optimum human/machine interface conditions are well documented but not well perceived. A condensed version, "Ergonomics and Visual Display Terminals—A Guide for Managers" has been issued for use by all managers with employees using VDTs. The 13–page booklet addresses the ergonomic and environmental factors of posture, lighting, visual fatigue, and workstation design, together with other factors such as work design, training, and rest breaks. Internal "Question and Answer" packages are also available to managers as required.

Employees with, or needing, corrective eyeglasses in many visual tasks may find that they need to adopt uncomfortable postures in order to view their work satisfactorily. These individuals may need modifications either in their eyeglass prescriptions or in their eyeglass structure. Employees requiring such modifications are provided with them as part of the safety and special eyeglass program.

Medical Programs

Medical programs vary slightly at IBM locations around the world owing to varying customs, laws, and practices. In some countries annual medical examinations are legally required. In the U.S., employees over age 35 participate in a voluntary health screening program every five years. Jobs determined to present some hazard to employees have more frequently required medical exams and are monitored regularly by industrial hygienists. Any employee, of any age, with a work-related complaint, whether musculo-skeletal in nature, attributable to improper posture, or vision-related, receives appropriate medical evaluation. All plant, laboratory, and major administrative locations have staffed medical facilities. Smaller locations have contracted medical services coordinated by IBM area medical directors.

SUMMARY

All applications of any tool, particularly of a new technology, need to take certain factors into account. In the case of VDTs, these include:

- Proper attention paid to the individual physiological and anthropometric requirements in workplace design, particularly if the VDT is used over prolonged periods.
- Design of the task to recognize the employee's needs for job challenge, control, and feedback.
- Careful introduction of changes in both the way the task is performed and the physical layout of the workstation, with the cooperation and

training of those affected and comfortable integration of such changes into the organization.

- Recognition that the new information systems affect the behavior of both individuals and organizations, in that they change both values and structural relationships (Keen, 1981, pp. 24-33).
- Recognition of the new systems as providing a positive addition to, and extension of, our human capability.

REFERENCES

Anon. Idndustrialization of America. *Business Week.* June 30, 1980.

Barlow, H. B., and Andrews, D. P. 1973. The site at which rhodopsin bleaching raises the scotopic threshold. *Vision Research* 43:903–8.

Bertinuson, J. 1981. Job design and organizational aspects. In *VDTs and vision of workers symposium.* Proceedings of the National Academy of Sciences. Washington, D.C.

Branscomb, L. 1982. Bringing computing to people—the broadening challenge. *Computer* 15:68–75.

Campbell, F. W., et al. 1979. Fluctuations of accommodation under steady viewing conditions. *Journal of Physiology* 145:579–94.

Canadian Council on Working Life and the International Council for the Quality of Working Life. 1981. QWL and the 80s. *An International Conference on the Quality of Working Life.* Toronto. 1981.

Dainoff, M. 1981. A review of research on visual effects of VDT use. In *VDTs and Vision of Workers.* Proceedings of the National Academy of Sciences Symposium. Washington, D.C.

Dainoff, M. J.; Happ A.; and Crane, P. 1981. Visual fatigue and occupational stress in VDT operators. *Human Factors* 23:421–38.

Gould, J., and Grischkowsky, N. 1982. Doing the same work with hard copy and computer terminals. In *Proceedings of the Human Factors Society 26th Annual Meeting.* Seattle, WA.

Grandjean, E., and Vigliani, E., eds. 1980. *Ergonomic aspects of visual display terminals.* Proceedings of the International Workshop. Milan: Taylor and Francis.

Gunnarsson, E., and Soderberg, I. 1980. *Eyestrain resulting from VDT work at the Swedish Telecommunications Administration.* Stockholm, Sweden: National Board of Occupational Safety and Health.

Hackman, J. R., and Oldham, G. R. 1975. Development of the job diagnostic survey. *Journal of Applied Psychology* 60:159–70.

Hamasaki, D. 1956. Amplitude of accommodation in presbyopia. *American Journal of Optometry* 33:3–14.

Hamrin, R. D. 1981. *The information revolution: changing employment trends in the information society.* Adherent.

Holmes, T. H., and Rahe, R. H. 1967. The social readjustment rating scale. *Journal of Psychosomatic Research* 2:213–18.

Hunting, W., Laubli, T. L., and Grandjean, E. 1981. Postural and visual loads at VDT workplaces I: constrained postures. *Ergonomics* 24:917–31.

International Business Machines (IBM). 1979. *Human factors of workstations with display terminals.* IBM document no. G320–6102–1, 2nd ed. IBM Corp, White Plains, N. Y.

Keen, P. G. W. 1981. Information systems and organizational change. *Communications of the ACM* 24:1:24–33.

King, V. 1981. Aspects of lighting and reflection. In *VDTs and vision of workers symposium*. Proceedings of the National Academy of Sciences. Washington, D.C.

Laubli, T. L., Hunting W., and Grandjean, E. 1981. Postural and visual loads at VDT workplaces II: lighting conditions and visual impairment. *Ergonomics* 24:933–44.

Macleod, D. I. A. 1978. Visual sensitivity. *Annual Review of Psychology* 29:613–45.

McCormick, E. J. 1979. *Job analysis: methods and applications*. American Management Association, New York.

Mills, T. 1975. Human resources—why the new concern? *Harvard Business Review* 53:120–34.

Myers, M. S. 1970. *Every employee a manager*. New York: McGraw–Hill.

National Academy of Sciences Institute of Medicine. 1981. *Research on stress and human health*. Publication no. 10M 81–05. Washington, D.C.: National Academy Press.

Norman, C. 1981. The new industrial revolution. *The Futurist*. February 1981.

Petersen, R. C. M.; Weiss, M.; and Minneci, G. 1980. *Nonionizing electromagnetic radiation associated with video display terminals*. Society of Photo–Optical Instrumentation Engineers (SPIE). Bellingham, Washington.

Rahe, R. H. 1972. Subjects' recent life changes and their near–future susceptibility. *Advances in Psychosomatic Medicine*, vol. 8: Psychosocial Aspects of Physical Illness, ed. Z. J. Lipowski. Basel, Switzerland. Skanger.

Ratliff, F. 1972. Contour and control. *Scientific American* 226/6:91–101.

Rogowitz, B. E. 1982. *The final interface—the human visual system*. Proceedings of the SID Seminar. San Diego.

Rush, H. M. F. 1969. *Behavioral science, concepts, and management applications*. The Conference Board. New York.

―――. 1971. *Job design for motivation*. The Conference Board. New York.

Sauter, S. L.; Gottlieb, M. S.; Jones, K. C.; Dodson, V. N.; and Rohver, K. M. 1983. Job and health implications of VDT use. *Communications of the ACM* 26:284–92.

Sayls, L. R., and Strauss, G. 1981. *Managing human resources*. Englewood Cliffs, New Jersey: Prentice-Hall.

Smith, A. B.; Tanaka, S.; Halperin, W.; and Richards, R. D. 1982. *Cross-sectional survey of VDT users at the Baltimore Sun*.

Smith, M. J.; Cohen, B. G. F.; and Stammerjohn, L. W., Jr.   1981a. An investigation of health complaints and job stress in video display operators. *Human Factors* 23:387–400.

——— . 1981b. Evaluation of workstation design factors in VDT operations. Ibid. 23:401–12.

Steers, R. W., and Porter, L. W. 1979. *Motivation and work behavior.* New York: McGraw-Hill.

U.S. Department of Health and Human Services (NIOSH). 1981. *Potential health hazards of video display terminals.* Publication no. 81–129. Washington, D.C.

U.S. Department of Health and Human Services (NIOSH). 1981. *An evaluation of radiation emission from video display terminals.* Bureau of Radiological Health. Publication no. 81–8153. Washington, D.C.

Walton, R. E. 1974. Innovation restructuring of work. *The Worker and the Job*, ed. J. M. Rossow. Englewood Cliffs, New Jersey: Prentice-Hall.

Weiss, M. M., and Petersen, R. C. 1979. Electromagnetic radiation emitted from video computer terminals. *American Industrial Hygiene Association Journal* 40:300–9.

Werblin, F. S. 1973. The control of sensitivity in the retina. *Scientific American* 228/1:71–9.

Werblin, F. S., and Copenhagen, D. R. 1974. Control of retinal sensitivity. *Journal of General Physiology* 63:88–110

Wolbarsht M. L., and Sliney, D. H. 1980. *Electromagnetic emission from visual display units: a non-hazard.* Society of Photo-Optical Instrumentation Engineers (SPIE). Bellingham, Washington.

Young, F. A. 1977. The nature and control of myopia. *Journal of the American Optometric Association* 48:451–7.

INDEX

AFTERWORD:
The Horseless Carriage

In its earliest days, the automobile looked much like the horse-drawn carriage that it was gradually to replace. So close was the resemblance that craftsmen in Chicago, Hoboken, and Denver did a brisk business in building mechanical horses to "trot" in front of these startling vehicles.

The "horseless carriage" was so revolutionary that it frightened people. A conveyence that moved without a horse aroused justifiable but exaggerated concern for the safety of both operator and bystander. Because of these anxieties, early designers and users sought some means of making the new appear like the old and familiar; hence, the mechanical horse. The episode seems humorous to us now, so accustomed are we to vehicles that move under their own power. But at the time, the automobile was not only a radical innovation itself; it was a symbol of the technical, social, and economic changes to come, and naturally provoked initial anxiety among those people who encountered it.

The development of the visual display terminal parallels that of the automobile. Where VDTs are concerned, we have just left the era of the horseless carriage. Only in recent years have we begun to see workstations that no longer resemble an ungainly merger of the typewriter with the television. (The television, another innovation that has spawned great social change, shares with the typical VDT an unfortunate characteristic: the low-resolution cathode ray tube. We use the term "visual display terminal" to remind ourselves that there are other display technologies available.) Display terminals with high-resolution screens, alternative input devices (such as the mouse), and convenient communications options (built-in modems and telephone handsets) are still rare sights in today's offices.

The evolution of the VDT, like that of the automobile, has been driven by the demands of the marketplace. Those demands have called for small incremental changes, rather than great leaps forward. And like the early cars built of modified carriage parts, VDTs need to be compatible with what went before.

A premise of this book is that most workstations currently in use were designed without proper attention to basic human needs, thereby causing unnecessary physiological and psychological problems. The negative effect of poorly-designed VDTs on computer applications is less obvious. We can only speculate on how the acceptance of computer applications has been hindered by uncomfortable workstations.

Computer terminals have become a symbol—like the automobile—of sweeping changes in our society that mark the coming of the information age. Change is always accompanied by anxiety. In this case, the fears have a basis in fact: many VDTs are uncomfortable to work with; existing workplaces were not designed with terminals in mind; and computers are changing the nature of work.

The early users of VDTs were willing to put up with whatever it took to do their jobs. Early users included computer professionals, such as systems programmers and engineers, who were tolerant of the technology, and data entry clerks, who had little choice in what tools they used to perform their work. Today's users are less knowledgeable about the seemingly limitless technology descending on them, but are more demanding. Ironically, Stanford University's clerical workers were considering unionization during the production of this book, and one of their rallying cries was the hazardous nature of working at a VDT. Workers should be concerned about working with terminals. But as this book suggests, much of the outcry is based upon anxiety rather than evidence of physical harm.

With these thoughts in mind, we have presented the reader not with a volume about the physical characteristics of the VDT itself—the screen, the keyboard, and their housings. Rather, we have presented current knowledge about what lies on either side of the screen: on one side the physiological and psychological capabilities and the concerns of the VDT operator; on the other, the interface to computer hardware and software that should serve as a tolerant and helpful servant to humankind.

John Bennett
Donald Case
Jon Sandelin
Michael Smith

ABOUT THIS BOOK

From the very beginning we intended to produce this book ourselves—that is to provide the publisher final camera-ready copy. There were two reasons for this decision. First, we believed with the tools available to us, we could create the typeset, ready-to-print pages more quickly, and thus have the book "on the shelf" much sooner. Second, we felt we could learn from the experience and apply what we learn towards improving emerging computer-based tools for book production. We did not finish this book as quickly as we initially planned but we did create it in less time than typically taken for texts of this type; and we certainly learned a great deal about the many tasks required in producing a book from start to finish!

The tools we used were developed at Stanford University. They included the Context system, with software specially designed by Pentti Kanerva for scholary writing and TeX, an elegant typesetting language developed by Professor Donald Knuth. These systems were hosted on a DEC 2060 computer and provided capabilities for editing text from inexpensive computer terminals at various locations (including at home), for communicating via electronic mail, for designing special characters if needed, and for producing high-quality final typeset copy. An inexpensive laser printer provided draft typeset copy for a few pennies per page so we could preview chapters before committing to final typesetting.

We learned that moving text from brand X computer to our DEC 2060 computer was hard to do. Each of the chapters was written on a different computer, i.e., the author's favorite system. And each author provided us a "computer-readable" copy, either on magnetic tape, on a diskette, or by transfering over an electronic network. For several chapters, we found it was faster and cheaper to retype the material into our system from a printed copy rather than struggling with the many annoying and time consuming problems involved when trying to move text between dissimmilar computer brands.

We learned also that the computer has a long way to go before book production is truly "automated". Although computer-based tools like the Context authoring system and the TeX typesetting system are an important step forward, the areas of book design, copyediting, indexing, and typesetting required skilled human beings. In our case, a number of people were involved: Susan True (book design), Bonnie Bernstein and Claire Delgado (copyediting), Susan Riggs (indexing) Dikran Karagueuzian, Jonni Kanerva, and Chip Haven (typesetting). Although Context and TeX helped supplement their skills to produce a finished work in an accelerated timeframe, a good deal of human labor was still required to produce a final camera-ready manuscript.

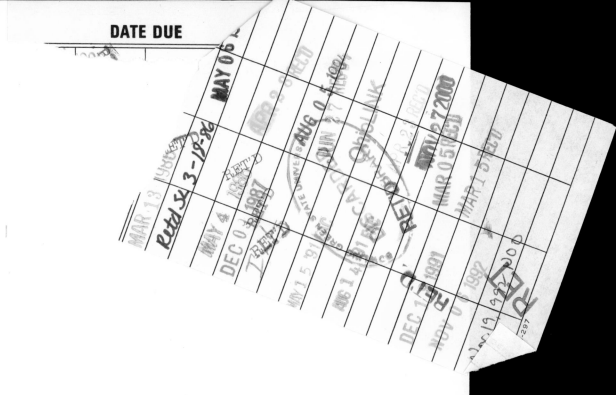